Routledge Revivals

Adulescentia

Adulescentia

The Eclogues of Mantuan

Baptista (Spagnuoli) Mantuanus

Edited, with an English
Translation, by
Lee Piepho

First published in 1989 by Garland Publishing, Inc

This edition first published in 2018 by Routledge
2 Park Square, Milton Park, Abingdon, Oxon, OX14 4RN
and by Routledge
52 Vanderbilt Avenue, New York, NY 10017

Routledge is an imprint of the Taylor & Francis Group, an informa business

Publisher's Note
The publisher has gone to great lengths to ensure the quality of this reprint but points out that some imperfections in the original copies may be apparent.

Disclaimer
The publisher has made every effort to trace copyright holders and welcomes correspondence from those they have been unable to contact.
A Library of Congress record exists under ISBN:

ISBN 13: 978-0-367-18029-4 (hbk)
ISBN 13: 978-0-367-18031-7 (pbk)
ISBN 13: 978-0-429-05920-9 (ebk)

WORLD LITERATURE
IN TRANSLATION

Adulescentia
The Eclogues of Mantuan

BAPTISTA (SPAGNUOLI) MANTUANUS

Edited, with an English Translation, by
LEE PIEPHO

GARLAND PUBLISHING, INC.
NEW YORK & LONDON 1989

Library of Congress Cataloging-in-Publication Data

Baptista Mantuanus, 1448–1516
[Adulescentia. English & Latin]
Adulescentia: the eclogues of Mantuan/Baptista Mantuanus; edited, with an English translation, by Lee Piepho.
p. cm.—(Garland library of world literature in translation; v. 14)
Bibliography: p.
ISBN 0-8240-3309-4
1. Pastoral poetry, Latin (Medieval and modern)—Translations into English. 2. Pastoral poetry, English—Translations from Latin (Medieval and Modern) 3. Pastoral poetry, Latin (Medieval and modern) I. Piepho, Lee. II. Title. III. Series.
PA 8463.B7A3813 1989
872'.01—dc20 89-16967

Book and cover design by
Renata Gomes

The volumes in this series have been printed on acid-free, 250-year-life paper.
Published in the United States of America

BAPTISTA MANTUANUS

A terracotta bust of Mantuan, probably taken from a copy based on a life–mask of the poet. Along with a bust of Virgil, it originally adorned the arch of the Porta Nuova at Mantua, refurbished by Mantuan's friend, Battista Fiera, in 1514. An inscription (ARGVMENTVM VTRIQUE INGENS SI SECLA COISSENT) under the bust of Marchese Francesco Gonzaga, whom the other busts flank on either side, favorably compares Mantuan's poetic powers with those of his distinguished fellow citizen. (*Foto Giovetti, Mantua*)

TABLE OF CONTENTS

PREFACE

Facile, precor gelida quando quando pecas omnia ruminat, and so forth.
. . .Old Mantuan, old Mantuan! who understandeth thee not, loves thee not.

When in *Love's Labor's Lost* Holofernes misquotes the first line of the *Adulescentia*, Shakespeare could still rely on his audience's widespread familiarity with the eclogues of "good old Mantuan" to catch the error of his foolishly pedantic schoolmaster. Indeed, it is partly because of Holofernes' real–life counterparts in the grammar schools that Mantuan's eclogues played such a crucial role in the culture of western Europe during the sixteenth and seventeenth centuries. That these poems are, despite W. P. Mustard's admirable edition, less well known today among students of the Renaissance is doubtless due to the decline of the study of Latin in the twentieth–century curriculum and to the lack of a modern translation of the entire collection. What follows is an attempt to rectify this situation. The primary aims of my translation have been utility and fidelity to the Latin text; only accidentally are they concerned with stylistic elegance. I have been less given to paraphrase than my two English predecessors, George Turberville and Thomas Harvey, and my medium has been prose rather than verse—a treatment under which Mantuan suffers a good deal less than does Virgil.[1] My version has been affected by the notes on vocabulary and syntax in Mustard's edition as well as in the Renaissance commentaries of Jodicus Badius and Andreas Vaurentinus, but no effort has been made to incorporate this material into my own annotation. The voluminous notes on verbal echoes of ancient and medieval writers in the eclogues have likewise been excluded, except in cases (e.g., II, 103n) where they are immediately and strikingly contextual. Given the widespread use of Badius' commentary in the Renaissance, however, I have included a selection, with translation, of his interpretative notes, in particular his important introductory discussions of the first and seventh eclogues.[2]

[1] Translations from ancient authors follow, as indicated, the versions in the Loeb Classical Library. Translations from the Bible are from the Douay-Rheims Version.

[2] In annotating the eclogues, I have tried to credit the commentator to first document a specific literary echo, determine a particular interpretation, and the like. Whenever possible, line numbers parallel the original annotation, the annotator being named in each note or indicated in parentheses by an initial (e.g., **B**=Badius; **M**=Mustard).

The facing–page Latin text of the *Adulescentia*, based on the first printed edition of the eclogues (the Mantua edition of 1498), is Mustard's and follows his modifications in spelling and punctuation. Mustard's edition has grown scarce and difficult to obtain, and, given the many citations that have been made to it over the years, it seemed desirable to make his text widely available again. More importantly, his pedagogical aim of keeping Mantuan's eclogues as a living document for twentieth–century readers of Latin continues to seem a laudable and more attainable goal with his text. In cases such as the texts printed in my first appendix, where the interest is more specialized and scholarly, I have retained the orthography and punctuation of the original.

Since the publication of Mustard's edition, the research of Ludovico Saggi and Graziano di Santa Teresa in particular have virtually transformed our knowledge of Mantuan's life and career. While I have taken their work into account, my introduction and notes focus only on those biographical aspects immediately relevant to the composition and publication of his *Adulescentia.*

Mantuan's request in his dedicatory letter to Paride Ceresara that all manuscript copies of earlier versions of his eclogues be destroyed has until recently proved so effective that information on the composition and publishing history of the *Adulescentia* has remained scattered and sketchy. To rectify this situation, in the Introduction and first appendix I have printed and discussed transcriptions of manuscript versions of the ninth and tenth eclogues as well as newly discovered excerpts from the original, unprinted collection. In addition, the Introduction and a second appendix supplement Edmundo Coccia's bibliography in order to more fully document the publishing history of the *Adulescenitia*. Finally, I have, unlike Mustard, taken note of an important letter from Mantuan to his father that, written when he was at work on the first version of his eclogues, sheds important light on the circumstances of their composition.

Comments on the style, theme, and organization of Mantuan's *Adulescentia*, set forth in the Introduction, are elaborated in the notes to the individual eclogues. In discussing literary conventions and backgrounds, my annotation goes somewhat beyond what Mustard took for granted in an earlier day. (It is still assumed, of course, that interested students will consult *The Oxford Classical Dictionary* as well as *The Oxford Companion to Classical Literature* and other reference works in the field.) In particular, I have presented more of the Carmelite heritage that informs the revised version of Mantuan's collection.

The work of Mustard and other scholars on the influence of the *Adulescentia* on European culture and literature has been incorporated into the introduction and notes to the individual eclogues.[3] In many ways, this

[3] I have taken what seems to me most useful in Mustard's survey. Some of the echoes he hears (e.g., Candidus' complaint against niggardly patrons [V, 145 f.] in Thomas Lodge's *Fig for Momus*) are too general to admit a particular influence. Others are too imperfectly or inaccurately documented to be traceable (e g., his discussion [pp. 44-45] of quotations from the

remains the most dated aspect of Mustard's edition. A good deal of critical endeavor has been expended since 1911 on the influence of the *Adulescentia*. The need now would seem to be for a full-scale treatment of the place of Mantuan's eclogues within European literature. This is clearly an aim outside the bounds of an edition. For all that, if my endeavor succeeds in encouraging such an undertaking, what follows will have more than served its purpose.

****

In the arduous task of checking references I have had the able assistance of the staffs at the Folger Shakespeare Library, the Library of Congress, the Newberry Library, the New York Public Library, the libraries at Yale, Michigan, Columbia, North Carolina, and Virginia as well as the Cochrane Library at Sweet Briar. Katherine Pantzer, Harriet Jameson, Giulia Bologna, Carla Bonanni Guiducci, and John Morrison were all very kind in answering questions and providing material to resolve an array of bibliographic problems. I am grateful to the Bodleian Library, Oxford, as well as to the Vatican Library and Collegio di Sant' Isidoro, Rome, for permission to print transcriptions from manuscripts in their collections. Thanks also are due to the editors of *Renaissance Quarterly* and *Renaissance Studies* for permission to print material that first appeared in their pages. To the staffs of the Folger Library (especially Laetitia Yeandle and Nati Krivatsy), the Bodleian Library, and the libraries at Virginia and North Carolina—at all of which places work on this edition was carried out—as well as to John Jaffe and Christoper Bean at the Sweet Briar Library I owe a deep and longstanding debt of gratitude.

Grants from the National Endowment for the Humanities and the Southeastern Institute of Medieval and Renaissance Studies helped to support work on this edition under the sympathetic encouragement of Jean-Claude Margolin and Louis Martz. Portions of the manuscript were read at different times by them and by Charles Fantazzi, Laetitia Yeandle, Herbert Matsen, and the late Calvin Anderson (who generously opened to me the hospitality of Whitefriars Hall, Washington, and the treasures of its library). John B. Dillon saved me from a number of errors by his careful reading of an earlier version of the entire manuscript. (He also communicated material, so marked, on literary influences on the *Adulescentia*, based on an annotated copy of the eclogues made by Howard T. Easton, Mustard's pupil at Johns Hopkins during the 1920s.) Catherine Cravens assisted in preparing the final version, which was gone over by Scott Bentley at Garland. To Robin Nisbet of Corpus Christi College, who read and offered numerous suggestions on the translation, I owe a further debt of gratitude for his having originally helped me to discover the delights of

eclogues in Burton's *Anatomy of Melancholy* and a treatment [p. 47] of borrowings from the eclogues in Otto Melander's *Iocorum atque seriorum . . . centuriae aliquot iucunda*).

Virgil and pastoral poetry during a sabbatical year at Oxford University. Last but not least, I owe a continuing indebtedness to the interest and support of my wife, a twentieth-century woman of science intrigued, if sometimes puzzled, by the world of *quattrocento* Italian humanism.

L. P.

Sweet Briar, Virginia
February, 1989

ABBREVIATIONS OF WORKS FREQUENTLY CITED

A Florido Ambrogio. *De rebus gestis ac scriptis operibus Baptistae Mantuani cognomento Hispanioli, Carmelitae.* Turin: Ignatius Soffietti, 1784.

Ad Baptista Mantuanus. *Adulescentia,* in *Secundus operum B. Mantuani tomus.* Paris: Badius Ascensius, 1513.

AOC *Analecta Ordinis Carmelitarum.*

AOCD *Analecta Ordinis Carmelitarum Discalceatorum.*

BC Cosma de Villers. *Bibliotheca Carmelitana.* Edited by Gabriel Wessels. Rome: Collegium S. Alberti, 1927.

C Edmondo Coccia. *Le edizioni delle opere del Mantovano.* Rome: Institutum Carmelitanum, 1960. (Unless otherwise noted, cited by item number: e.g., C130.)

CH Benedictus–Maria a S. Cruce (Zimmerman). "Les carmes humanistes." *Études Carmélitaines,* 20 (1935). 19–93.

Col Publius Vergilius Maro. *Eclogues.* Edited by Robert Coleman. Cambridge University Press, 1977.

Cos Mario C. Cosenza. *A Biographical and Bibliographical Dictionary of the Italian Humanists . . . 1300–1800.* 5 volumes. New York: G. K. Hall, 1962.

G Graziano di Santa Teresa. "Nuova cronologia della vita del B. Battista Mantovano." *Ephemerides Carmeliticae,* 9 (1958). 423–42.

Gir Rodolfo Girardello. "Vita e testi del beato Battista Spagnoli." *Carmelus,* 21 (1974). 36–98.

GW *Gesamtkatalog der Wiegendrucke.* 1928; rpt. New York: H. P. Kraus, 1968. (Unless otherwise noted, cited by item number: e.g., GW3470)

LR Alessandro Luzio and Rodolfo Renier. "Cultura e relazioni letterarie d'Isabella d' Este." *Giornale storico della letteratura italiana,* 34 (1899). 59–70.

M Baptista Mantuanus. *The Eclogues of Baptista Mantuanus.* Edited by Wilfred P. Mustard. Baltimore: Johns Hopkins University Press, 1911.

MHC *Monumenta historica Carmelitana.* Ed. Benedictus–Maria a S. Cruce (Zimmerman). îles de Lerins: ex typis Abbatiae, 1905-07.

NUC *The National Union Catalogue: Pre–1956 Imprints.* London: Mansell, 1968–85. (Cited in all cases by item number: e.g., NB0100954.)

Opera Baptista Mantuanus. *Opera Omnia.* Ed. Laurentius Cuperus. Antwerp: Joannes Bellerus, 1576. (Volume four is paginated in two formats [e.g., IV, ii, 235–70 or IV, i, 179–83], two printers having set it. The resulting sigla *i* and *ii* are mine.)

P1 Lee Piepho. "Mantuan and Religious Pastoral: Unprinted Versions of His Ninth and Tenth Eclogues." *Renaissance Quarterly*, 39 (1986). 644–72.

P2 ________ . "Versions by Thomas, Lord Fairfax of Some Poems by Mantuan and Other Italian Neo–Latin Writers." *Renaissance and Reformation*, n. s. 7 (1984). 114–20.

S Ludovico Saggi. *La congregazione mantovana dei Carmelitani sino alla morte del B. Battista Spagnoli (1516).* Rome: Institutum Carmelitanum, 1954.

V Harry Vredeveld. "Pastoral Inverted: Baptista Mantuanus' Satiric Eclogues and Their Influence on the *Bucolicon* and *Bucolicorum Idyllia* of Eobanus Hessus." *Daphnis*, 14 (1985). 461-96.

Var *The Works of Edmund Spenser: A Variorum Edition.* Eds. Edwin Greenlaw et. al. Baltimore: Johns Hopkins University Press, 1932–49.

Z1 Vladimir Zabughin. "Un beato poeta (Battista Spagnoli, Il Mantovano)." *AOC*, 4 (1917–1922). 125–57.

Z2 ______________. *Vergilio nel rinascimento italiano.* Bologna: Nicola Zanichelli, 1921–23. Volume I, pages 243–46, 269–72.

Abbreviations of Latin or Greek works and authors are those used in Lewis and Short, *A Latin Dictionary* and in the *Oxford Classical Dictionary*. Other abbreviations follow the conventions of the *MLA International Bibliography*.

INTRODUCTION

Life

Baptista Spagnolo,[1] who took his more familiar name, Mantuanus ("Mantuan" in England since the Renaissance), from his birthplace, the city of Mantua, was born on April 17, 1447,[2] perhaps illegitimately,[3] of a distinguished Spanish family that after 1435 had settled in northern Italy.[4] The most outstanding of several children conspicuous in their service to church and state,[5] Mantuan from early youth had his father's encouragement in his study of the liberal arts.[6] At Mantua he was the pupil

[1] The name is sometimes encountered as "Spagnulo" or "Spagnoli:" **Gir** 39. For the "Johannes" occasionally found with Mantuan's name, see **S** 116, n. 122 and **Gir** 40, n. 23.

[2] Following the great eighteenth-century scholar, Girolamo Tiraboschi, Mustard (11) gives Mantuan's birth date as 1448. On the basis of the Harley documents in the British Library, Zimmerman (**MHC** 262) dated his birth in 1447, however, and Saggi (**S** 121) has supported this latter date, arguing for the improbability of ordination before Mantuan's twenty-third birthday, or of his becoming prior of the monastery at Parma at the age of twenty-two. 1447 has also been accepted as Mantuan's year of birth by **G** (428), Coccia, *Bibliotheca sanctorum* (Rome: Instituto Giovanni XXIII, 1961–), XI, 1340, and **Gir** (40).

[3] The claim of illegitimacy goes back to a statement made in the sixteenth century by Paolo Giovio in his *Elogia veris clarorum virorum imaginibus* (*Gli elogi degli uomini illustri*, ed. Renzo Meregazzi [Rome: Instituto Poligrafico dello Stato, 1972; = *Pauli Iovii opera cura et studio Societatis Historicae Novocomensis denuo edita*, VIII], 88). More recently, the charge has been supported by Stefano Davari (*Della famiglia Spagnola, quale risulta dai documenti dell' Archivio Storico Gonzaga* [Mantua: eredi Segna, 1873], 5–6) but rejected by Florido Ambrogio, (*De rebus gestis ac scriptis operibus Baptistae Mantuani* [Turin: Ignatius Soffietti, 1784], 11–15) and Gabriel Wessels (*AOC*, 4 [1917–22], 6–8).

[4] Both his father, Pietro, and his grandfather, Antonio, were originally taken prisoner by the Genoese in a naval battle off Gaeta. A nobleman from Granada, Pietro lost his family name ("Modover" or "Moduer") and gained "Spagnolo" from the name of his country. He eventually settled in Mantua (where in 1460, with his family, he was granted citizenship) and served Lodovico as advisor and diplomatic representative, subsequently enjoying the favor of Federico and Francesco, Lodovico's successors as marquises of Mantua, before dying there early in 1494 (**M** 18–19; Davari, *op. cit.*, 4).

[5] Foremost among Mantuan's ten brothers and sisters were Tolomeo, who served as confidential secretary to Francesco, Marquis of Mantua, and Alessandro, a famous lawyer and canon there. Late in Mantuan's life (ca. 1509) Tolomeo published a learned defense of his works, *Apologia contra detrahentes operibus Baptistae Mantuani*. (**M** 20–22)

of Giorgio Merula and notably of Gregorio Tifernate[7] (reflected in Mantuan's eclogues in the figure of Umber), and afterwards he studied philosophy at Padua where he attended the lectures of Paolo Bagelardi.[8] Unsuccessful in following his father's advice to exchange an early love of the muses for the study of "knotty sophistries (*nodosa sophismata*)," he composed the first version of his eclogues[9] as well as a collection of unprinted elegiac verse during these years.[10] Poverty seems to have compelled him to leave Padua, however, and a serious quarrel on returning home, coupled with a growing, mystically based sense of vocation, led Mantuan early in 1463 to enter the reformed Carmelite monastery at Ferarra.[11] During his novitiate there he composed *De vita beata*, a dialogue on the religious life (**S** 122). In 1464 he began teaching rhetoric and the following year was appointed to study logic at the monastery (**S** 122). At the General Assembly of the Congregation in May 1466 he delivered the official

[6] Late in Mantuan's life, Pietro is remembered for this early encouragement in a passage in Mantuan's *Vitae suae epitome* quoted by Mustard (19).

[7] Born ca. 1415 in Città di Castello, Gregorio Tifernate counted Vittorino da Feltre and Manuel Chrysoloras among his teachers. After studying at Perugia, he spent several years in Greece, returning to teach Greek at Naples. From 1449 to 1455 he served Nicholas V, for whom he translated several Greek prose works into Latin. After 1456 Gregorio was in France at the court of Charles VII. Later, as Professor of Greek at the University of Paris, he played an important role in introducing Italian humanism into Northern Europe. By September, 1459 he had returned to Italy From April, 1460 to December, 1461 he taught at Mantua before moving on to spend the rest of his life at Venice, where he died ca. 1466 (**M** 131; **Cos** IV, 3412–14). Originally Gregorio's pupil, Giorgio Merula was at Mantua from 1460 to as late as 1465: Ferdinando Gabotto and A. B. Confalonieri, *Vita di Giorgio Merula* (Alessandria: Jacquemod Giovanni, 1893), 31, 37. In a letter (quoted by Gabotto and Confalonieri, *ibid.*, 34–35), Merula praises Gregorio for requiring students not simply to repeat what they had been taught but to present their own arguments buttressed with evidence and clear reasoning for all their decisions. In this way he thought that Gregorio had avoided the superficiality that characterized so many students at the time. For Gregorio Tifernate and Umber in Mantuan's eclogues, see IV, 81 f. and notes.

[8] A many-sided man, Bagelardi was famous for weaving the other *artes liberales* into his lectures on philosophy: see Ettore Bolisani, "Scholaro a Padova," *Padova*, 4 (1956), 22.

[9] For the circumstances surrounding the composition of this first version, see Mantuan's prefatory letter to Paride Ceresara as well as "Composition and Publication of the *Adulescentia*."

[10] **Gir** (42–43), who prints this collection of elegies (75–95).

[11] **S** 121; **Gir** 44–46. Thus began his lifelong association with the Congregation of Mantua, otherwise known as the Mantuan Reform. Beginning at the convent of Le Selve, outside Florence, this movement instituted a series of reforms regarding tenure of office, residence within the convent, and the possession of private property. Over the years the Congregation grew to include houses at Mantua and Gironda, until in 1442 it achieved quasi-autonomy under a vicar general. By Mantuan's time it had brought under its authority a number of other houses in northern and central Italy. Ludovico Saggi's *La congregazione Mantovana* is the standard work on this movement. Zimmerman (in **MHC** 483–90) prints the text of an important letter written to Mantuan's father soon after he had entered the monastery at Ferarra in which Mantuan recounts the events and reasons leading to his decision: see "Composition and Publication of the *Adulescentia*" below.

oration (G 429)—striking evidence of Mantuan's solid training in rhetoric and of his precocity. In June of 1469 he completed his studies and was appointed *baccalarius* at Ferarra (G 429). By 1470 he seems to have been ordained, perhaps at Bologna,[12] and was at once elected prior of the chapter at Parma (G 429). In June of the following year he returned to Bologna where he served as *clavarius*[13] at the monastery of San Martino and began his studies in theology at the *studium generale* there.[14] In 1473 he taught rhetoric in the convent (A 28), completing his studies in theology at the *studium* in April, 1475.[15] In 1475 and again in 1477 he was chosen *regens*[16] at the monastery of San Martino (G 430, 431). Twice during Mantuan's years at Bologna, plague drove him from the city. Between 1478 and 1481 we find him first outside Bologna at the villa of Giovanni Baptista Refrigerio[17] where he worked on *De calamitatibus temporum,* his influential, often reprinted attack on the waywardness of the times, and then at Mantua.[18] Again, in 1482, Refrigerio and another friend, Ludovico Foscarari, spirited him to safety outside the town after his monastery had been quarantined because of the death of a monk. In gratitude Mantuan dedicated to Refrigerio and Foscarari his *Parthenice Mariana,* the first and most distinguished of a series of poems by him on various saints and the Virgin Mary.

After May, 1479 he was prior and *regens* at the convent at Mantua as well as tutor to the children of the Marchese Federico.[19] By mid–1481 Mantuan was back at Bologna, however, where, first designated *regens* at San Martino, in July he was appointed head of the college of theologians (S 127; G 433). In this latter office Mantuan took part in the inquisition of Giorgio di Novara, who was convicted and executed on a charge of heresy.[20] First elected vicar general of the Carmelite Congregation at Mantua in 1483,

[12] S 125. Graziano di Santa Teresa cites (G 429) a document dated 13 April 1470 in which Mantuan appears towards the head of a list of names as *"fr. baptista petrj de spagnolis de mantua."*

[13] G 429. The *clavarius* was an administrator under the prior of the monastery: see S 125, n. 131.

[14] S 125; Gir 49. A portion of one of Mantuan's disputations is printed in *AOCD,* 7 (1932), 173–74.

[15] Notice of the *privilegium doctoratus* is printed by C. Piana in *Ricerche su le Università di Bologna e di Parma nel secolo xv* (Florence: S. Bonaventura, 1963), 133. The *studium* at San Martino was linked to the University through the Faculty of Theology (Gir 48).

[16] As *regens* Mantuan would direct the programs of studies and watch over the progress of students at San Martino.

[17] For Refrigerio, see "Composition and Publication of the *Adulescentia.*"

[18] A letter to Refrigerio puts him in Mantua as early as December, 1478 (G 432).

[19] In May 1479 he was elected prior and *regens* at Mantua (G 432). The tradition that he had charge of the education of Federico's children dates from Louise de S. Thérèse, *La succession du S. Prophète Elie en l'Ordre des Carmes et en la réforme de S. Thérèse* (Paris: G. Sassier, 1662), 585-86.

[20] S 127. In *De patientia* Mantuan speaks at length about this inquisition (*Opera,* IV, ii, 138–146).

he was reelected to this office five times—each time for a period of two years, with an interval of four years—in 1489, 1495, 1501, 1507 and 1513.[21]

Soon after his election in 1483 Mantuan made his first official journey to Rome, where before Sixtus IV he pleaded the Congregation's case regarding the color of the Carmelite habit.[22] Following a period in Bologna after his first term as vicar general,[23] we find Mantuan back in Rome in 1486, where he succeeded in acquiring San Crisogono in Trastevere as a seat for the Mantuan Congregation in the papal city (**S** 131). In this action he was aided in part by Falcone de' Sinibaldi (**S** 131), along with Bernardo Bembo the foremost, from the standpoint of their role in the eclogues, among a large group of ecclesiastical and literary acquaintances that Mantuan made during his residence at Rome.[24]

From May 1487 to 1489 Mantuan was prior of the newly established house at Rome, during the second year also serving as *regens* there (**S** 131; **G** 435–36). At this time a number of his works, which (*De vita beata* excepted) had previously appeared only in manuscript copies, were first printed at Bologna.[25] A sermon delivered before Innocent VIII on All Saints' Day, 1488, attacks corruption within the Papal Curia in terms reminiscent of the ninth eclogue. Christ, Mantuan warns the prelates, dressed in simple attire and ate his bread, most often begged for, in the houses of other men. The cardinals before him, on the other hand, consume at a single meal fish, flesh, and fowl, caring little or not at all for God's law, for scandal, or for the needs of the wretched of the earth. Delivered less than three decades before the coming of Luther, Mantuan's warning at the conclusion of this oration—that both the weeds and good grasses have grown so closely together that they must both perish before the mower's scythe—has an ominous ring. But by concluding with a prayer advocating spiritual renewal within the Church,[26] he sharply

21 **A** 63, 69, 77, 78, 81, 84. Since the statutes mandated a two-year term followed by four years of ineligibility, Mantuan in effect held the office the maximum allowable period—ample testimony to the Congregation's respect for his effectiveness as its leader.

22 **S** 129–30. For the dispute on the color of the habit and its significance in Mantuan's eclogues, see "Themes, Style, and Organization."

23 On 3 May 1485 he was appointed *regens* at San Martino and also appears as *clavarius* in May and October of that year (**S** 131; **G** 435).

24 For Falcone and Bembo, see "Composition and Publication of the *Adulescentia*." Mustard lists (22–24) Mantuan's friends and acquaintances at Bologna, Mantua, and Rome and reprints (24–25) portions of a lively correspondence carried on in the 1490s with Giovanni Pico della Mirandola and his nephew, Gianfrancesco.

25 In a letter written in October 1490 Mantuan claims that their appearance sprang from the efforts of well-meaning friends at Bologna who, during his absence in Rome, sent the works to the printer without his knowledge (**MHC** 494). These friends might plausibly include Refrigerio and Foscarari as well as Filippo Beroaldo (to whom Mantuan was both friend and confessor) and the Bolognese notary Caesare de' Nappi (an acquaintance of Refrigerio) in whose autograph manuscript, *Palladium eruditum*, a number of Mantuan's works appear (Ludovico Frati, *Studii italiani*, 16 [1908], 129–38).

26 Edited by Gabriel Wessels as "B. Baptistae Mantuani oratio habita coram Innocentio VIII et Cardinalibus in Basilica Vaticana," *AOC*, 6 (1927–29):

marks himself off from Protestant reformers who subsequently embraced him as one of their prophets.[27]

In 1489 he travelled from Mantua to Loreto at the head of a company of Carmelite friars who had been put in charge of the *santa casa*, the reputed house of the Virgin, located there.[28] Between 1490 and 1492 Mantuan was at Bologna and Rome,[29] but from the middle of 1493, when he was appointed prior and *regens* at Mantua (G 437), he was to spend more and more of his time there. In October, 1493 he delivered a funeral oration at Mantua mourning the death of Eleonora of Aragon, mother of Isabella d' Este (M 16), and during the later years of his life we catch glimpses of his participation in an "Accademia de Santo Pietro" instituted by Isabella and overseen by Mario Equicola, Matteo Bandello, and at times by Castiglione and Pietro Pomponazzi.[30]

Bad health plagued Mantuan through much of his life, and during the first decade of the sixteenth century, representatives were often sent on his behalf to assemblies and on visitations to monasteries within the Congregation (S 132–33; G 440). Nonetheless, we should not underestimate the energies of a man who twice during this period could serve as vicar general of the Congregation. In an election dominated by Leo X and Sigismondo Gonzaga, Mantuan's old pupil and now Cardinal Protector, in 1513 he was chosen general of the entire Carmelite order, a position he held until his death.[31] During his brief tenure in office, his foremost accomplishment was his assistance in consolidating the Congregation of Albi,

---

Christus per omnem vitam una et ea quidem humili veste contentus in alienis semper aedibus pane, ut plurimum mendicato, vescebatur. Nos autem dum quicquid errat in terris, quidquid natat in undis, quicquid volat in aëre una mensa consumimus, nulla de Dei lege, nulla de scandalo, nulla vel certe postrema est cura de miseris. . . . Zizania ista, quae super bonum semen jecit inimicus, extirpare nequeunt. Heu, quam metuo, ne brevi totus ager iste demetatur! Nam mala gramina tam alte fixere radices, sic cum bonis graminibus, si quae supersunt, sese complicuere, ut dum secerni non possunt a messoribus, omnia simul oporteat interire.

Quod ne fiat ad sanctissimum illud coelestis patriae collegium, cuius hodie festa celebrantur, conversis animis et sursum cordibus elevatis, omnipotentem Deum Patrem, Filium et Spritum Sanctum deprecemur, ut pacem ecclesiae, praelatis lumen intelligentiae, principibus nostris de infidelibus victoriam, et tandem catholicis omnibus coelestem patriam multiplicatis intercessoribus largiatur. (p. 134)

27 On this aspect of Mantuan's reputation, see the introductory note to "Eclogue IX" and P2 116–18.

28 A, 69–70. See also *Opera*, IV, i, 216, 220, 222.

29 In the Assembly held May, 1490, Mantuan was appointed *regens* at San Martino (G 436). For a year beginning May, 1491 he was prior at San Crisogono in Rome before again being appointed *regens* at San Martino in 1492 (G 437).

30 LR 2–22, 35–41, 59. Among his acquaintances at Mantua, the most important from the standpoint of the *Adulescentia* is Paride Ceresara, to whom Mantuan dedicated the printed version of his collection (see "Composition and Publication of the *Adulescentia*" below).

31 S 133–35. Mantuan seems to have been reluctant to accept the position and refused to travel to Rome to attend the chapter.

a French imitation of the Mantuan Reform.[32] On the twentieth of March, 1516, he died in the city that had given him his name.

Composition and Publication of the *Adulescentia*

In dedicating the first printed edition of his collection to Paride Ceresara,[33] Mantuan tells him that he composed the eclogues long ago when he was a student at Padua (whence the title, *Adulescentia* [*Youth*], that he gave to them at the time). Believing that, as immature work, they had disappeared many years before, he describes how, when passing through Bologna in 1497, he had unexpectedly come on a manuscript copy of the collection. He soon finds that too many copies are in circulation to call them all in and therefore resolves to revise the poems, adding to the end of the collection two eclogues that he composed after entering religious orders. In this version, the entire collection was first printed at Mantua in September 1498, the only edition of his eclogues to appear there.[34]

Written long after the event, Mantuan's dedicatory letter gives no

[32] Leo Van Wijmen, *La congregation d'Albi (1499–1602)* (Rome: Institutum Carmelitanum, 1971), 65–71. Mantuan was named to, but apparently never attended, the Lateran Council of 1513 (S 139). In 1515 he was involved in an attempt made by Leo X to arrange peace between Francis I and the Duke of Milan (S 140–41).

[33] Born in 1466 of a noble family in Mantua, Ceresara was a lawyer distinguished for his great wealth and learning. He composed sonnets (one of which survives), translated Plautus' *Aulularia* and (perhaps) a Greek comedy, was noted for his erudition in Greek and Latin, and had a passing knowledge of Hebrew (**LR** 87–90; F. R. de' Angelis, in *Dizionario biografico degli italiani*, dir. Alberto M. Ghisalberti [Rome: Instit. della Enciclopedia Italiana, 1960–], XXIII, 720–21). A member of Isabella d' Este's circle, Ceresara devised the programme for Lorenzo Costa's *The Garden of the Peaceful Arts* and Perugino's *Battle between Love and Chastity*, paintings intended for her *studiolo* and *grotta*: *Splendours of the Gonzaga*, eds. David Chambers and Jane Marineau (London: Victoria and Albert, 1981), 52, 165. In his old age he studied astrology and acquired a notable posthumous reputation for having predicted the accession to the papacy of Paul III (1534–1549): Lynn Thorndike, *A History of Magic and Experimental Science* (New York: Columbia Univ. Press, 1923–58), V, 256. This being so, he is perhaps to be identified with Patritio Tricasso da Ceresari, author of *Epitoma Chyromantico* (printed at Venice in 1538), a highly systematized treatise of astrology and fortune-telling: F. R. de' Angelis, *op. cit.*, 720–21. In his lifetime Ceresara came to be considered a necromancer, so that his splendid home, built in 1527, was called "the Devil's house" (Thorndike, *op. cit.*, V, 256).

[34] Printed, according to the colophon, by Vincenzo Bertocchi (**GW**3244). As Mustard notes (35), sometime during the course of printing the day of the month, 16 September (*"sexto decimo Kalendas Octobres"*), was added. A 1498 edition appeared after 16 September at Milan (**GW**3245). A curious edition finished, according to the colophon, on 25 August 1525 (*"per Ludovicum Britannicum. Die XXV. Augusti. MDXXV"*) announces in its title that it has been "diligently corrected and revised (*diligenter emendata atque revisa*)" and opens with a dedicatory epistle addressed to Julianus Calinus and dated 1 August 1525 (Mantuan had been dead over nine years at this time). Aside from the substitution of Calinus' name for Paride Ceresara's, the letter is identical with that printed in the 1498 edition, and the text of the eclogues contains no significant variants.

indication of the personal turmoil that surrounded the composition of the original collection. For this, we must look to an earlier, quite remarkable letter written by Mantuan to his father soon after he had begun his novitiate at Ferarra.[35] Here he chronicles the spiritual crisis in the midst of which the poems were composed and which concluded by leading him to enter the Carmelite order. Early in his youth, he confesses, he had done things so shameful that (as he puts it) he had been unable even to face the paintings in the churches. After an abortive attempt to enter a local monastery, he had gone to study at Padua, but falling into a life of poverty and servitude there, he returned home only to find himself banished from the house by his suspicious father. Since the world hates him, Mantuan concludes, he has resolved to hate the world. But he is not, he assures his father, abandoning it simply because he is afraid of failing in life. The decisive factor leading him to make his choice, he declares, has been the personal intervention of the Virgin Mary. Falling dangerously ill during an epidemic of plague at Padua, he was saved from death, he claims, only after he had prayed to the Virgin for deliverance. In return, he had vowed eternal service. But, as Mantuan tells his father, he held back from carrying out his pledge until, during a journey by boat from his native city to Venice, the Virgin raised a tempest on the waters in order that his vow might recur to him and lead him to act on it.[36]

[35] A note in an early version of Mustard's introduction to the eclogues indicates that he knew of this letter but dismissed its authenticity because of an error in the article on Mantuan in the *Catholic Encyclopedia*: "'In a letter addressed to his father (1st April, 1464), and in his first publication, *De vita beata,* he gave an account of his previous life and of the motive which led him to the cloister.' So the *Catholic Encyclopedia*. But the *De vita beata* contains nothing of the sort, and one would like some other authority for the letter and its date." "On the Eclogues of Baptista Mantuanus," *TAPA*, 40 (1909), 150. Mustard seems never to have consulted the text of the letter itself, which in his time had been printed in MHC by Zimmerman (author of the *Catholic Encyclopedia* article) as well as earlier in Latin and in French and Spanish translations (C502, C503, C504, C507). The original version appears in a notebook, now in the Bodleian Library (MS. Selden Supra 41), compiled by John Bale, for whom see below. Saggi (S 122), noting that Bale's manuscript records the day and month but not the year of publication, first suggested that the letter was written, like *De vita beata,* in 1463 during Mantuan's novitiate at Ferarra.

[36] MHC 484–86, as transcribed by Zimmerman:

> *Et hiis* [Mantuan's dissolute youthful companions] . . . *magis quam Omnipotenti Deo placere studens, me quoque interserebam, ut postea ad me rediens tanta efficerer verecundia quod nequibam sanctorum imagines in templis pictas respicere. . . . Tunc, ut nosti, Paduam perrexi. Ubi anxietates varias passus sum, scilicet sitim, famem, nuditatem et servitutem. Rursus Mantuam reversus omnia perturbata reperi et suspicionem falsam piget dicere, sed dicam, quae me per diversa pericula extra limen paternum rejecit et quasi sub pelagi fluctibus submersum. Hoc demum concludere possum, ubicumque fuerim me semper adversam habuisse Fortunam . . . et me forte in desperationem compulisset, nisi Omnipotentis Dei validissimum illud antidotum prius recepissem. Hoc est: si vos de mundo essetis, mundus quod suum esset diligeret. Sed quia de mundo non estis vos mundus odio habet. Et habeat; par pari referens ego quoque illum odio habebo. . . . Ego pauper, despectus, pannosus procul a turbis hominum degam, ut tandem cœlestem adipiscar patriam. . . . Nec volo existimes me naufragii timore id voluisse. Et tamen quoniam ex voto feci si libet audire causam voti tibi recludam.*

As the subtitle of Mantuan's seventh eclogue suggests, the material in this letter can be seen refracted in Pollux's experiences in the *Adulescentia*.[37] In all likelihood, Mantuan (despite references to the cruelty of Pollux's parents in VII, 59–64) revised out some of the eclogue's passion and immediacy in preparing it for printed publication. It would seem equally likely that, as in the case of the prayer and *kalendarium marianum* in the eighth eclogue (lines 122–51, 177-219), he also projected into Pollux some of his own subsequent poetic accomplishments and ambitions.[38] Above all, the final version of the collection clearly reflects the religious spirit and many of the traditions of the Carmelite order that Mantuan had subsequently entered.[39]

His request in the dedicatory letter that all manuscript copies of the eclogues be destroyed has in the past made it difficult to trace the history of his collection before its first printing.[40] Thanks to the recent discovery of manuscript copies of the ninth and tenth eclogues[41] and to the perhaps unexpected diligence of John Bale, originally a Carmelite monk before becoming a staunch defender of the English reformation,[42] we are now, however, in a better position to follow the outlines of this history.

Granting the widest latitude to the period Mantuan spent at Padua,[43] it nonetheless seems improbable that all eight eclogues in addition to his unprinted collection of elegies date from this time. It seems more likely that the eclogues had their beginnings at Mantua, perhaps with the

---

Patavii eram et ibidem contagiosa pestis dominabatur. Ecce nescio quo dierum instar glandis sinistro in femore mihi intumescit. Quid facerem nisi timerem. A quo auxilium peterem nisi ab illo inexhaustæ pietatis fonte Maria Virgine? Petivi. Impetravi. Nonne æquum est ut servem pactum? Justum est utique. Petieram enim ea conditione ut si me liberaret, Illi in perpetuum servirem. Volui illico religionem induere, sed nescio quibus retentus laqueis distuli. Et cum a patria Venetias iterum navigarem Salvatrix mea negligentiam meam intelligens, fluctus maris proram misere ferientes in oculos meos excitavit, ut in memoriam voti redirem, nec amplius differrem.

37 Badius first noted the link between Mantuan's life and Pollux's resolve in VII, 59 f. to flee the harshness of his life at home.

38 See the introductory note to "Eclogue VIII."

39 For which, see "Themes, Style, and Organization."

40 The account in Mantuan's letter is taken at face value by, e.g., Mustard, 35; **BC** col. 233; and **Gir** 70.

41 Printed with a discussion of their date of composition by Lee Piepho, in "Mantuan and Religious Pastoral: Unprinted Versions of his Ninth and Tenth Eclogues," *RQ*, 39 (1986), 644–72, on which the following account is partly based.

42 The following discussion of the extracts from the eclogues made by Bale and of their implications for the date of publication of Mantuan's collection is based in part on Lee Piepho, "Mantuan on Women and Erotic Love: A Newly Discovered Manuscript of the Unprinted Version of His Eclogues," *Renaissance Studies*, 3 (1989), 13–28.

43 1461–1463, according to Graziano di Santa Teresa (**G** 428), who finds it difficult to compress the events described in Mantuan's letter into a shorter span of time. But this dating would make Mantuan's apprenticeship under Giorgio Merula and Gregorio Tifernate (who began teaching at Mantua in April 1460) unrealistically short.

encouragement of the humanist Gregorio Tifernate, and that at least the seventh and eighth eclogues may have received their final form as late as Mantuan's novitiate or soon afterwards. On the basis of John Bale's work, we can say with confidence that the collection existed in published form by 1476 when the Flemish Carmelite Adrien van Eckhoute made a transcription of it at Padua from Mantuan's personal copy.[44]

The original title was not *Adulescentia,* as Mantuan claims in his letter to Paride Ceresara, but *Suburbanus* (*The Rustic*).[45] Like his *Parthenice Mariana* and several other works published in manuscript form[46] during the 1470s, it was dedicated (in this case by means of a prefatory poem) to Giovanni Baptista Refrigerio, Mantuan's admirer and protector during times of plague at Bologna.[47] Given that we find Mantuan at Bologna

[44] See "Appendix I," where Bale's extracts and the glosses (all apparently by Mantuan) from van Eckhoute's manuscript are printed with translation from Bodleian Library MS. Selden supra 41. The form in which the extracts appear, indeed their very existence is explained by Bale's interests in the 1520s, when most of Bale's manuscript was compiled. (For a discussion, with references, of the history of Bale's compilation, see Leslie Fairfield, *John Bale: Mythmaker for the English Reformation* [West Lafayette: Purdue Univ. Press, 1976], 9, 159–61.) During this period Bale as a Carmelite monk was studying at Cambridge and at Toulouse and Louvain, with an active interest in the history and personages of the order. In gathering material for what were projected to become two accounts—one a chronicle history, the other a biographical history of the order's saints and great men—Bale visited the convents of France and the Low Countries, copying out extracts from the documents he found there. As his colophon indicates, Bale came on a transcription of Mantuan's copy of the eclogues, most likely among van Eckhoute's library in the convent at Ghent. (Brief accounts of van Eckhoute's life are found in CH 77–78 and *Nouvelle bibliothèque Carmélitaine,* in *Études Carmélitaines* 3 [1913], 15–16.) A Carmelite in Padua during the 1470s, van Eckhoute formed a friendship with Mantuan recorded in two letters (portions of which are reproduced in CH 77–78) to him from the Italian poet, and it is doubtless at this time that, as Bale claims, he was given access to Mantuan's copy of the original collection. Van Eckhoute's transcription seems to have disappeared when his library was burned by Protestants, who ravaged the convent at Ghent in 1578 (*Nouvelle bibliothèque Carmélitaine,* 16, reconfirmed in correspondence with Gilbert Tournoy of the Katholieke Universiteit Leuven).

[45] With the incipit *Faustus adit segetes,* the title is recorded in Johannes Trithemius' survey, made in 1494, of Mantuan's works: *De scriptoribus ecclesiasticis* (Basel: Johann Amerbach, 1494), fol. 132. The original title appears in reference works as late as Johann Fabricius' *Bibliotheca ecclesiastica* (Hamburg: Liebezeit and Felginer, 1718), 218.

[46] For information on the publication of manuscripts, see Pascale Bourgain, "L'édition des manuscripts," in *Histoire de l'édition française,* eds. Henri–Jean Martin, Roger Chartier, and Jean–Pierre Vivet (Paris: Promodis, 1982–6), I, 55.

[47] Ludovico Frati in his "Notizie biografiche di Giovanni Battista Refrigerio," *GSLI,* 12 (1888), quotes part of a dedicatory letter by Refrigerio in which he speaks of how he daily absorbs Mantuan's teachings (*eius disciplinas quotidie haurio*) (327), a description which may, as Frati believes (326–27), imply formal instruction. In 1479, during a time of plague, Refrigerio spirited Mantuan out of the city to his villa at Claterna, between Imola and Bologna (Frati, 327–28). Mantuan in the *Villa Refrigerii* (*Opera,* III, 233–38) leaves behind an attractive picture of the house, modelled, as he claims, on ancient Roman houses, its dining room frescoed with scenes of Parnassus and Olympus, its library well supplied with the works of Plato, Plutarch, Strabo, Livy, Sallust, Pliny, Cicero, Virgil, and Horace. In the *Porretane* Sabadino praises Refrigerio's vernacular poetry and prose as well as his skill in Latin prose composition

on a regular basis only after 1470, it therefore seems most likely that his collection of eclogues had a gestation period during the 1460s, circulating individually or together (perhaps in an earlier form),[48] before being published and dedicated to Refrigerio sometime between June 1471, when we first find Mantuan at San Martino, and 1476.

Mantuan's ninth and tenth eclogues were composed, according to his letter to Paride Ceresara, after entering religious orders and, it would seem on the basis of manuscript copies, well after the publication of *Suburbanus*.[49] What became "Eclogue IX" is dedicated as a *strena* (a New Year's gift to a patron)[50] in a letter to Falcone de' Sinibaldi as "Protonotary and Papal Treasurer (*protonotario ac thesaurio apostolico*)," a description that dates Mantuan's letter from some holiday season between 1484, by which time, as papal treasurer, Falcone had resigned his office as *clericus Camerae* (S 130), and 1491, the last new year's season before his death.[51] Since his last major service—assistance in acquiring San Crisogono for Mantuan's congregation—was completed in 1486 (S 131), circumstances would favor the mid-1480s as a composition date for both Mantuan's letter and the eclogue.[52]

The first version of Mantuan's tenth eclogue would now seem to have been composed sometime during the latter half of the 1480s. In its manuscript title it is dedicated to Bernardo Bembo,[53] father of the famous

(Frati, 325-26). Among other works, twenty *strambotti* and a collection of Italian poems survive, along with an assortment of letters written in Latin. Sabadino, in a passage from the *Porretane* quoted by Mustard (27), includes Mantuan's *Suburbanus* among a group of works dedicated to Refrigerio.

48 In a prose gloss recorded by Bale (fol. 35), Mantuan speaks of the poems as having had wide circulation under his name before he decided to publish them.

49 See "Appendix I," where manuscript copies of these eclogues are printed with translation.

50 For the *strena*, see H. W. Garrod, "Erasmus and his English Patrons," *The Library*, 5th ser., 11 (1949), 11–12.

51 Walter von Hofmann, *Forschungen zur Geschichte der Kurialen Behörden vom Schisma bis zur Reformation* (Rome: von Loescher, 1914), II, 113.

52 As *clericus Camerae* under Sixtus IV, Falcone had also worked to facilitate approval of the reformed Carmelite habit (S 131, 103): see "Themes, Style, and Organization." He evidently aspired to a cardinalate (S 130), and Mantuan's high hopes for him and gratitude are recorded not only in the ninth eclogue but in his *Epigrammata ad Falconem*, a collection of epigrams dedicated to Falcone. Filippo Baveria, Falcone's brother (S 131) and a follower of the Roman humanist Pomponio Leto (**BC** col. 221), is remembered for a favor in one of the epigrams (*Opera*, I, 111v) and mourned in death in Mantuan's *Ad D. Falconem de morte Phil. Baveriae Querimonia* (*Opera*, I, 113).

53 Thus comfirming Mustard's conjecture (26) that the figure of Bembus in the eclogue is connected with Bembo. Together with a highly respectful autograph letter, Mantuan sent Bembo a copy of his sermon for All Saints' Day, Bembo being noted for his erudition—Mantuan addresses him as *"hominem litteratissimum"* (*AOC* 6 [1927–29], 130)—and for his eloquence in oratory. *Parthenice Catharina*, a versified life of Saint Catherine of Alexandria and the second of Mantuan's *parthenices*, was dedicated to Bembo in an edition first printed at Bologna in 1489 (**GW**3290). (An elegy by Pietro praising Mantuan is included in this edition, perhaps the first printed poem by Bembo's famous son: Nella Gianetto, *Bernardo Bembo: umanista e*

cardinal and poet, as "Venetian orator to Pope Innocent VIII (*Venetorum ad Innocentum VIII summum pontificem Oratorem*)." Bembo held this office from November 1487 to October 1488, during which time, like Bembus in Mantuan's poem, he displayed his skills as an arbitrator, helping to settle a short but bloody war between the Venetians and the forces of the Archduke Sigismondo.[54] October 1488 is therefore the *terminus ad quem* of Mantuan's eclogue, and his dedication would favor a date of composition at some time during the preceding two years.

Spanning over twenty years in its original composition and, to all appearances, heavily revised before its printed publication,[55] Mantuan's *Adulescentia* can thus, despite its title, hardly be considered solely the work of his youth. And in spite of the apparent modesty of his dedicatory letter, in placing the eclogues at the beginning of the 1502 edition of his collected works, the only edition of his *Opera* that he personally oversaw (**LR** 67), Mantuan clearly indicates that he knew their worth. From their first printing, they were immensely popular throughout western Europe—indeed, based on a survey of printings,[56] more so north of the Alps than in his native land. Between 1498 and 1600, the period during which most editions of the *Adulescentia* were produced, only ten of the 165 extant printings appeared in Italy. At Paris, on the other hand, the widely reprinted commentary by Jodocus Badius (Josse Bade) was published in 1502 (C22),[57] less than four years after the first printed edition of Mantuan's eclogues; and the next year, 1503, saw the first publication of the Alsatian humanist Jakob Wimpfeling's popular edition (C29),[58] by which time editions had already appeared at Cologne (C2), Erfurt (C6), Deventer (C15), and Leipzig (C21). In time, notes

politico veneziano [Florence: Leo S. Olschki, 1985], 193, 199.) The dedicatory letter to Bembo, respectful but formal, has none of the personal warmth that marks Mantuan's letter to Refrigerio and Foscarari dedicating his *Parthenice Mariana* to them.

54 A. Ventura and M. Pecoraro, in *Dizionario biografico degli italiani*, VIII, 105.

55 See the discussion in "Appendix I."

56 See Edmundo Coccia, *Le edizioni delle opere del Mantovano* and "Appendix II."

57 Printed by André Bocard for Jean Petit and the de Marnef brothers. A letter by Badius, dated 27 March 1502 (reprinted in Philippe Renouard, *Bibliographie des impressions et des œuvres de Josse Badius Ascensius* [1908; rpt. New York, Burt Franklin, n. d.], II, 110–11), dedicates the work to Ladislas and Clément, sons of Jean Alexandre, a bookseller at Anjou for an edition of Badius' commentary on the *Parthenice Mariana* printed in June of that year (*Répertoire bibliographique*, vol. XXVI, p. 30). From the time of his printing of an edition of Beroaldo's *Orationes* in 1492, French Carmelites came to regard Badius, as James Wadsworth remarks, "almost as their official publisher": *Lyons 1473–1503: The Beginnings of Cosmopolitanism* (Cambridge, Mass.: Medieval Academy of America, 1962), 47. For further information on Badius, also called Ascensius, see Renouard, *op. cit.*, vol. I, passim and Wadsworth, 43–68.

58 Besides the *Adulescentia* with Badius' commentary, the first version of this successful school edition included a poem by Mantuan on John the Baptist, *In laudem Ioannis Baptistae pro natali eius carmen*. In 1504 *De vita beata* was added, in which form it was often printed at Strasbourg (C52, *Index aureliensis* 112.425, C90, C103, C143, C220, C235, C254, C255, C291, C321) as well as by Thomas Anshelm at Tubingen (C197, C213, C234, C277) and Haguenau (C294).

were added by Guilielmus Rameseus[59] and Joannes Murmellius;[60] and a second, much less widely circulated commentary by Andreas Vaurentinus made its first appearance at Lyons in 1517 (C302).[61]

Not, of course, that the *Adulescentia* went unvalued in Italy. In 1504, four years after their initial publication, his eclogues appeared in company with those of Virgil, Calpurnius, Nemesianus, Petrarch, and Boccaccio in a handsome Giuntine edition printed at Florence (C48).[62] The title of an edition published at Turin in 1520 is particularly expansive in its praise, proclaiming that in the *Adulescentia* the reader will discover the life of man portrayed more fully than in Virgil's bucolics, setting aside (the publisher concedes) the loftier grandeur of the Roman poet's verse.[63] Mantuan's amatory eclogues seem to have been of particular interest.[64] The titles of the Milan edition of 1498 (GW3245) and the Brescia edition of 1502 (C13) announce the first eclogue "with another eclogue opposing love newly added (*cum quadam alia ægloga contra Amorem nouiter addita*)," [65] though both editions (*pace* Coccia, p. 113) include the entire collection; and both versions conclude not with Mantuan's tenth eclogue but with his *Elegia contra amorem*.[66]

59 Printed in C209, dated 19 November 1512, or perhaps somewhat earlier in an undated version (NUC NB0100954) estimated to have been printed after 1509.

60 First printed, according to GW (vol. III, col. 315), at Deventer in 1508. This is probably the edition recorded by *Index aureliensis* (see "Appendix II").

61 Originally *argumenta* and additions to Badius' commentary, Vaurentinus' notes were first expanded to a full commentary in 1519 (C320). They were printed alone (C320, Adams M393) or joined with the annotations of Joannes Coroneus Carnutensis (C351, C370, C387, *Répertoire bibliographique*, vol. III, p. 21), Remundus Lauganus de Alta Ripa (C351, C366, C370, C387, *Répertoire bibliographique*, vol. III, p. 21), Bertocus Casalusmagnus Sparro (C388), as well as with Rameseus' notes (C302, C350, C365) and Badius' commentary (C350, C365). In *Neo-Latin and the Pastoral* (Chapel Hill: Univ. of North Carolina Press, 1965), W. Leonard Grant speaks of a commentary by Beroaldo on the eclogues (p. 126), but none is recorded in *Gesamtkatalog der Wiegendrucke*, Coccia, or the reference works consulted for Appendix II.

62 The first three eclogues were included in an immense collection of pastoral poetry selected by Gilbert Cousin of Noseroy, Erasmus' one-time secretary, and printed by Oporinus at Basel in 1546 (C399). None found its way, however, into the selections from Mantuan included by Gruterus in his *Delitiae poetarum Italorum* (C452).

63 *In [Mantuani bucolico carmine] Humanae conditionis vitam planius expressam inuenies quam aut apud Vergilium citra tamen Carminis ipsius Poetae Maiestatem : vel Calpurnium Siculum siue Nemesianum : vel etiam apud Franciscam Petrarcam Bucolicae scriptores. Tu legens idem comprobabis.* (*Index aureliensis*, 112.697)

64 Significantly, John Bale's "*notabilia* (noteworthy passages)" are all extracted from Mantuan's eclogues on love and women.

65 Despite the authority of Mantuan's prefatory letter, the title of his collection varies, especially among earlier editions where, in addition to *Æglogae . . . de honesto amore et foelici eius exitu quadam alia ægloga contra amorem noviter addita*, we commonly find the following titles: *Carmen bucolicum*, *Æglogae Vergilii neoterici*, and *Bucolica seu Adulescentia in decem æglogas divisa*.

66 Likewise, a German collection of Ovid's amatory pieces included Mantuan's *Contra poetas impudice loquentes* (*Against Poets' Shameless Talk*) (C454); and—a reversal of the pattern—

The principle reason for the massive number of printings of the *Adulescentia* is, of course, that quite early the collection established itself as a textbook in the grammar schools of Europe. A letter by Wimpfeling prefacing his edition stresses the correctness of Mantuan's Latin and his safe treatment of subject matter that, in the case of the first four eclogues, was obviously interesting to young students.[67] The English schoolmaster Charles Hoole has left behind a good account of what this must have meant in practice in the classroom.[68] At each lesson students were to take six lines of a given eclogue and, first committing them to memory, were to construe and parse them. Then the master was to "help them to pick out the Phrases and Sentences; which they may commit to a paper–book; and afterwards resolve the matter of their lessons into an English period or two, which they may turn into proper and elegant Latine, observing the placing of words, according to prose." To illustrate this process, Hoole takes the first five lines of Mantuan's first eclogue, thus rendering them in English prose:

> Shepherds are wont sometimes to talke of their old loves, whilest the cattel chew the cud under the shade; for fear, if they should fall asleep, some Fox, or Wolf, or such like beast of prey, which either lurk in the thick woods, or lay wait in the grown corn, should fall upon the cattel. And indeed, watching is farre more commendable for a Prince, or Magistrate, then immoderate, or unseasonable sleep.[69]

---

a French translation of Enea Silvio Piccolomini's *De remedio amoris* with a selection of similar pieces from Mantuan (C313, C397) was joined in a later edition with a version of the *Ars amatoria* (C411).

67 *"Baptistam mantuanum extollo tum in poematibus suis tersis & puris quae absque veneno a maturo praeceptore iuuentuti tradi possunt."* (*Bucolica* [Strasbourg: Joannes Prüss, 1503], sig. a1v). In his dedicatory letter Badius similarly praises Mantuan's eloquence and good sense in treating delicate subject matter (*"Est . . . vir ille ut disertissimus et ditissima vena prædítus, ita optimis institutionibusque præter cæteros ornatus. Norit enim, ut est prudentissimus, quam periculosum imo perniciosium sit lasciva canere, perinde anxie cavit ne quid divo Paulo indignum emittat, quippe qui rectissime a Catullo catullisque similibus dissentit."*): Philippe Renouard, *op. cit.*, II, 111. John Colet included Mantuan in the curriculum at Saint Paul's, numbering him among "goode auctors suych as haue the veray Romayne eliquence joyned withe wisdome, specially Cristyn auctours that wrote thyre wysdome with clene and chast laten": as quoted by J. H. Lupton in his *Life of Dean Colet* (London: George Bell and Sons, 1887), 279. (Mustard questions whether Colet might not have in mind some of Mantuan's religious poems [37–38], but de Worde's editions of the *Adulescentia* in 1523 and 1526, coupled with the complete absence of English editions of Mantuan's other works during this time, suggest that the eclogues rather than some other work by him was in fact being read at Saint Paul's.)

68 In addition to being prescribed by statute in the influential curriculum at St. Paul's School in 1518, Mantuan's eclogues, as Mustard documents (37–39), were set by school orders at the King's School, Durham, in 1593 and were in use at the Free School of St. Helens, ca. 1635. To these, Joan Simon adds the grammar schools at Canterbury in 1541 and Worcester in 1544: *Education and Society in Tudor England* (Cambridge Univ. Press, 1966), 186.

69 *A New Discovery of the Old Art of Teaching Schoole* (1660; rpt. Menston: Scolar Press, 1969), 65-66. The title page announces that Hoole's book was "Written about Twenty three yeares ago, for the Benefit of Rotherham School, where it was first used." As Hoole remarks

Small wonder, given this procedure, that we hear so much in the Renaissance about "morall Mantuan"![70]

As with many of his works, the number of printings of the *Adulescentia* begins to decline during the 1530s. Here, England is the striking exception. The only work by Mantuan to gain any number of printings there, editions of the *Adulescentia* intensify in number after John Kyngston's in 1569[71] until, eventually passing into the English Stock, at least forty printings appeared before 1700.[72] By Doctor Johnson's account, the *Adulescentia* was still being taught in some of the grammar schools in Britain during the early eighteenth century.[73]

Themes, Style, and Organization

Despite much of their secular subject matter, no understanding of Mantuan's eclogues can be complete without some knowledge of the traditions and religious spirit of the Carmelite order, especially the ideals of the reform movement for which he was to become chief defender.[74] The

(300), Mantuan's eclogues were taught in the fourth form at Rotherham before he came as master there.

70 As in, e.g., Michael Drayton's *The Owl* in *Works*, eds. William Hebel, Kathleen Tillotson and Bernard Newdigate (Oxford: Shakespeare Head Press), 1931–41, II, 497, and George Puttenham's *Arte of English Poesie* (in G. Gregory Smith's *Elizabethan Critical Essays* [Oxford Univ. Press, 1904], II, 40).

71 The third English printing, after two by Wynkyn de Worde in the 1520s. A hiatus in English printings between 1526 and 1569 should be weighed against use of the *Adulescentia* at Canterbury and Worcester in the 1540s and the appearance of George Turberville's translation in 1567 (C421), indications of continuing interest in Mantuan's eclogues during this intervening period.

72 De Worde's editions aside, English printings of the *Adulescentia* adopt various arrangements of the following material: Johannes Murmellius' *annotatiunculi* in a letter to Paulus Ruremundensis, together with an *adelon* incorporating comments on style abstracted from Badius' dedicatory epistle, which Murmellius' letter replaces; Mantuan's letter to Paride Ceresara; the text with Murmellius' *argumenta* and Badius' commentary; and an index by Bartholomaeus Laurentis.

73 *Lives of the Poets* (Oxford Univ. Press, 1906), II, 389. The last extant English printing of the complete *Adulescentia* appeared in London in 1707 (NUC NB0101010). In the early sixteenth century Michel d' Amboyse translated all ten eclogues into French as *Les bucoliques de frère Baptist Mantuan. . . .* Paris: Alain Lotrian and Denys Janot, 1531 (C372), and Laurent de la Gravière has versions of the first four eclogues and the sixth in *Les Églogues de frère Baptiste Mantuan. . . .* Lyons: Jean Temporal, 1558 (C413). In 1567 the first nine eclogues in Mantuan's *Adulescentia* were translated into English fourteeners by George Turberville in an edition (C421) reprinted in 1572 (C427) and 1594 (C444); and all ten were finally translated in the seventeenth century by Thomas Harvey as *The Bucolicks of Baptist Mantuan in Ten Eclogues* (London: Humphrey Mosley, 1656) (C474). William Bewick in *Several Letters and Miscellany Poems*, 2nd ed. (Newcastle: James Fleming, 1742), 71, speaks of having made a translation of Mantuan's eclogues, but only his versions of the first four eclogues seem to have survived as *Faustus, Fortunatus and Amyntas* (London: T. Warner, 1718) and *Alphus* (London: T. Warner, 1718) (C488).

Carmelites often claimed to be the oldest of the religious orders, and we should not be surprised that, writing well before the Bollandists, Mantuan left behind several accounts defending these claims.[75] Following an old tradition, he identified Elijah as one of the order's founders and placed its beginnings in the religious community which, originally settled beside the Jordan, later moved to establish itself around the well of Elijah on Mount Carmel. According to Mantuan, these "sons of the prophets" (as they were called from their Elian origins) continued on Mount Carmel through the time of Christ when they were converted, subsequently dedicating to the Virgin a chapel on its slopes. Henceforth Carmelites made their vows to both God and Mary and jealously defended their title of "brothers of the Blessed Virgin Mary of Mount Carmel." After the fall of Acre in 1291 they were compelled to abandon the site, dispersing thereafter throughout western Europe; and with this move came fundamental changes in the nature of the order. Most important, the original rule of Saint Albert was modified under Innocent IV in 1247 so that the order was in effect granted mendicant status and allowed to establish itself in urban areas. Hence arose a continuing conflict within the Carmelites between the contemplative ideal and the life of apostolic and clerical activity that the order came increasingly to pursue in succeeding ages.

The reform issue most immediately evident in Mantuan's *Adulescentia* involves the color of the Carmelite habit.[76] In his tenth eclogue as well as his prose writings Mantuan variously insisted that the original color of the habit had been white, light brown, or grey (*Opera* IV, i, 260; S 280–81), and the oldest extant document related to the subject does in fact prescribe a grey, apparently undyed tunic which had replaced the striped mantle worn in the Holy Land. Over the years, however, difficulty in obtaining material of the same color led to the occasional practice of dyeing the habit black. The issue came to a head when a papal bull of 1483 reaffirmed the black habit decreed by the prior general of the order eleven years before. As vicar general of his congregation, Mantuan appealed the case before Sixtus IV in an action that led the following year to adoption of an undyed grey habit such as (according to the decision of the Diet at Bologna) "old constitutions of the Carmelite order mandate and all the blessed brethren within the aforementioned ancient order observed of old."[77]

---

74 The following account of Carmelite traditions and the religious spirit of the order is based on: Titus Brandsma, "Carmes," *Dictionnaire de spiritualité*, eds. M. Viller et al., (Paris: Beauchesne, 1937–), II, 158–72; Joachim Smet, "The Carmelites," and Efren de la Madre de Dios and Otger Steggink, "Carmelite Spirituality," *New Catholic Encyclopedia* (New York: McGraw–Hill, 1967), III, 114–18, 118–21; Rudolf Hendricks, "La succession héréditaire," *Études Carmélitaines*, 35 (1956), 34–81; *The Rule of Saint Albert*, trans. and eds. Hugh Clarke and Bede Edwards (Aylesford: n. p., 1973); and S 3–24.

75 *De vita beata*, in *Opera*, IV, ii, 178–230; *De laudibus ordinis fratrum Carmelitarum*, in *Opera*, IV, i, 250–72; and a letter (apparently written late in life) to Sigismondo Gonzaga, printed in S 279–84.

76 For which, see S 98–106.

At first glance the whole dispute is apt to seem trivial and slightly Byzantine. For Mantuan, however, the change in the color of the habit was less an issue of expediency than a symbol of the decadence that he saw overtaking the order. As he was to remark later in life, "we were wearing white, that true and ancient color; the others continued just as they sought to be—utterly blackened."[78]

The choice that the Virgin Mary urges on Pollux in the seventh eclogue reflects a number of ideals embraced by the Carmelite order, ideals Mantuan often defended after entering it. Pollux's choice of Mary echoes, for instance, the Carmelites' special devotion to the Virgin, and Mantuan's stress on his decision to leave his parents and native land to enter the silent cloisters calls attention to an aspect of the order going back to the rule of Saint Albert.[79] In *De vita beata* Mantuan echoes the Carmelite rule in making Pollux's chastity a basic requirement of the religious life;[80] and on several occasions later in life he traced chastity as an ideal within the order back to Elijah and his early followers (*Opera* IV, i, 255; IV, ii, 209v). Finally, Pollux's retirement from the world is basic to the Carmelite idea of retreat into the "desert" or "wilderness" of the monastery,[81] an ideal reaffirmed in Mantuan's accounts, written well after ordination, of how early members of the order had forsaken the city to live in caves on the slopes of Mount Carmel (*Opera* IV, i, 242; S 279).

Deeply rooted in monastic tradition,[82] this ideal of eremitic withdrawal stands in part behind the antipathy expressed towards the city in Mantuan's ninth and tenth eclogues. Petrarch's example is also broadly influential here: writing to his brother about the meaning of the first eclogue in his *Bucolicum carmen*, he explains that he has chosen the name "Sylvanus" for himself "partly because I have always felt from earliest childhood a hatred of cities, implanted in me by nature, and a love of sylvan life which has led many of our friends to call me 'Sylvanus' far more often than 'Francesco.'"[83]

---

77 "*. . . sicut antique . . . ordinis Carmelitarum constitutiones mandant et omnes sancti patres antiqui predicti ordinis observaverunt,*" as quoted in S (104).

78 "*. . . nos subfusco, vero et antiquo colore uteremur, alii autem sicut petierant remanerent, omnino denigrati.*" Quoted in S 281–82.

79 *Rule of Saint Albert*, 90; see also *New Catholic Encyclopedia*, III, 115.

80 *Opera*, IV, ii, 184v-85; see *Rule of Saint Albert*, 78.

81 *Dictionnaire de spiritualité*, II, 161–62; *New Catholic Encyclopedia*, III, 114; and, more generally, George H. Williams, *Wilderness and Paradise in Christian Thought* (New York: Harper and Row, 1962), 38–46.

82 See, e.g., St. Jerome's famous 125th epistle: "Others may think what they like and follow each his own bent. But to me a town is a prison and a solitude, paradise." Quoted in Williams, *op. cit.*, 43.

83 "*. . . tum propter insitum ab ineunte etate urbis odium amoremque silvarum, propter quem multi ex nostris in omni sermone sepius me Silvanum quam Franciscum vocant . . .*" *Le familiari*, ed. Vittorio Rossi (Florence: Sansoni, 1933–42), II, 305–6. Antipathy towards the city also appears in Boccaccio's eclogues: see, e.g., XII, 107, 119–27.

This fierce antagonism towards cities is a feature of post–classical pastoral quite alien to Virgil. If the niggardliness of town merchants in part prevents Tityrus from amassing the means sufficient to purchase his liberty, Virgil's first eclogue nonetheless reminds us that it is Octavian, leader of a city whose grandeur far surpasses Tityrus' previous experience, who has the power to protect the lands he relies on to gain his freedom.[84] At times, Mantuan is capable of such equipoise, most notably in a lovely passage in his eighth eclogue (VIII, 184–89) that portrays as complementary the relationship between pastoral Loreto and the urban pilgrims who flock to it. But far more often he condemns the city on moral and spiritual grounds—the home of shysters, quacks, and libertines (VI, 118–215), a den of predatory monsters (IX, 141–52)—that Mantuan's years at Rome doubtless helped to aggravate. Not that country life is soft or wholly attractive in either Virgil's eclogues or the *Adulescentia*. Candidus' idyllic account of it (IX, 67–77) is, like Meliboeus' lyrical description in Virgil's first eclogue (lines 51–58),[85] less the product of fact than of his present situation. Nevertheless, a spirit of *contemptus mundi* permeates Mantuan's pastoral world to an extent quite alien to the Roman poet: as Fortunatus puts it in the second eclogue, "all good fortune has its joyless sequel" (line 26).

Readers accustomed to Virgil's eclogues will find numerous stylistic qualities that distinguish the eclogues in the *Adulescentia* from ancient pastoral. Unlike Virgil's bucolics, Mantuan's pastorals are all fully dramatized dialogues, by far the most common form in post–classical Latin pastoral. In particular, the fifth, sixth, and tenth eclogues in the *Adulescentia* betray their formal origins in medieval debate literature.[86] Like Mantuan's numerous catalogues of phrases and epithets and his massive accumulation of grotesque exempla—a device which has its formal origins not in pastoral but in the satires of Juvenal[87]—the rhetorical edge inherent in the debate form results at times (as in the latter half of the sixth eclogue) in arid stretches of invective and in a strident tone utterly foreign to Virgil's sense of proportion and use of understatement.

[84] **Col** 79. Coleman's introduction contains a good survey (pp. 1–14, 21–36) of the conventions and major developments in ancient pastoral.

[85] For which, see **Col** 23.

[86] In Latin pastoral the debate form goes back to Theodulus' eclogue, a commonly used school text in the Middle Ages: see George L. Hamilton, "Theodulus: A Medieval Textbook," *MP*, 7 (1909), 174. The subject matter of Mantuan's tenth eclogue—the differences between the observant and nonobservant Carmelites—has its precedent in works such as the *Dialogus inter Cluniacensem et Cisterciensem de diversis utriusque ordinis observantiis* and *Dialogus de clericis sæcularibius et regularibus*: H. Walther, *Das Streitgedicht in der lateinischen Literatur des Mittelalters*, Quellen und Untersuchungen zur lateinischen Philologie des Mittelalters, vol. 2 (Munich: C. H. Beck, 1920), 163. The topic announced in the subtitle of Mantuan's sixth eclogue—the virtues and vices of the city and countryside—is, however, one familiar in Roman culture (see headnote to "Eclogue VI").

[87] Cf., e.g., Juvenal *Sat.* VI, 582–91, 610–26 and Mantuan IV, 151–70 and VI, 198–207. Similar catalogues are found in Petrarch's eclogues (e.g., IV, 45–49).

"Herds grow by piety (*pietate peculia crescunt*)" (VIII, 157), "counsel after action is like rain after harvest time (*consilium post facta, imber post tempora frugium*)" (II, 93)—like his diction,[88] these sometimes mordant aphorisms contribute to a degree of rustic realism in the *Adulescentia* unprecedented in Latin pastoral before his time. It has long since been customary to stress the role of close personal observation in creating this effect.[89] More recently, however, Helen Cooper has suggested some of the ways in which Mantuan's rustic realism participates in a widespread literary trend expressed in France and England in the literature of *bergerie*. Indeed, at times the two influences become difficult to disentangle. Faustus' description of Tonius, the drunken bagpiper of the first eclogue (lines 163–71), has, for instance, been praised as an accurate description of an Italian rustic type.[90] But the bagpipes, along with the feasting and dancing that accompany Faustus' wedding, can all be equally well paralleled in French and English *bergerie* literature.[91]

There is an earthiness and workaday quality about Mantuan's shepherds more pervasive and striking than anything found in previous Latin pastoral. Arcadia's gentle shepherds never castrate sheep and swine (VIII, 19), nor are any of them so explicit about the demands of nature (IV, 87–88). Akin to this workaday aspect, a note of social realism is struck at times—most strikingly in the sixth eclogue (lines 225–33) in the *contadino* Cornix's justification of stealing from predatory city-dwellers—that is unprecedented even in contemporary Italian pastoral. And (a gentler strain) in Pollux's prayer as well as in the description of the statue of the Virgin surrounded by votive offerings (VIII, 122–51, 116–18), Mantuan has introduced elements of the popular religion of his own day[92] to create a pastoral world quite different from Virgil's Arcadia.

But if Mantuan has a keen eye for rustic ways and often delights in them, suffusing the *Adulescentia* there is also the detachment of a sensibility bred in different circumstances and destined for different ends. Most often this attitude shows up in a comic treatment, sometimes light, sometimes

[88] Tolomeo in his *Apologia contra detrahentes operibus B. M.* (*Opera*, IV, i, 102–3) defends his brother's diction as being appropriate to the comic roughness of his speakers. And Badius likewise contends that, on the basis of his diction, Mantuan maintained a more consistent level of pastoral decorum than his master, Virgil (Renouard, *op. cit.*, II, 111).

[89] See, e.g., **Z1** 148.

[90] Francesco Arnaldi, "Introduzione," *Poeti latini del quattrocento* (Milan/Naples: Ricciardi, 1964), xl–xli.

[91] Helen Cooper, *Pastoral: Medieval into Renaissance* (Ipswich: D. S. Brewer, 1977), 55, 56–57. The comic and domestic tone unique in earlier Latin pastoral to Boccaccio's eclogues may, as Janet Smarr suggests, have encouraged Mantuan's extensive use of anecdotes, homey images, and humorous turns of phrase: Giovanni Boccaccio, *Eclogues*, trans. Janet Levarie Smarr (New York: Garland Pub., 1987), lxiii.

[92] See the headnote to "Eclogue VIII." Hans Trümpy has inquired into this subject in his edition of Mantuan's *Fausti* (also known as *De sacris diebus*): *Die Fasti des Baptista Mantuanus von 1516 als volkskundliche Quelle* (Nieukoop: de Graaf, 1979).

more heavy–handed, of characters and situations in the eclogues (e.g., I, 148–51; IV, 87–88). At times, however, one can hear the severer accents of the well–bred city–dweller's patronizing tone (e.g., VIII, 28–39) and even the scorn of the nascent monk (e.g., II, 66–75).

Mantuan's pastoral world is a more localized realm than is Virgil's blending of Sicily, Greece, and northern Italy. Characters are associated with specific regions—Aegon of Val Sasina, Harcules returning from Verona—and Mantuan catalogues the landscape surrounding his native city far more thoroughly and consistently than does Virgil. Yet, more often than not, these details serve purposes other than simply helping to establish a scene. At the beginning of the second eclogue, for instance, Fortunatus' description of the Po's overflowing presents an image of turmoil introductory to the account of Amyntas' spiritual disorder. And Amyntas' sojourn through "Coitus" (II, 40) to Solferino, that "tower of sulphur," sets up signposts that foreshadow his downfall.[93]

There are, in fact, three Arcadias in Mantuan's eclogues. In addition to the realm of Faustus, Fortunatus, and their like, we find, for one, the primitive Carmelite community described in the seventh and tenth eclogues (VII, 124–31; X, 70–73, 145–53). Long since woven by the Church Fathers into their vision of the monastic life,[94] the main precedent in ancient pastoral for this second Arcadia is Virgil's messianic fourth eclogue. But where Virgil's Golden Age is to be embodied in this world, the monastic life urged on Pollux in the seventh eclogue is only partial and provisional,[95] a paradise that is meant to lead to a third, otherworldly Arcadia (VII, 132–40)[96] whose nymphs

---

[93] A similarly symbolic function is served by the storm that closes the second eclogue—a purpose obscured by Zabughin (Z_2 245), who stresses the specific and concrete qualities that distinguish it from the conclusions of Virgil's eclogues.

[94] See, e.g., Basil the Great, the organizer of Eastern monasticism:

> I am living . . . in the wilderness wherein the Lord dwelt. . . . Here is Mount Carmel where Elijah abode and pleased God. Here is the plain whither Ezra withdrew, and at God's bidding poured forth from his mouth all his divinely inspired books. Here is the wilderness where the blessed John ate locusts and preached repentance to men. Here is the Mount of Olives, which Christ ascended and there prayed, teaching us how to pray. . . . Here is the narrow and strait way that leadeth to life. Here are teachers and prophets, "wandering in deserts, in mountains, and in dens, and in caves of the earth" [Heb. 11:38]. Here are apostles and evangelists and the life of monks, citizens of the desert.

Quoted in Williams, *op. cit.*, 39.

[95] Conversely, by cutting Bembus' concluding vision (lines 122–34, in "Appendix I") from the revised version of his tenth eclogue, Mantuan intensifies the emphasis on constant, long term struggle to achieve an eremitic paradise within this world: see "Appendix I."

[96] A description based on the fusion of Christ's words on the cross, "this day thou shalt be with me in paradise" (Luke 23:43), the myth that placed the earthly paradise on a high mountain (see VIII, 44–46n) and the specific significance of Mount Carmel in Mantuan's religious order (*Dictionnaire de spiritualité*, II, 157–58). Within pastoral poetry Boccaccio had already portrayed an otherworldly mountaintop paradise (*Ecl.* XIV, 170–96; XV, 156–64, 179–88). The implied link in Mantuan's eclogues between paradise and the monastic cell, seen also in, e.g., Radbert's *Ecloga duarum sanctimonialium* (lines 98–99, in *Seven Versions of*

inhabit celestial groves.

For all this, Mantuan is at least as interested in life here and now as in the next world. A main theme of the *Adulescentia,* announced in the first lines and reiterated throughout the collection, is the constant need for toil and vigilance in a difficult, often dangerous world. Leisure has its proper time and function—it can even be used to insure watchfulness (I, 1–5)—but it should always be blended with labor (X, 18) and, indeed, labor and hardship sweeten it (VI, 42). The prime force disturbing toil and watchfulness in Mantuan's eclogues as in Virgil's is love. Not only, as Fortunatus argues, does it impede the acquisition of wealth and land (II, 115–19); in the shepherds' world where existence itself is always in doubt, love can lead to starvation and ruin (III, 57–88). Against Fortunatus' arguments are placed Amyntas' description of love as the union of two hearts (III, 93–102) and the opposition he draws between free love and honor (II, 156–67). While this opposition introduced into pastoral poetry elements of a so-called "soft primitivism" that were to find their best known expression in the first chorus of Tasso's *Aminta,*[97] it nonetheless seems clear that Mantuan by no means intended his reader to accept them uncritically. In distorting psychological probabilities by having Amyntas speak of spiritual union with a girl who doesn't even know he loves her (III, 128–29), Mantuan is stressing the extent to which love can become a selfish infatuation that makes a man look like a fool. In this respect Jannus' tale of the lovesick shepherd boy (IV, 20–75) functions as a pendant to Amyntas' tragedy, the foolish state the boy finds himself in, having fallen into a wolfpit, functioning as a farcical restatement of the condition to which Amyntas has been driven. But like Jannus' boy Amyntas has also become less than a man, figuratively a wild beast. Much more insistently than do Virgil's eclogues, Mantuan's *Adulescentia* stresses that love is a hidden fire, a madness that, blinding the eye of reason, cancels out the faculty separating men from wild animals.

Women set off this process: as Umber remarks, they are the Medusas who change men to stone (IV, 239–41). Although there are occasional strains of misogyny in ancient pastoral,[98] to Mantuan belongs the dubious honor of having introduced misogynistic satire wholesale into the genre. Nonetheless, despite Umber's notorious attack on women in the fourth eclogue (lines 110–241)[99] —a tirade ranging far beyond their direct effect on men—women

Carolingian Pastoral, ed. R. P. H. Green [Univ. of Reading Press, 1980], 23), dates back to Jerome and the Eastern Church Fathers: see Williams, *op. cit.,* 38–46 and Gerhart Ladner, *The Idea of Reform: Its Impact on Christian Thought and Action in the Age of the Fathers* (Cambridge: Harvard Univ. Press, 1959), 77–78, 147.

[97] *Aminta,* ed. Luigi Fassò, 5th ed. (Florence: Sansoni, 1963), 35-38. Citing this link with Mantuan's eclogue, Mustard points out (57) that Tasso's chorus was translated into English by Samuel Daniel (*Works,* ed. A. B. Grosart [London: Hazell, Watson and Viney, 1885–96], I, 260–62). Henry Reynolds also has a translation (reprinted with a discussion of the topic by Frank Kermode in *English Pastoral Poetry: From the Beginnings to Marvell* [London: George Harrap, 1952], 81–83, 241), and Thomas Carew adapted Tasso's first chorus in his "A Rapture" (*Poems,* ed. Rhodes Dunlap [Oxford: Clarendon Press, 1949], 49–53).

[98] See Calp., III, 10 and Virg., *Ecl.* VIII, 47–50; also *G.* III, 212–18.

cannot ultimately be held responsible for the foolishness and suffering that in the *Adulescentia* almost invariably accompany them. In the final analysis, Faustus, Amyntas, and Jannus' shepherd boy are all fallible and all choose their own lot. They become the makers of their folly rather than simply Love's passive victims.

And, of course, not all kinds of love are destructive or culpable in the *Adulescentia*. The titles that Mantuan gives to the first three eclogues indicate a distinction that he established between Amyntas' self–destructive passion and Faustus' honorable love (*honestus amor*) that finds its end in marriage. Indeed, in forging a reconciliation between pastoral love and marriage in "Eclogue I," Mantuan boldly entered onto ground that Virgil had left untrodden. But, for a full evaluation of Faustus's love, one must look beyond the opening eclogues to the design of Mantuan's collection as a whole.

Despite the episodic nature of its composition, a number of threads unite the published text of the *Adulescentia*. Themes and images recur: love, founts and streams, the city and the countryside, mountains and lowlands, hellish and bestial places, a fondness for the old days and ways, and reverence for the wisdom of our fathers. Moreover, the settings of the eclogues are so arranged as to give a roughly sequential and comprehensive impression of the countryman's life at various seasons of the year.[100] The pivot on which the collection as a whole turns is the seventh eclogue, which initiates a development of viewpoint carried through the succeeding eclogues by no single character but, as the headnotes indicate ("Eclogue VII" being composed "when the author is already aspiring to enter religious orders," the ninth and tenth eclogues "after his entry into religious orders"), by Mantuan as the implied author of the *Adulescentia*.[101] In the seventh and eighth eclogues Pollux embodies the first stage of this development as, discovering the wellspring of his salvation in the Virgin Mary's warning and exhortation, he reorients himself from an exclusive concern with this world towards a discovery of the full importance of the life of the spirit. From this movement inwards, Candidus and especially Batrachus in the last two eclogues initiate a movement outwards, attempting to find a life on earth fully consonant with

[99] The passage embarrassed even Mantuan's English translators. As George Turberville notes, drawing a distinction absent from Alphus' report: "Let never honest Lucrece lowre, / let not Grisell grutch: / For neither Alphus here, nor I / the modest matrone toutch." *The Eclogues of Mantuan*, ed. Douglas Bush (New York: Scholars' Facsimiles and Reprints, 1937), sig. E3v.

[100] The first three eclogues are all set in springtime (I, 172–73; II, 12–13). "Eclogue V" is suffused with the impending physical hardships of late autumn (see, e.g., line 24), and the sixth eclogue announces that winter has arrived in earnest (lines 1–27). The eighth and ninth eclogues bring us back to late spring and summer (VIII, 1; IX, 94–101); and, balancing the first eclogue's vernal setting, "Eclogue X" returns us to a wintry scene (lines 13–17).

[101] For a further discussion of the organization of Mantuan's collection, see Lee Piepho, "The Organization of Mantuan's *Adulescentia* and Spenser's *Shepheardes Calendar*: A Comparison," in *Acta Conventus Neo–Latini Bononiensis: Proceedings of the Fourth International Congress of Neo–Latin Studies*, ed. R. J. Schoeck (Binghamton, N. Y.: Medieval and Renaissance Texts and Studies, 1985), 577–82.

the soul's demands. The description of Mount Carmel in Mantuan's seventh eclogue (lines 124–40) holds the key to the conclusion of this development, as, first juxtaposed in the ninth eclogue with the scorched earth of a degenerate Rome, in the tenth eclogue it is explicitly developed by Batrachus in the primitive ideal which the Carmelite order must struggle to recapture and institute among themselves in this world.

Seen from the point of view of these concluding four eclogues, Amyntas' frantic ramblings (III, 144) thus take on more serious overtones, recalling as they do the goal toward which Pollux was moving (VII, 106–8) and Bembus' concluding admonition to call home flocks that are wandering among the haunts of savage beasts (X, 202–3). Indeed, even Faustus' *honestus amor* must finally concede higher place to the religious devotion exemplified by Pollux in the later eclogues. Compared with the exalted tone that characterizes his encounter with the Virgin Mary, the amused, slightly detached tone in which Faustus' affair is presented (e.g., I, 148–51) conveys a qualitatively different evaluation of the two kinds of love.[102]

Especially in comparison with much of Mantuan's later verse, the *Adulescentia* is one of his most unified and polished pieces. It is also, as the headnotes and the letter to his father indicate, a quite personal work. Yet the relation between Mantuan's seventh eclogue and the material in his letter is by no means a simple one. Setting aside discrepancies in detail, the conversion pattern uniting the experiences of Pollux and the young Mantuan has what is surely an intentional ring of familiarity to it. In part, this sense of *dejà vu* confirms that God's ways of choosing his elect repeat themselves throughout history, a seal that identifies Pollux and Mantuan as belonging to that line of elect spirits that stretches back to Augustine, Jerome, and Paul. And in Pollux's case this recurrence of similar elements is a pledge, a promise that as God has repeated himself in the past, so he will continue to extend his hand in recognizable because similar ways to present and future generations. Experience then both in Mantuan's letter and the seventh eclogue is significant as the revelation of general patterns and, more, as testimony to the link binding earth and heaven, this life with the world to come.[103] Mantuan's letter to his father is openly rhetorical, a singleminded effort to convince him of the wisdom of his choice; and in its revised form Mantuan's collection of eclogues also has designs on the moral and visionary resources of its readers. A diversity of subjects—the poverty of poets, the ways of erotic

102 Mantuan's exaltation of devotion to the Virgin Mary over erotic love may, as Janet Smarr points out (*Boccaccio's Eclogues*, lxiii), have been influenced by a similar structural displacement of erotic by divine love in Boccaccio's fourteenth eclogue. The distinction Mantuan draws in the opening three eclogues between good and bad erotic love is to be contrasted with the obsessively otherworldly mood that suffuses Boccaccio's displacement of erotic love, however, as is his concern with worldly corruption and an achievable eremitic ideal in the last two eclogues of the *Adulescentia*.

103 For the background of this redemptive power of historical events as they are recreated in the lives of individuals, see A. C. Charity, *Events and their Afterlife: The Dialectics of Christian Typology in the Bible and Dante* (Cambridge Univ. Press, 1966), 8, 158–64.

love, the origins of country folk—enriches the eclogues. And more important, a diversity of qualifying, sometimes conflicting perspectives informs the collection. Women may seem frivolous, but the men who encourage them are still more fallible (I, 79–80, 85–87). Mountains may be holy places, but the people who dwell there lead difficult, desperate lives (VIII, 42–59, 63–66). For all this, in its final form the *Adulescentia* shows Mantuan's overriding concern, as he expressed it late in life, to bring poetry in all its winding ways back again to serve the teachings of Christ.[104]

Granted this essential unity of intention, the impression of diversity within the collection nevertheless remains. That the eclogues were composed at different periods in Mantuan's life accounts only in part for this multifaceted quality. More important is his seemingly insatiable curiosity to try out different styles, material, and points of view—coupled at times, the reader might feel, with a lack of proportion or due consideration for unity of effect. From romantic love to corruption within the Papal Curia, from the allegorical technique popularized by Petrarch and Boccaccio to the rustic realism of the literature of *bergerie*, Mantuan's *Adulescentia* develops most of the possibilities open to pastoral in his time. For this very reason it became along with Virgil's eclogues a textbook within the developing educational program of the Northern humanists used in part to teach what pastoral should be. In time, however, the extremes of realism and allegory came to offend. Scaliger complains that Mantuan's world is too rustic for pastoral,[105] and Fontenelle is repelled by the corporeal realism of his description of Galla.[106] Pope finds the religious eclogues too allegorical,[107] and Doctor Johnson thunders against shepherds who are priests in poetic disguise.[108] At this point, the influence and esteem accorded to Mantuan's *Adulescentia* have at long last come to an end.

---

104 *"Multivagam Christo feci servire poesim. . . ."* From the *Vitae suae epitome* (*Opera*, II, 387).

105 The main point of his influential attack on Mantuan's poetry: see Fred J. Nichols, "The Development of Neo-Latin Theory of Pastoral in the Sixteenth Century," *HumLov*, 18 (1969), 112.

106 In his "Discours sur la nature de l'eclogue," *Œuvres* (Paris: n.p.,, 1790–92), V, 9. Alphus' sojourn in IV, 87 likewise drew Fontenelle's disapproval.

107 In his "Discourse on Pastoral Poetry," *Poems*, ed. John Butt (New Haven, Yale Univ. Press, 1963), 122.

108 As a necessary condition for good pastoral Johnson notes that

> . . . the occasion which is supposed to produce it, be at least not inconsistent with a country life, or less likely to interest those who have retired into places of solitude and quiet, than the more busy part of mankind. It is therefore improper to give the title of pastoral to verses, in which the speakers, after the slight mention of their flocks, fall to complaints of the errors in the church. . . .

Works, vol. III (*The Rambler*), eds. Walter Jackson Bate and Albrecht B. Strauss (New Haven: Yale Univ. Press, 1969), 204–5.

TEXT AND TRANSLATION

Frater Baptista Mantuanus Carmelita
Paridi Ceresario D. S.

Audi, o Pari, aenigma perplexum quod Oedipodes ipse non solveret. ego quinquagenarius et iam canescens adulescentiam meam repperi, et habeo adulescentiam simul et senectam. sed ne longa ambage te teneam, nodum hunc dissolvo. anno praeterito, cum Florentia rediens Bononiam pervenissem, intellexi apud quendam litterarium virum esse quendam libellum meum quem olim ante religionem, dum in gymnasio Paduano philosophari inciperem, ludens excuderam et ab illa aetate Adulescentiam vocaveram. carmen est bucolicum in octo eclogas divisum, quod iam diu tamquam abortivum putabam abolitum. ubi id rescivi, Saturnina fame repente sum percitus, et cogitavi quonam pacto possem proli meae inferre perniciem. iuvantibus ergo amicis libellum meum vindicavi, ut perderem quem suspicabar erratis non posse non scatere. at ubi intellexi et alia quaedam exemplaria superesse, visum est praestare hoc quod vindicaram emendare emendatumque edere, ut eius editione cetera quae continent multa nimis iuvenilia deleantur. hoc igitur sic castigatum duabus aliis eclogis quas in religione lusi in calce subiunctis tibi, o Pari, iuvenis antiquae nobilitatis et studiorum ac omnium bonarum artium amantissime nostraeque urbis decus egregium, libentissime dono, ut, quando tetricis illis philosophiae ac theologiae lucubrationibus quibus assidue vacas fatigatus fueris, habeas iucundulam hanc lectiunculam qua tamquam ludo quodam blandulo sed liberali lassum legendo reparetur ingenium. omnes autem penes quos immatura illa sunt exemplaria quae dixi rogatos volo ut, si quid umquam fuit eis dulce meum, confestim exurant nec ullo pacto superesse permittant. accipe ergo, Pari suavissime, libellum et auctorem, et ambobus tamquam rebus tuis tuo deinceps utaris arbitrio. vale. Kalendis Septembris, MCCCCLXXXXVIII.

To Paride Ceresara
Baptista Mantuanus O. C.
Sends His Greetings

Hearken, oh Paride, to an entangled ænigma that Oedipus himself might not have unraveled. Fifty years old and already growing grey, I have found my youth again and simultaneously possess both youth and old age. But lest I detain you with a lengthy digression, I shall unravel this knot. Last year when returning from Florence I had come to Bologna, I understood that there was in the house of a certain man of letters a small book of mine that long ago, before I had entered religious orders, when I was beginning my studies in philosophy at the school at Padua, I had composed as a diversion and had called *Youth*, taking the title from that period in my life. The collection of poems is bucolic in character and is divided into eight eclogues. Born prematurely, as it were, it is a work that I thought had been destroyed long ago. So, when I learned of it, I was suddenly roused by Saturn's hunger and pondered the means by which I might be able to bring about my progeny's obliteration. Thus through the help of friends I laid claim to my little book in order to suppress it, a work that I suspected could not help but abound in errors. But when I learned that certain other copies also existed, it seemed better to emend the one I had laid claim to and publish it so that through its publication the other copies, which contain much that is too youthful, might be destroyed. Therefore, this work, thus corrected with the addition at the end of two other eclogues that I composed after entering religious orders, I present with the greatest pleasure to you, oh Paride—youth of ancient nobility, deeply devoted to learning in all the liberal arts, outstanding ornament of our city—so that when you have been wearied by those philosophical and theological works to which you continually devote yourself, you might have this pleasant book as light reading, a work by which, as by an agreeable yet honorable diversion, you might renew your wearied mind. Moreover, I desire everyone possessing those copies that I have called premature, if anything of mine has ever been pleasing to them, to burn those copies forthwith at my request and by no means to allow them to survive. Take then to yourself, most delightful Paride, this little book, and its author, and may you employ both of them in turn according to your judgment as though they were your own. Farewell.

September 1, 1498

ECLOGA I
FAUSTUS
De honesto amore et felici eius exitu

Fortunatus Faustus

For. Fauste, precor, gelida quando pecus omne sub umbra
ruminat, antiquos paulum recitemus amores,
ne, si forte sopor nos occupet, ulla ferarum
quae modo per segetes tacite insidiantur adultas
saeviat in pecudes; melior vigilantia somno.
Fau. Hic locus, haec eadem sub qua requiescimus arbor
scit quibus ingemui curis, quibus ignibus arsi
ante duos vel (ni memini male) quattuor annos;
sed tibi, quando vacat, quando est iucunda relatu,
historiam prima repetens ab origine pandam.
Hic ego, dum sequere primis armenta sub annis,
veste solo strata sedi iacuique supinus
cum gemitu et lacrimis mea tristia fata revolvens.
nulla quies mihi dulcis erat, nullus labor; aegro
pectore sensus iners, et mens torpore sepulta
ut stomachus languentis erat quem nulla ciborum
blandimenta movent, quem nulla invitat orexis.
carminis occiderat studium, iam nulla sonabat
fistula disparibus calamis; odiosus et arcus,
funda odiosa, canes odiosi, odiosa volucrum
praeda, nucum calyces cultro enucleare molestum;
texere fiscellam iunco vel vimine, piscem
fallere, scrutari nidos, certare palaestra,
sortiri digitis res iniucunda, voluptas
magna prius, tanti dum mens erat inscia morbi.
colligere agrestes uvas et fraga perosus
maerebam ut pastu rediens philomena cibumque
ore ferens natis, vacuo sua pignora nido
cum sublata videt: rostro cadit esca remisso,
cor stupet et contra nidos super arboris altae
fronde sedet plorans infelices hymenaeos;
seu veluti amisso partu formosa iuvenca
quae, postquam latos altis mugitibus agros
complevit, residens pallenti sola sub umbra
gramina non carpit nec fluminis attrahit undam.
Sed quid circuitu pario tibi taedia longo,
dum sequor ambages et verba et tempora perdo?
summa haec: vitales auras invitus agebam.
quod si forte volens cognoscere singula dicas,
"Fauste, quis in syrtes Auster te impegerat istas?"

ECLOGUE I
FAUSTUS
Honorable Love and Its Happy Outcome
Fortunatus Faustus

For. Faustus, while the cattle all lie chewing their cud in the cool shade, I pray you let us tell a little about our loves of old lest, if sleep perchance overwhelm us, any of the wild beasts that now lurk secretly in ambush within the ripened wheat fields should rage against the herd. Watchfulness is better than sleep.
Fau. This place, this very tree beneath which we are resting, knows with what cares I sighed, with what fires I burned two or (unless memory fails me) four years ago. But since there is time and the tale is pleasing to tell, going back to its beginnings, I will lay open my story for you.

[11] Here, when in my youth I followed the herd, I sat on my coat spread upon the ground and lay on my back, pondering my sad fate with many a sigh and tear. No repose or toil was sweet to me. My emotions were dulled by a sickness of heart, my mind was overcome by torpor, like the stomach of a sick man that none of food's enticements arouse, that no appetite attracts. [18] My love of song had perished, my pipe's uneven reeds sounded no more. Hateful too was my bow, hateful my sling, hateful my hounds and the spoils of my birds; irksome it was to pick out nutmeats with my knife. Weaving a basket with rushes or twigs, ensnaring fish, searching out birds' nests, competing at wrestling and *morra*—unpleasant things now, these were all great pleasures before, when my heart knew not such a sickness. Loathing to gather wild grapes and strawberries, I lamented like a nightingale returning from feeding and bearing food in her beak for her young when she sees that her darlings have been borne away from the empty nest. The food falls from her loosened beak, her heart is struck dumb and, facing the nests, she perches on the branch of a tall tree lamenting her ill-fated marriage. Or like a comely heifer when her calf has been lost: after filling the wide fields with her low bellowing, down she sinks alone in the wan shadows, and does not crop the grass or drink the waters of the stream.

[36] But why am I causing tedious ramblings, while I digress and waste both words and time? The sum of the matter is this: against my will I breathed the life-giving breezes. But if, desiring perchance to know the details, you should ask: "What manner of south wind dashed you against those sandbanks?" my

me mea (verum etenim tibi, Fortunate, fatebor)
me mea Galla suo sic circumvenerat ore
ut captam pedicis circumdat aranea muscam.
namque erat ore rubens et pleno turgida vultu
et, quamvis oculo paene esset inutilis uno,
cum tamen illius faciem mirabar et annos,
dicebam Triviae formam nihil esse Dianae.
For. Ludit Amor sensus, oculos praestringit et aufert
libertatem animi et mira nos fascinat arte;
credo aliquis daemon subiens praecordia flammam
concitet et raptam tollat de cardine mentem.
nec deus (ut perhibent) Amor est, sed amaror et error.
Fau. Adde quod optatis nec spes erat ulla potiri,
quamvis illa meo miserata faveret amori
monstraretque suos oculis ac nutibus ignes.
nam, quocumque isset, semper comes aspera: semper
nupta sequebatur soror et durissima mater.
sicque repugnabant votis contraria vota
non secus ac muri catus: ille invadere pernam
nititur, hic rimas oculis observat acutis.
For. Qui satur est pleno laudat ieiunia ventre,
et quem nulla premit sitis est sitientibus asper.
Fau. Tempus erat curva segetes incidere falce
et late albebant flaventibus hordea culmis.
affuit (ut mos est) natis comitata duabus
collectura parens quae praeterit hordea messor,
ignorabat enim vel dissimulabat amorem;
dissimulasse puto, quoniam data munera natae
noverat, exiguum leporem geminasque palumbes.
For. Pauperies inimica bonis est moribus; omne
labitur in vitium, culpae scelerumque ministra est.
Fau. Farra legens ibat mea per vestigia virgo
nuda pedem, discincta sinum, spoliata lacertos,
ut decet aestatem quae solibus ardet iniquis,
tecta caput fronde intorta, quia sole perusta
fusca fit et voto facies non servit amantum.
iam tergo vicina meo laterique propinqua
sponte mea delapsa manu frumenta legebat.
nec celare suas nec vincere femina curas
nec differre potest; tantum levitatis in illa est.
For. Quisquis amat levis est, nec femina sola sed ipsi
quos sapere et praestare aliis mortalibus aiunt,
quos operit latus fulgenti murice clavus,
quos vidi elatos regali incedere passu.
tu quoque sic affectus eras dementior illa
forsitan et levior. virgo data farra legebat,

Galla (for indeed, Fortunatus, I will confess the truth to you), my Galla thus ensnared me with her looks as a spider encircles a captured fly with its snares. For her face was ruddy and stout, and though she was almost blind in one eye, all the same when I marveled at her good looks and youth I used to say that in comparison triform Diana's beauty was of no account.

For. Love deceives the senses, blinds the eye, steals away the mind's freedom, and bewitches us with his wondrous art. I am convinced that some demon, stealing into our hearts, stirs up a flame there and unhinges our ravished thoughts. Nor is love a god (as men say) but bitterness and error!

Fau. [53] Add to this that there was no hope of possessing what I desired though, having pitied my love, Galla looked with favor on it and by glances and nods revealed the fires of her love. For wherever she went, there always went a stern companion: always her married sister and strict mother followed her. Thus desire opposed desire as a cat does a mouse: the mouse strives to get at the ham; keen–eyed, the cat watches over the chinks in the wall.

For. The well–fed commend fasting. Those whom no thirst oppresses are cruel towards the thirsty.

Fau. [63] It was the season to mow the crops with our curved scythes, for far and wide the barley grains seemed white on their golden stalks. As is the custom, Galla's mother was there, accompanied by her two daughters, to glean the barley that the reaper had passed over. For she was either ignorant of our love or hid her knowledge of it. I think that she hid her knowledge since she knew of the gifts—a small rabbit and twin wood–pigeons—I had given her daughter.

For. Poverty is the enemy of good character. It lapses into every vice and ministers to guilt and crime.

Fau. [72] Gleaning grain, the girl followed my footsteps: barefoot, her dress loosened at her breasts, her arms stripped bare as befits summer when the sun blazes cruelly. A twisted garland of leaves covered her head, since a sunburned face becomes swarthy and does not serve a lover's wishes. Now at my back and near my side Galla gleaned the grain that I willingly let slip from my hand. A woman is unable to hide, overcome, or put off her love—so much is the frivolity in her.

For. [81] Whoever falls in love is frivolous: not women alone but even those who people say are wise and surpass other mortals, men cloaked in a broad stripe of gleaming purple, proud men whom I have seen walk with a regal step. You too, thus afflicted, were more mad and perhaps more frivolous than Galla. The girl gathered the grain given to her, but you gave

at tu farra dabas; dic, quae dementia maior?
perge; opus est verbis aliquando arcere soporem.
Fau. Continuo aspiciens aegre tulit aspera mater
et clamans "quo," dixit, "abis? cur deseris agmen?
Galla, veni, namque hic alnos prope mitior umbra,
hic tremulas inter frondes immurmurat aura."
o invisa meis vox auribus! "ite," precabar,
"ite, malam venti celeres dispergite vocem."
si quis pastor oves ad pinguia pascua ducat
et vetet adductas praesens decerpere gramen,
vel si iam pastas potum compellat ad amnem
et sitibundo ori salientem deneget undam,
nonne importunus, naturae inimicus et excors?
illa mihi vox visa Iovis violentior ira
cum tonat et pluvius terris irascitur aer.
non potui (et volui) frontem non flectere; virgo
demissi in cilium de sub velaminis ora
me aspiciens motis blande subrisit ocellis.
id cernens iterum natam vocat improba mater;
Galla operi magis intendens audire recusat.
ut pede, sic animo sequitur. tum providus ipse
(namque dolos inspirat Amor fraudesque ministrat)
nunc cantu, nunc sollictans clamore metentes
velamenta dabam sceleri, quo credere possent
et soror et mater non audivisse puellam.
falce repellebam sentes, ne crura sequentis
levia, ne teneras ausint offendere plantas.
For. Quisquis amat servit: sequitur captivus amantem,
fert domita cervice iugum, fert verbera tergo
dulcia, fert stimulos, trahit et bovis instar aratrum.
Fau. Tu quoque, ut hinc video, non es ignarus amorum.
For. Id commune malum, semel insanivimum omnes.
Fau. Hoc animi tam triste bonum, tam dulce venenum,
cottidie crudele magis crescebat in horas,
ut calor, in nonam dum lux attollitur horam.
pallebam attonito similis, lymphaticus, amens,
immemor, insomnis. nec erat res ardua morbi
nosse genus; frons est animi mutabilis index.
ut pater advertit, mitem se praebuit ultra
consuetum, quod et ipse suos expertus amorum
sciret onus, blandoque loquens humaniter ore
"dic," inquit, "dic, Fauste, quid hoc quod pectore volvis?
infelix puer, haec facies testatur amorem.
dic mihi; ne pudeat curas aperire parenti."
For. Sit licet in natos facies austera parentum,
aequa tamen semper mens est, et amica voluntas.

her the grain. Tell me, which was the greater madness? But go on—at times we need words to keep slumber away.

Fau. [89] Immediately seeing Galla, her cruel mother was vexed and shouting said, "Where are you going? Why are you leaving the group? Come, Galla, for here near the alders the shade is gentler, here the breezes murmur among the trembling leaves." Oh voice hateful to my ears! "Go, swift winds," I prayed, "go and scatter her harmful words!" If a shepherd should lead his sheep to fertile pasture lands and at once forbid them to graze; or if, having already pastured them, he should drive them to the river to drink and deny the dancing waters to their thirsty mouths, wouldn't he be selfish, stupid, and contrary to nature? [100] That voice of hers seemed more savage to me than Jupiter's rage when he thunders and the rain–filled air rages at the earth. I couldn't help but turn my face (and I wanted to), and the girl, gazing from under the edge of her chaplet, smiled alluringly at me with her dancing eyes. Seeing this, Galla's mother (that wretch!) called her again. Galla, applying herself still more to her task, refused to hear. As with her feet, so with her thoughts she followed me. Then, having become cautious myself (for Love inspires trickery and provides for deception), urging on the mowers now with a song, now with a shout, I so veiled our crime that both her sister and mother might believe that the girl hadn't heard them. With my scythe I drove back the brambles lest they dare strike her smooth legs or tender feet as she followed me.

For. [114] He who loves also serves: he follows his lover as a captive, endures the yoke on his conquered neck, endures her sweet scourging and goading, and like an ox he draws the plow.

Fau. You too, as I perceive from this, are not ignorant of love.

For. 'Tis a universal evil. We have all been crazy once.

Fau. [119] This treasure so grievous to my mind, this venom so sweet grew daily more cruel with each hour, like heat when the sun reaches its height at midday. Like a dazed man I became pale, frenzied, distracted, forgetful, and sleepless. Nor was it hard to learn what kind of illness it was. The face is the changeable indicator of our thoughts. When my father observed this, he became gentler than usual since, having experienced love, he too knew its burden. And speaking gently to me with encouraging words he said, "Tell me, Faustus, what is this that you are pondering in your heart? Unhappy lad, this look of yours bears witness to your love. Tell me, don't be ashamed to reveal your cares to your father."

For. [131] Though parents' looks may be harsh towards their children, their thoughts are always kind and their dispositions friendly.

Fau. Ut facilem pater affectum prae se tulit, ultro
rem confessus opem petii. promisit; et ante
quam brumale gelu Borealibus arva pruinis
spargaret, agnati unanimes cum patre puellam
despondere mihi. nec adhuc sine testibus illi
congrediebar; eram medio sitibundus in amne
Tantalus. o quotiens misso cum bobus aratro,
ut vacuis aliquando esset sola aedibus, ibam!
omnia causabar, stivam, dentale iugumque,
lora iugi, rullam; deerant quaecumque, petebam
e soceri lare. sola tamen deerat mihi virgo.
non deeram mihi; piscator, venator et auceps
factus eram, et sollers studia intermissa resumpsi.
quidquid erat praedae, quidquid fortuna tulisset,
ad soceros ibat; gener officiosus habebar.
nocte semel media subeuntem limina furtim
(sic etenim pactus fueram cum virgine) furem
esse rati invasere canes; ego protinus altam
transiliens saepem vix ora latrantia fugi.
His tandem studiis hiemem transegimus illam.
ver rediit, iam silva viret, iam vinea frondet,
iam spicata Ceres, iam cogitat hordea messor,
splendidulis iam nocte volant lampyrides alis;
ecce dies genialis adest, mihi ducitur uxor.
sed quid opus multis? nox exspectata duobus
venit, et in portum vento ratis acta secundo est.
tum bove mactato gemina convivia luce
sub patula instructis celebravimus arbore mensis.
affuit Oenophilus multoque solutus Iaccho
tempestiva dedit toti spectacula vico.
et cum multifori Tonius cui tibia buxo
tandem post epulas et pocula multicolorem
ventriculum sumpsit, buccasque inflare rubentes
incipiens oculos aperit ciliisque levatis
multotiensque altis flatu a pulmonibus hausto
utrem implet, cubito vocem dat tibia presso.
nunc huc, nunc illuc digito saliente vocavit
pinguibus a mensis iuvenes ad compita cantu
saltidico dulcique diem certamine clausit.
et iam tres hiemes abiere et proximat aestas
quarta: dies rapidis, si qua est bona, praeterit horis.
si qua placent, abeunt; inimica tenacius haerent.
For. Fauste, viden? vicina percus vineta subintrat;
iam (ne forte gravi multa taxemur) eundum est.

Fau. When my father had shown his sympathy, I asked his help, having freely confessed my love. He gave his promise, and before the chill of winter had sprinkled the fields with Boreas' hoarfrost, my relatives together with him betrothed the girl to me. And I still was not meeting with her unescorted—I was Tantalus, parched by thirst in the middle of a river. Oh, how many times did I go, having left the plow and oxen, wishing for her to be alone at some time or other in the empty house! [141] I made all sorts of excuses: the plow–handle, the share–beam, the yoke and its straps, the plowstaff—whatever was lacking I sought from her father's house. All the same, I still lacked her presence alone. Yet I was not lacking to myself: I became a fisherman, hunter, and fowler and skillfully took up pursuits again that I had interrupted. Whatever game I caught, whatever good fortune brought me went to her family—I was thought a dutiful son–in–law. At midnight once when secretly approaching her door (for I had agreed to this with Galla) the dogs, having taken me for a thief, set upon me. At once, clearing a high hedge, with much ado I fled their barking jaws.

[152] With such activities we at length passed that winter. Spring returned, now the woods grew green again and the vineyards leafy; now the wheat put forth its ears, and now the reaper gave thought to his barley, and now the glowworms flew about at night on their little glimmering wings. And behold! our wedding day arrived, my wife is brought to me. But why say more? The night hoped for by both of us arrived, and my bark was driven into port by favorable winds. Then, having slain an ox, we celebrated with a two–day feast at tables prepared under a broad–spreading tree. [161] Oenophilus was there and, freed from cares by drinking a good deal of wine, provided fit cheer for the whole village. And when Tonius, whose pipes are made of many–holed boxwood, after feasting and drinking took up his varicolored bagpipe, and, beginning to puff up his reddening cheeks, opened wide his eyes and when, having raised his eyelids and many times drained the breath from the depths of his lungs, he had filled the bag, the pipe, pressed by his elbow, gave out its sound. [169] His fingers dancing here and there, he called the lads and lasses from their richly provided tables to the crossroads with a song for dancing, and with friendly contests he thus closed up the day. And now three winters have gone and a fourth summer approaches—if a day is fortunate, its hours pass swiftly away. If a thing pleases, it passes away. Hostile things cling closer to us.

For. [175] Faustus, do you see? Our herd is stealing into the neighboring vineyards! Now, lest perchance we be punished with a heavy fine, we must go!

ECLOGA II
FORTUNATUS
De amoris insania
Faustus Fortunatus

Fau. Cur tam serus ades? quid te (iam septima lux est)
detinuit? gregibusne nocent haec pascua vestris?
For. Fauste, Padus nostros qui praeterlabitur agros
creverat et tumidis ripas aequaverat undis;
nos, cura gregis omissa, privata coegit
publicaque utilitas ripam munire diurnis
nocturnisque operis fluviumque arcere furentem.
Fau. Fert Padus exundans mala saepius omina: noster
Tityrus est auctor, qui pascua dixit et arva.
For. Forsitan id verum, quando extra tempora et ultra
mensuram atque modum subito concreverit aestu.
nunc autem id poscit tempus, nam liquitur altis
nix hiberna iugis, implent cava flumina montes.
Fau. Se exonerant fluviosque onerant. sic flumina rursum
se exonerant pelagusque onerant; hominum quoque mos est
quae nos cumque premunt alieno imponere tergo.
For. Sed iam contractum revocat suus alverus amnem.
Fau. Decrescente Pado (dictu mirabile) noster,
Fortunate, lacus maioribus aestuat undis.
urbs natat, obscurae fiunt cellaria fossae.
lintre cados adeunt; labens ad vina minister
ridet, et ex imis fertur gravis obba lacunis.
multa, licet nati fuerint melioribus horis,
multa et magna ferunt aliquando incommoda cives.
For. Commoditas omnis sua fert incommoda secum,
et sorti appendix est illaetabilis omni.
Fau. Hactenus Eridanus; nostros repetamus amores,
quandoquidem nunc alma Venus movet omnia, caelum
luce tepet nitida, tellus viret, arva volucres
cantibus exhilarant vernis, nunc omnia fetant.
For. Tu tua lusisti, sed nos aliena sequamur.
namque tibi noti referam pastoris amores,
ut doceam Veneris nihil esse potentius igne.
Pauper et infesto sub sidere natus Amyntas
sex vitulos totidemque pares aetate iuvencas
armentique patrem ducens in pascua taurum
venerat ad Coitum, nitidis ubi Mincius undis
alluit herbosos fugiens perniciter agros.
arx nova propter aquas pinnatis ardua muris
est Coitus, campo moles fundata palustri.

ECLOGUE II
FORTUNATUS
Love's Madness
Faustus Fortunatus

Fau. Why are you so late in coming? What kept you? ('Tis now the seventh day.) Are these pastures harmful to your flock?
For. The Po, Faustus, that glides past my fields had risen and with its swollen waters had reached the level of its banks. My flock's care put aside, my own and others' self–interest drove me, serving night and day, to fortify the bank and repulse the raging river.
Fau. When it overflows, the Po too often brings omens of evil. Thus our Tityrus taught, who sang of the pastures and fields.
For. [10] Perhaps this is true when, heedless of the season and beyond measure and bound, it swells with an unexpected surge. But now the season requires these things: for the snows of winter are melting on the high ridges and the mountains are filling the deep–channelled rivers.
Fau. They disburden themselves and fill up the rivers. Likewise the rivers disburden themselves and fill up the sea. So too it is with the ways of men: whatever weighs us down we load on another man's back.
For. But in fact, having already subsided, the river is being summoned back by its channel.
Fau. [18] Ah, Fortunatus (wondrous to tell!) though the Po is waning, our lake now swells with greater waves. The town is afloat now, our cellars have become concealed drains. Men approach their wine casks in skiffs. Gliding towards his wine the steward laughs when a heavy jar is borne from the depths of a pool. Though they might have been born for happier hours, townsmen at times endure many and great misfortunes.
For. Each advantage brings its disadvantages with it. All good fortune has its joyless sequel.
Fau. Thus much for Eridanus. Let us return to our old loves, since now indeed life–giving Venus moves all things and warms the sky with her radiant light, now the earth is green, birds gladden the fields with their spring–songs, and all creatures are bringing forth their young.
For. [31] You sang of your love, but let me speak of another man's love. For I will recount the love of a shepherd we know to show you that nothing is mightier than Venus' flames.

Poor and born under a hostile star, Amyntas, leading to pasture six calves and the same number of heifers equal in age along with a bull, the sire of the herd, came to Coitus where the Mincio, swiftly fleeing, washes against the grassy fields with its glistening waves. A wondrous, lofty stronghold with pinnacled walls near the water is Coitus, a massive structure founded on the

hic igitur recubans vitrei prope fluminis undam,
vitis ubi amplectens longis dumeta lacertis
in vada curvata ripae supereminet umbra,
piscibus insidias tendebat harundine et hamo.
messis erat: solis rapidi violentia campos
sciderat arentes, finem philomena canendi
fecerat, et neque lux, passim morientibus herbis,
pascere oves poterat neque nox umore cicadas.
dumque incumbit aquis studioque intendit inani,
taurus (ut auditum est) primum vexatus ab oestro,
mox canibus, demum furaci a milite silvis
abditus ex toto confestim evanuit agro.
    Quod puer ut novit, tumulum conscendit et alta
voce bovem clamans longo rura omnia visu
prospicit. ut frustra niti se comperit, arcum
corripit et pharetram sequiturque per invia taurum.
illum per caulas et per stabula omnia quaerens
per colles, Benace, tuos, per consita olivis
iugera, per virides ficis et vitibus agros,
venerat ad sublime iugum quod sulphuris arcem
sustinet et longis aperit prospectibus illinc
Benacum, hinc campos longe lateque patentes.
lux ea sacra fuit Petro: frondente sub ulmo
mixta erat ex omni pubes post prandia vico
ducebatque leves buxo resonante choreas.
Fau. Rustica gens, nulla genus arte domabile, semper
irrequietum animal, gaudet sudore. peracto
mane sacro festa (quando omnibus otia) luce
ipsa oti ac famis impatiens epulatur et implet
ingluviem. audito properat tibicine ad ulmum;
hic furit, hic saltu fertur bovis instar ad auras.
quam rastris versare nefas et vomere terram
calcibus obduris et inerti mole fatigat
ac ferit, et tota Baccho facit orgia luce
vociferans, ridens, saliens et pocula siccans.
For. Stulte, quid haec faris? solatia rustica damnas
rusticus ipse? tuis malus es, tibi pessimus ipsi.
Fau. Dicta ioco fuerint; nostrum repetamus Amyntam.
For. Continuit gressum baculoque innixus acerno
intermisit iter, donec mitesceret aestus.
ah puer infelix, aestus te maior in umbra
corripiet. nudam videas ne in fonte Dianam,
claude oculos, blandis neu des Sirenibus aurem.
sors tua Narcisso similis: Narcissus in undis
dum sedare sitim properat, sitit amplius; at tu
exteriorem aestum fugiens intrinsecus ardes.

marshy plain. [41] Reclining here nigh the waters of the glassy river where a vine embracing the hawthorn with its long arms overshadows curving shallows, he laid out his trap—rod and hook—for the fish. It was harvest time. The vehemence of the scorching sun had levelled the parched fields, the nightingale had ceased her singing and, the grass everywhere dying, neither could day pasture the sheep nor night feed the cicadas with dew. And while Amyntas bent over the water and turned to his foolish doings, his bull suddenly disappeared from the field, vexed first (so they say) by gadflies, then by dogs, and finally hidden in the woods by a thievish soldier.

[53] When the lad discovered this, he mounted a hill and, calling his bull with a loud voice, surveyed the entire countryside. When he found that his efforts were in vain, he snatched up his bow and quiver and searched for the bull among trackless places. At every enclosure and stable he sought him, among your hills, Benacus, among acres of land planted with olive trees and fields green with fig trees and vines. At last he came to an elevated ridge that lifts up a tower of sulphur and reveals on one side a distant view of Benacus and on the other side plains stretched out far and wide. The day was consecrated to Saint Peter: under a leafy elm young men from throughout the village had come together after their midday meal and frivolously danced to the re-echoing pipe.

Fau. [66] Rustics—a race tamable by no art, creatures forever restless—these people delight in the sweat of toil! When on a feast day (a day of rest for all) the morning service has been completed, impatient with rest and fasting they feast and cram their maws. Having heard the piper, they hasten to the elm, and here they rage and leap into the air like bulls. The earth, sinful to turn then with the hoe and plow, they weary and strike with their hard heels and clumsy bulk; and all day long they keep Bacchus' orgies, shouting, laughing, dancing, and draining their cups.

For. Fool, why are you talking like this? You condemn rustic pleasures, though a rustic yourself? Unfaithful to your own race, you are most disloyal to yourself!

Fau. These things may be spoken in jest—let us return to Amyntas, our fellow.

For. Amyntas stayed his course and, leaning on his maple staff, interrupted his journey until the heat of the day grew less severe. Ah, unfortunate lad, within the shade a greater heat will lay hold of you! Close your eyes lest you see Diana naked in the fountain, lend not your ear to the seductive Sirens. Your fate is like Narcissus'. When he hastened to ease his thirst within the waters, Narcissus thirsted still more. You, however, fleeing an outward heat,

quam melius fuerat (nisi te sic fata tulissent)
ad reliquum rediisse pecus, servasse iuvencas,
amissi bovis aequo animo dispendia ferre
quam, dum conaris nil perdere, perdere te ipsum.
Fau. Sed post iacturam quis non sapit? utile non est
consilium post facta, dari quod oportuit ante.
consilium post facta, imber post tempora frugum.
For. Una puellares inter pulcherrima turmas
virgo erat, alba comas, aliis procerior, annos
nata quater quinos vel circiter, ore nitenti
urbanis certare potens et vincere nymphis.
aureolis radians guttis ad tempora limbus
ibat, et ad pectus clausum velamen aëno
claviculo; mediam fulgenti fibula ferro
stringit in angustum; nova candicat instita lapsu
linea rugoso pedibusque allabitur imis.
hanc puer ut vidit, periit flammasque tuendo
hausit et in pectus caecos absorbuit ignes,
ignes qui nec aquis perimi potuere nec umbris
diminui neque graminibus magicisve susurris.
oblitusque greges et damna domestica totus
uriter et noctes in luctum expendit amaras.
    Saepe gravescentem verbis compescere flammam
nixus et insanum iuvenis cohibere furorem
dicebam: "miserande puer, quis te deus istas
misit in ambages? sed non deus, immo Satanum
pessimus ex illis quos noctibus atque diebus
ter tribus in terras fama est ex aethere lapsos.
dic, age, si nosti quemquam, reminiscere si quem
videris hoc pacto ditescere, surgere in altum,
dilatare domum, maioribus horrea acervis
complere his studiis, extendere latius agros,
multiplicare greges, acquirere pascua bobus.
inter tot populos quot habet latissima tellus
sunt qui nostra ferant mensis epulanda cruentis
corpora et humanos absumant dentibus artus;
sunt, inquam, quos tanta malis tot vexet Erinys;
sed nullum est tam immane genus, tam barbara nusquam
gens, quae femineos non exsecretur amores.
hinc veniunt rixae, veniunt et iurgia et arma,
saepe etiam dirae multo cum sanguine mortes;
hinc quoque deletis eversae moenibus urbes.
ipsae etiam leges rubrisque volumina loris
clausa vetant scelus hoc et detestantur amores."
    Ut leges audivit, ad haec respondit Amyntas
(civis enim fuerat puer et versatus in urbe)

will burn inwardly. How much better had it been (had not fate thus carried you off) to have returned to your abandoned herd, watched over your heifers, and endured the cost of your lost bull, than, in trying to lose nothing, to lose your very self!

Fau. [91] But after a loss who isn't wise? Advice that must be given before an action is useless after it. Counsel after action is like rain after harvest time.

For. Among a company of young women there, one girl was most beautiful: blond, taller than the others, some twenty years old, able with her radiant face to vie with and overcome the nymphs of the city. The fringe of her veil, glittering with gold flecks, was pulled back towards her temples and fell on a breast enclosed by the bronze clasp of her robe; a clasp of polished iron squeezed together her waist; and a pleated border of fresh white linen hung down at her feet. [103] When the lad saw her, he perished. Beholding her, he drank in love's flames and swallowed down its unseen fires into his heart, fires that can be neither extinguished by water nor lessened by shade or herbs and magical murmurings. Forgetting his herd and the losses to his household, he was wholly consumed by the fires of love and spent his bitter nights in sorrow.

[109] Having often tried with words to curb Amyntas' worsening flames and restrain his insane rage, I said, "Pitiful lad, what god cast you into this confusion? Nay, no god but Satan, the worst of those who men say fell thrice three nights and days from heaven to earth. Tell me if you know, if you can recall anyone who grew rich in this way, who rose in the world, increased his household or heaped his granaries higher by such interests, who enlarged his fields or multiplied his herds or acquired pasturelands for his cattle? [120] Among the many peoples who dwell on this broad earth there are those who carry in men's bodies to be feasted on at bloodstained tables and who crush human limbs with their teeth; peoples, I say, whom such a Fury vexes with so much wickedness. But there is no race so monstrous, no people so barbarous that they do not curse the love of women. Hence springs brawling. Hence comes strife in arms and often deaths fearful and bloody. Hence too come cities overthrown, their walls destroyed. Moreover, the laws themselves written in volumes enclosed by red leather bindings forbid this crime and abhor love."

[131] When he heard me speak of the law, Amyntas (for as a boy he had been a townsman and passed his time in the city) answered my words: "You

"his monitis prudens et circumspectus haberi
niteris et sensu tetricos anteire Catones.
error hic, haec passim sapiens dementia regnat.
ipse sibi blanditur homo sollersque putari
vult animal; tamen incautus sibi multa tetendit
retia et in foveam cecidit quam fecerat. ante
liber erat; servile iugum sibi condidit ipse;
pondus id est legum (vidi ipse volumina) quas nec
antiqui potuere patres, nec possumus ipsi,
nec servare aetas poterit ventura nepotum.
aspice quam stulta est hominum prudentia: caelum
sperat et esse sibi sedem inter sidera credit;
forsitan in volucrem moriens transibit et altum
spiritus assumptis tranabit ad aethera pennis."
Tunc ego: "quid latras? legum Deus auctor, et ipis
non parere sapit magnam nimis impietatem."
Fau. Grandia de magnis haec sunt certamina rebus.
For. Quid fuerim reris? quamvis pannosus et asper
sim modo, tunc animo, tunc vi, tunc ore valebam,
nec mihi sese alius poterat componere pastor.
Fau. Nunc quoque, si rectus vultu gradiare supino,
alter eris Marius; raso ore videbere Carbo.
For. Talia respondit sic obiurgatus Amyntas:
"facto homini Deus invidit (concessa voluptas
visa bonum nimis excellens) et vota repressit
legibus inventis, ut equi ligat ora capistro,
ne quocumque libet flectat vestigia, sessor.
quae mea sit me cogit amor sententia fari,
liberaque ora facit: qui non communicat usum
coniugis invidus est; livorem excusat honestas
introducta usu longi livoris iniquo.
nam dum quisque sibi retinet sua gaudia, nec vult
publica, communis mos ac longaevus honestas
factus, et hunc morem fecit dementia legem.
invida res amor est, res invidiosa voluptas."
Tunc ego non audens hominem contendere contra
amplius insano rediens ab amante recessi.
Fau. Cernis ut hic malus affectus sic lumina mentis
claudat, in errores ut sponte feramur apertos?
For. Cernis ut a summo liventia nubila Baldo
se agglomerent? oritur grando; ne forte vagantes
tempestas deprendat oves, discedere tempus.

are trying to be thought prudent and cautious with these warnings and striving to excel the stern Catos in judgment. Far and wide, this delusion, this shrewd–seeming madness reigns supreme. Man flatters himself and wants to be thought a clever creature, but heedlessly he spreads many nets for himself and tumbles into pitfalls that he himself has dug. Before now, he was free, but he fashioned a servile yoke for himself. This is the burden of those laws (for I too have seen those volumes) that neither our fathers of old could observe nor we ourselves or our children in ages to come can uphold. [143] Behold how foolish is man's wisdom! He hopes for heaven and trusts that there is a place for him among the stars. Perhaps when he dies, he will be changed into a bird and his spirit will rise high into the air on newly acquired wings!"

[147] Then I replied, "Why are you ranting this way? God created the laws and knows that impiety will not obey them when it waxes too great."

Fau. This was a great struggle about important matters!

For. What kind of man do you think I was? Though I might be ragged and rude now, then I was keen–witted, strong, and eloquent, then no herdsman could match himself against me.

Fau. Even now, if you walk erect with your head uplifted, you are Marius. With your face shaved you seem to be Carbo.

For. [155] Thus rebuked, Amyntas replied, "When man had been created, God envied him—for the pleasure He had granted to him seemed too great a good—and repressed man's desires by laws He invented: just as a rider halters his horse lest it be able to turn wheresoever it pleases. Love frees my tongue and compels me to speak my opinion. Whoever doesn't share the use of his wife is an envious man; and honor, introduced by the unjust practice of longstanding envy, frees that envy from blame. For when a man keeps his delights to himself, not wishing to share them with others, a custom—made universal and longstanding, having become 'honor'—madness makes into law. Love becomes an envious thing, pleasure a thing that is envied."

[168] At that moment, daring dispute no more with him, I withdrew from the further ravings of this man possessed by love.

Fau. Do you see how, affected thus, this wicked man can close the eye of reason? Do you perceive how we can freely be led into open error?

For. And do you see how, descending Baldo's peak, the darkening clouds are gathering? A hailstorm is stirring. Lest perchance the tempest overtake our wandering sheep, it is time to depart!

ECLOGA III
AMYNTAS
De insani amoris exitu infelici
Faustus Fortunatus

Fau. Illa hesterna ruens Baldi de vertice grando,
Fortunate, fuit nobis innoxia (divis
gratia nostrarum quibus est custodia frugum)
sed, veluti ex illis veniens ait Harculus oris,
Veronensem agrum, pecudes et ovilia sic est
demolita, casas et pastoralia tecta
sic evertit, ut agricolis spes nulla supersit.
agricolis etenim pecus est substantia, et arva
his subiecta malis; grandi thesaurus in arca
civibus est quem nulla queat contundere grando,
nulla pruina, gelu nullum, nullae aëris irae.
For. Nescio quis ventos tempestatesque gubernat;
id scio (sed neque si scio sat scio, sed tamen ausim
dicere—quid? vitane ideo multabor in ipsa?)
numina si, ut perhibent, orbem moderantur ab alto,
extimo nil duros hominum curare labores.
aspice quo tenuem victum sudore paramus,
quot mala pro grege, pro natis, pro coniuge pastor
fert miser, infestis aestate caloribus ardet,
frigoribus riget hibernis; dormimus ad imbrem
cotibus in duris vel humi; contagia mille,
mille premunt morbi pecudes, discrimina mille
sollicitant, latro insidias intentat ovili
atque lupus milesque lupo furacior omni.
ut manus assiduo detrita incalluit usu,
squaluit os, barba obriguit, cutis aruit aestu,
una repentino rapit omnia turbine grando.
hoc Superi faciunt quibus inclinamur ad aras
et quibus offerimus faculas et cerea vota.
nescio quae pietas et quae clementia tantis
cladibus involvat pastores omnium egenos.
Fau. Fortunate, scelus nobis haec omnia nostrum
ingerit; aetherei sententia Iudicis aequa est.
For. Quod scelus? an fuimus Christi vitae insidiati?
Fau. Iurgia, furta, irae, Venus et mendacia, rixae.
For. Quid meruere boni? nec enim scelus orbruit omnes,
et tamen una omnes pariter pessumdat Erinys.
Fau. Heu nescis male de Superis sentire nefandum?
his igitur quae scire nefas, nescire necesse est,
posthabitis curas iterum repetamus Amyntae

ECLOGUE III
AMYNTAS
The Unhappy Outcome of Mad Love

Faustus Fortunatus

Fau. That hailstorm yesterday, Fortunatus, that came tumbling down Baldo's peak did us no harm (all thanks to the gods who watch over our crops). But just as Harculus coming from the region claims, it so ravaged Verona's fields, livestock, and sheepfolds, overthrew so many of its cottages and shepherds' huts that the farmers there have no hope left them. For indeed livestock are the farmer's riches, livestock and the fields subjected to these misfortunes. But the townsman has a hoard laid up in a large coffer, a treasure that no hailstorm, frost, cold, or airy tempest can batter.
For. [12] I know not who rules the winds and storms. This I do know. (But though I know this, I know not enough. And yet might I dare speak? What will I say? Will I therefore be punished in my lifetime?) If, as is claimed, divine powers rule the world from above, I reckon that they care not at all for the hard labors of men. Look with what sweat we gain our meager living, how many evils the shepherd bears (poor wretch!) for his flock, children, and wife. [19] In summer he burns in its harmful heat. He is numbed by the frosts of winter. In the rain we sleep on hard flints or on the ground. A thousand contagions, a thousand sicknesses oppress our sheep, a thousand dangers harass them. The thief threatens the flock with his snares, the wolf too and the soldier, more thievish than any wolf. When our hands have become calloused, worn by constant use, when our faces have become dirty, our beards stiff, our skin dried out by the heat, then a single hailstorm suddenly snatches up everything with its whirling winds. The gods above do this, the gods before whose altars we bend in honor and to whom we dedicate our little torches and waxen offerings. I don't know what kind of affection and mildness could overwhelm with so many calamities shepherds who lack all the necessities of life.
Fau. [32] Our crimes, Fortunatus, bring all these things on us. The sentence of Heaven's judge is just.
For. What crimes? Did we plot against Christ's life?
Fau. Our quarrels, thefts, anger, and lust, our lies and brawling.
For. But why have even good men deserved this? For truly crime overwhelms not all men, yet one scourge equally destroys all of us.
Fau. Ah! don't you know that it is impiety to speak wickedly of the gods above? These matters, impious to know, it is thus necessary not to know. Putting them aside, let us turn again to the cares of Amyntas, cares we too

quas sumus experti, quas ignorare negatum est;
res vulgaris amor, studium commune iuventae.
For. Maeror et affectus alii de cardine mentem
saepe levant; animo sermo venit aeger ab aegro.
Fau. Intellecta licet pro re, pro tempore fari
(sic habitus Cosmas sapiens) incognita numquam.
For . Fauste, sapis; notos igitur repetamus amores.
restat Amyntaeos postrema in fata furores
ducere et in misero lacrimas impendere casu.

Praeteriens illac parvo post tempore rursum
insanire hominem video et miseratus amantem
"o," iterum dixi, "mens inconsulta veneno
ebria fatali. populo iam fabula factus
non resipiscis adhuc, et adhuc in amore sepultus
te ruis atque tuos, pecus atque mapalia, tecum
ut quondam moriens rapuit secum omnia Samson.
cum senio curvatus eris (si forte senectam
fata tibi dederint) quis sustentabit inertem,
somnolentum, inopem, cum iam defecerit omne
robur et ingenium, sensusque recesserit omnis?
haec tibi cuncta feret (nisi mors praevenerit) aetas.
esto domi, vigila, observa, super omnia semper
prospice quo tendas, et quo venisse dolendum est
ire cave. discerne vias hominemque memento
non ad delicias, non ad muliebria natum
blandimenta levi tam perniciosa iuventae.
ipse ego cui pecudes, cui lac, cui caseus, aegre
vitam ago; tanta agros omnes invasit egestas,
tot duri rerum eventus, incommoda passim
tanta, tot adversis totus convolvitur orbis.
accipe rem non auditam, non tempore factam
praeterito, sed quam lux haec mihi protulit ipsi.
ut mos, autumno pecudes crescente totondi.
mane foro exposui lanae venalia pondo
sexaginta hodie, grande aes conflare putabam;
vix vitam gregis eduxi, vix pabula possum
mercari hibernis nivibus; quo cetera pacto
sit victura domus nondum mihi constat, Amynta.
quisquis amat dominae munuscula mittat oportet;
tu vero cui vix tectum fortuna reliquit
sub quo luce habitat, sub quo pernoctat egestas,
quid poteris cupidae gratum donare puellae?
mittere mala decem satis esse solebat amanti,
purpurei flores et raptus ab arbore nidus,
gramen odoriferum, memini quo tempore magnae
credebantur opes; ventum est a gramine ad aurum.

have known and cannot be ignorant of. Love is common to all of us, an interest shared by all young men.

For. [43] Often grief and other feelings unhinge our judgment. Troubled words oft issue from a troubled mind.

Fau. Things we understand may be spoken according to circumstance and time (in this way was Cosmas thought wise), but what we don't understand must never be uttered.

For. Faustus, indeed you are wise. Let us return to love, a subject we know. It remains to present Amyntas' ravings during his last days and to devote a tear to his pitiable downfall.

[50] Passing that place again a little later I saw the man raging with love and pitying him I again said, "Oh, you of heedless mind, drunk with a deadly poison! Though the people gossip about you, you still haven't recovered your reason. Sunk still in love, you are ruining yourself and everything around you, both cattle and cottage, just as once long ago Samson in dying destroyed everything with him. When you are bent with age (if perchance destiny grants you an old age) who will support you, idle, dull, and weak, since all your strength and skills have already deserted you and your reason has wholly abandoned you? [61] All these afflictions old age (unless death precedes it) will bring to you. Stay at home, remain wakeful and watchful; above all, always look where you're heading and beware of going where it is grievous to enter. Distinguish between the various paths, and remember that man was not born for those feminine delights and allurements so ruinous to frivolous young men. I myself, who have cattle, milk and cheese, can scarcely make a living: such great want has ravaged all my fields; everywhere so many hardships, such great vexations, so many misfortunes are compacted within the world. [71] Hearken to a tale untold, a matter revealed to me not in the past but today. As usual, with autumn approaching I sheared my sheep. At the market this morning I offered for sale sixty pounds of wool and thought I would get a high price for it. I have supported my flock with difficulty; now, only with difficulty will I be able to buy food for them against the snows of winter. I can't see yet, Amyntas, how the rest of my household is going to live. [79] Every lover must send little gifts to his lady. But you, whom Fortune has scarce left a roof under which poverty dwells night and day, what gift will you be able to offer to a greedy wench? I remember when it used to be enough to send your lover ten apples, red flowers, a bird's nest snatched from a tree, and fragrant herbs. I recall when these were thought great riches. But now we have come from herbs to gold. In these times love is a regal

regia res amor est hac tempestate; recessit
mos vetus et quaedam mala lex inolevit amandi."
Talia suadenti torvo mihi rettulit ore:
"si cupis optatam mihi, Fortunate, salutem,
da quod amo; nostro haec una est medicina dolori.
cetera quae memoras mihi sunt tormenta. revelli
ex animo furor iste nequit; mea pectora imago
virginis obsedit, mecum est, mecum itque reditque,
excubat et dormit mecum; caput, ossa, medullas,
cor complexa potest cum sola excedere vita.
ac veluti quotiens aliena ex arbore secto
surculus inseritur trunco, natura duorum
iungitur et mixto coalescit corpore virga,
sic dominae dilecta mihi se immersit imago
et fecit duo corda unum, duo traxit in unum
pectora; sensus inest nobis et spiritus idem.
o me felicem, si, cum mea fata vocabunt,
in gremio dulcique sinu niveisque lacertis
saltem anima caput hoc languens abeunte iaceret;
illa sua nobis morientia lumina dextra
clauderet et tristi fleret mea funera voce.
sive ad felices vadam post funera campos,
seu ferar ardentem rapidi Phlegethontis ad undam,
nec sine te felix ero, nec tecum miser umquam.
o Dryades florumque deae Nymphaeque decentes,
o nemorum Silvane pater, servate (precamur)
collibus in vestris gelidisque in vallibus omne
silvarum rurisque decus; circumdate saltus
saepibus et prohibete pecus, ne floribus obsit;
ista (precor) dominae servate in funera nostrae.
tunc omnis spargatur humus; redolentia serta
texite, quae circa tumulum supraque iacentem
componantur heram. tristes ad busta puellae
Pierides arderunt et lamentabile carmen
ore canent madido signataque verba relinquent
ista sepulturae relegenda nepotibus olim:
HIC TEGITUR VIRGO CUI NIL QUIN DIVA VOCARI
DEBUERIT DEERAT, NISI DURA FUISSET AMANTI.
o virgo, si te tantus consumeret ardor,
per centum Scyllas ad te, per mille Charybdes,
tranarem laturus opem; tu saevior Hydra
me fugis. at culpae nihil est in virgine, nam me
nescit adhuc; si sciret enim, succurreret ultro,
nec puto sub miti tam ferrea pectora vultu.
signa tamen vultus fallacia; sub cute molli
mens fera, sub blanda sunt corda immania fronte.

thing. The old ways are gone and a kind of evil rule of love has arisen."

[89] And while I thus exhorted him, with a fierce look he replied: "If you wish my welfare, Fortunatus, give me what I desire. This is the one remedy for my heartache. The others you name are torments to me. This 'madness' can't be plucked from my thoughts. The girl's image dwells in my heart: she stays with me, comes and goes with me, wakes and slumbers with me. Twined round my heart, head, bones, and marrow, she can leave me only when my life departs. Just as wherever a scion cut from one tree is grafted onto the trunk of another, the nature of the two is joined and the slip, blended with the trunk, unites with it, [100] in the same way my lady's beloved image has plunged into my heart and drawn our two hearts together, making them one; the same feelings, the same soul dwells within us. Oh, how fortunate would I be if when death calls me I could at least lay my languishing head, my soul then departing, on her lap, sweet breasts, and in her snow–white arms! With her right hand she would close my dying eyes, and she would bewail my death with many a mournful cry. Whether after death I journey to the fields of the blessed or am borne to swift Phlegethon's burning waves, without you I will never be blessed, with you never be pitiable. [111] Oh you dryads, floral goddesses, and comely nymphs, oh Silvanus, lord of the groves, on your hills and within your cool valleys watch over, I pray you, each grace of the forest and fields. Enclose your groves with fences and keep out the herds lest they injure the flowers there. Keep those beauties, I pray you, for my lady's funeral rites. Then let the ground be wholly strewn with flowers, weave fragrant garlands and place them round her grave and over my mistress as she lies there at rest. [119] The Pierian maidens will be in mourning at her tomb and sing a song of lamentation, their cheeks moist with tears. And they will leave behind engraved on her tomb these words to be read by future ages: 'Here lies buried a maid who would have been called "goddess," had she not been cruel to her lover.' Ah maid, if such an ardent desire as mine consumed you, past a hundred Scyllas, a thousand Charybdises I would swim to help you; but you, more savage than the Hydra, flee me. And yet she is not to blame, for as yet she does not know of me. Indeed, if she knew, she would hasten unbidden to aid me; nor do I reckon that behind such a gentle visage can lie so iron–hard a heart. [131] All the same, looks are deceiving: fierce minds lie under soft skin, monstrous hearts

alloquar et faciam nostros intellegat ignes.
si tamen illa meos vultus averterit, ibunt
in lacrimas oculi, triste in suspiria pectus.
oderit illa licet semper fugiatque sequentem,
ista tamen, quocumque ferar, me cura sequetur.
ite procul medicae, non sum sanabilis, artes,
ite procul magico qui (quod nec credere dignum est)
carmine pallentes animas revocatis ab Orco,
ite procul vanis precibus qui flectere divos
creditis; adversum est et inexorabile caelum.
me rapit impatiens furor et iuvat ire per altos
solivagum montes, per lustra ignota ferarum."
Talia iactantem verbis conabar amicis
flectere, sed vulnus nihil insanabile curat.
illum per campos nox intempesta silentes,
illum exorta dies inter dumeta videbat
insomnem semper, raro silvestria poma
carpentem et potu contentum simplicis undae.
post longos gemitus exhaustaque lumina fletu
assiduo, post lamenta et convulsa frequenti
pectora singultu, moriens finivit amores.
exanimum corpus tumuli sine honore relictum
nocturnae absumpsere ferae volucresque diurnae.
Fau. Heu fenesta lues, fatalis machina passim
corda venenatis penetrans humana sagittis,
aequiperans hominem pecudi. quae pocula Circe,
quae peiora umquam potuit dare philtra Calypso?
quae Styx, quis Phlegethon gravior? quae maior Erinys?
o stulti, quicumque deum dixistis Amorem.
num natura nocens deus est? ubicumque locorum
sit deus, est homini clemens, innoxius, aequus.
For. Heu miserande puer tenera sublate iuventa,
quae tibi nascenti luxerunt sidera? quae tam
noxia pars caeli est, ut te nil tale merentem
laeserit et primis infortunarit ab annis?
nec tamen omnino caelum tibi defuit; omne
carmen et argutis quidquid modulamur avenis
doctus eras. nisi te mors immatura tulisset,
dignus eras hederis, dignus Parnaside lauro;
nec melius cecinit pugnas ac tristia bella,
hordea et agrorum cultus et pascua noster
Tityrus a magno tantum dilectus Alexi.
namque tui praecox animi sollertia nobis
cognita iam pridem magnam producere frugem
coeperat, et specimen tuleras virtutis et artis
non vulgare tuae; poteras iam gloria dici

behind a tranquil brow. I will speak to her and make her understand the fires of my love. And yet if she turns her face from mine, my eyes will melt in tears, my unhappy heart in sighs. Though she might forever hate and flee me, nonetheless wherever I am borne, my care for her will always pursue me.

Hence, you healing arts—I cannot be cured. Hence, you who with magic incantations (a thing unworthy of belief) recall pale spirits from Orcus. Hence, you who think the gods can be moved by your vain entreaties. Heaven is contrary and deaf to your prayers. An impatient rage now seizes me and bids me wander alone among mountain heights and the unknown haunts of wild beasts!"

[145] While thus he raged, with friendly words I tried to turn him from his purposes, but nothing can heal an incurable wound. The dead of night discovered him among the still fields. Among thickets of thorns the newly risen day viewed him always sleepless, now and then plucking an apple in the forest and content simply with a draught of water. After many a sigh, his eyes emptied by constant weeping, after lamentations and after his heart had repeatedly been shaken by sobbing, in dying he at last set a bound to his love. His lifeless body, abandoned without the honor of a grave, beasts devoured by night and birds by day.

Fau. [156] Alas, oh deadly plague, oh fateful weapon that pierces human hearts far and wide with poisoned arrows, that brings men to the level of beasts! What worse cup could Circe have offered? What love potion more evil could Calypso ever have given? What Stygian waves, what waters of Phlegethon are more grievous? What Fury is greater? Oh, fools you are, anyone who affirms Love to be a god! Can a nature that is harmful be a god? Wherever a god is, he is merciful, just, not harmful to men.

For. [164] Alas, pitiable lad felled in the tenderness of youth, what stars shone at your birth? What part of heaven is so harmful to you as to have afflicted you undeservedly and condemned you to misfortune in your youth? Nonetheless, the heavens were not wholly unforthcoming to you. You were expert in every kind of verse and in whatever we sang to the accompaniment of the clear-noted pipe. Had not an untimely death borne you off, you would have been worthy of the ivy, worthy of Parnassus' bays. Nor did Tityrus sing better of battles and unhappy war, of barley and pastures and the care of the fields—Tityrus, our fellow, greatly beloved by mighty Alexis. [175] For your early quickness of mind, long known to us, had begun to bring forth a bountiful harvest, and indeed you had borne an uncommon example of your excellence and artistry. You could already be called the glory of our fields and

ruris et aetatis decus indelebile nostrae.
te Padus et noster lugubri Mincius ore
cum Nymphis flevere suis, ut Thracius Hebrus
Orphea; te tristes ovium flevere magistri,
ut Daphnim luxisse ferunt; te pascua et agri
undique; et audita est totis querimonia campis.
spargite, pastores, tumulum redolentibus herbis
atque sacerdotum cantus ac tura quotannis
ducite, et aeternam requiem cantate poetae.
Fau. Tu tamen arva tenes patriae melioris et altum
incolis Elysium; nos hic te flemus, Amynta.
For. Flendum hodie nobis fuerat; nam tristia nocte
nescio quae maestis cernebam insomnia formis.
sed iam Vesper adest et sol se in nube recondens,
dum cadit, agricolis vicinos nuntiat imbres;
cogere et ad caulas pecudes convertere tempus.

ECLOGA IV
ALPHUS
De natura mulierum
Alphus Iannus

Alphus Ianne, caper (video) macer est tuus. esse solebat
acer et elatis in caelum cornibus ire;
nunc deiectus humi flaccis piger auribus herbam
olfacit et summis attingit gramina labris.
Iannus Languet, et ex isto languore facetia surgit
quae, quotiens memini, risum ciet. edita nondum est;
edita cum fuerit, totus mirabitur orbis.
Alphus Ianne, soles narrare sales lepidissime et ore
suaviloquo; dic ergo tuus cur langueat hircus.
Iannus Res non ficta (Deus testis) sed facta recenter.
at dulce id facinus non est narrabile gratis;
quid pretii sperare licet? quae dona reporto?
Alphus Ianne, ubi congessit nidos philomena docebo.
Iannus Qui leviter spondet promisso eludit inani.
Alphus Qui non credit, inops fidei. sed pignore tutum
te faciam; duo tela mea deprome pharetra.
Iannus Incipiam. Nymphae Parnasides, ora movete
et memorate mei dira infortunia capri,
ac philomenaeos Alpho concedite nidos.
Conductus mercede puer praefectus ovili
assidue pascebat oves, caprum atque capellas.

the imperishable ornament of our age. The Po and our Mincio with their nymphs wept for you, as Thracian Hebrus lamented Orpheus. The lords of the flocks in sadness wept for you, just as they are said to have mourned Daphnis. The pastures and fields everywhere wept for you, and lamentation was heard throughout the plains. Shepherds, strew his tomb with fragrant grasses, yearly lead in procession the priests' singing and incense, and hymn the poet's eternal repose.

Fau. [188] All the same, Amyntas, you have reached the fields of a better homeland and now dwell high on Elysium. We here on earth weep for you.

For. And today there was reason for us to weep: for at night in my dreams I have been seeing mournful apparitions. But now Vesper is here and the setting sun, hiding behind a cloud, announces an approaching rainstorm to the farmer. 'Tis time to gather the sheep together and drive them to the sheepfold!

ECLOGUE IV
ALPHUS
The Character of Women

Alphus Jannus

Alphus That goat of yours, Jannus, I see has grown gaunt. He used to be lively and walk with his horns raised skywards. But downcast now, his ears drooping, he dully sniffs the grass and only touches it with his lips.

Jannus Indeed, he languishes, yet from that languor of his arises a merry tale that, however often I recall it, rouses my laughter. As yet I've not recounted it, and when I have, all the world will wonder at it.

Alphus Jannus, you are wont to recount a jest most wittily and with pleasing words—tell me then why your goat droops.

Jannus [10] 'Tis no fable (God is my witness) but a recent event. Yet this delightful misdeed I can't recount for free. What reward can I hope for? What gifts shall I carry home?

Alphus I will teach you, Jannus, where the nightingale builds her nest.

Jannus He who promises lightly deceives with empty promises.

Alphus And he who mistrusts is mistrusted. But I will make your mind secure with a token of my promise: take two arrows from my quiver.

Jannus Then I will begin. Nymphs of Parnassus, rouse your voices. Recount my goat's dire misfortune and grant to Alphus the nests of Philomel.

[20] A lad I had hired to oversee my sheepfold used regularly to pasture my

servitium nobis pueri fuit utile, donec
virgine conspecta quae tum huc veniebat aquatum
tabuit. ex illo vecors iam tempore factus
frigidius curare gregem, contemnere caulas
coepit et exhausto subvertere cuncta cerebro.
cum sopitus erat, poterat vigil esse videri,
nugabatur enim; quando vigilabat, inerti
corporis officio volvebat somnia mente.
hunc ergo in saltu ludens per cornua caprum
viminibus validis inter dumeta ligarat
(quarta dies hodie) tentans an vincula possit
vincere cervice ac praedurae robore frontis.
quaesitum interea nidos nemus omne pererrat.
corda subit virgo, dilecta recogitat ora,
ora, sinus et quae fari pudor; omnia volvit.
lux fugit interea; capri redit immemor. alta
nocte recordatus surgit, pavidusque per umbras
dum graditur, ruit in foveam quae fronde saligna
captandis obducta feris et stramine sicco
instar erat putei fundo irremeabilis alto.
est caper in vinclis, puer est in carcere, pastor
nullus oves curat. iam tertia luxerat hora;
miror, oves resero ac numero caprumque requirens
obstupeo; puerum clamo, magalia lustro.
vera loquar: magicis ne forte liquoribus unctus
extimui ascenso migrasset in aëra capro.
namque striges tali fama est ope nocte vagantes
ad quaedam longinqua procul convivia ferri.
attonitus tandem pecudes ad pascua duco.
dumque pedum meditans subeo nemus, ecce per umbras,
ecce procul caper in dumis strepit atque reluctans
cornibus adversis contra sua vincula pugnat.
terruit incautum subito feralis imago
et nil tale ratum; firmato pectore tandem
nosco animal subiensque rubos seco vincula runca.
sero domum rediens video per pascua longe
turbam exsultantem risu iuveniliter alto.
ut prope constitimus meque agnovere, salutant
et "tuus ecce," aiunt, "puer hic, o Ianne, luporum
erutus e foveis. dum nocte perambulat agros,
incidit in casses." et sic inventus uterque,
et caper et pastor. caper haec incommoda passus
languet adhuc; puer imprudens insanior hirco est.
virgo superbivit mox, ut se audivit amari,
et pueri simulans curam ignorare pudorem
fingit, ut ad formam faciat pudor. ora sinumque

sheep and my he–goat and she–goats. The boy's service was useful to me until, having spied a girl who came hither to fetch water, he pined away. Driven mad from that moment he began to cool in his care for my flock, to pay no heed to the sheepfold and, his mind exhausted, to upset all manner of things. Whenever he slept, he could seem to be awake, for he used to babble; and when he was awake, he was listless and daydreamed. [30] Sporting once in a grove, with strong withes he bound this goat here by its horns among the thornbushes (that was three days ago) to see if it could overcome his bonds with its neck and the strength of its rock–hard horns. Meanwhile he roamed throughout the grove seeking the nests of birds. The girl's image had entered his heart. He reflected on her dear face; her face, her breasts, and parts it's shameful to speak of—he contemplated everything! Meanwhile the light of day fled and, his goat forgotten, he returned home. Remembering it in the dead of night he arose, and as he walked fearfully among the shadows he tumbled into a pitfall that, covered with willow branches and dry straw to catch wild animals, was like some inescapably deep dungeon. Thus my goat was in bonds, my boy in a prison, and no shepherd watched over my sheep!

[43] By this time the third hour of the day had come. I began to wonder. I released and counted the sheep and, searching for my goat, was struck dumb with amazement. I called after the lad and made the rounds of the huts. I'll speak truly: I feared lest, anointed perchance with some magic oil, he had mounted the goat and departed into the air. For it is said that by such magic, witches wandering at night are borne hence to their far–off revels. Puzzled, I at last drove my sheep to pasture. [51] And when, musing idly on my shepherd's crook, I entered the grove—lo! among its shadows my goat raised a ruckus far off within the thornbushes and with its horns struggled against its bonds. Not expecting such a sight, I was terrified by this sudden spectral image. But plucking up my courage at last, I recognized the animal and, entering the brambles, cut its bonds with my billhook.

[57] Returning home late I spied far off in the pasture a crowd exulting with boyish laughter. When we had drawn near and they had recognized me, they greeted me and said, "Behold your boy here, oh Jannus, plucked out of the wolfpits. While he was roaming the fields at night, he fell into a trap." And thus were found both goat and shepherd. Having borne these troubles, my goat droops yet; but the callow boy has less sense than the goat. The girl soon grew proud when she heard she was loved and, pretending not to know of his love, feigned coyness so that it might add to her beauty. She decked out

ornat et in terram versis incedit ocellis
callida; vulpina rem simplicitate gubernat.
haec studia, hi casses, haec sunt mulieribus arma.
ille sua sperans Galatea aliquando potiri
contempta mercede suos sectatur amores.
propterea plaustro, stiva bobusque relictis
ad pastoris opus redeo; subiecta furori
ista iuventutis levitas rura omnia vexat.
Alphus Quod nequit ingenium, casus facit. o stupor, o sors
ingeniosa, o res risu celebranda bimestri!
Ianne, fides servanda; tibi philomena laborat.
sed quod tam vafro memoras de virginis astu
rettulit in mentem quae psallere saepe solebat
carmina femineis olim de fraudibus Umber.
Iannus Dic Umbri, dic, si quid habes. meditare parumper
et verba et numeros; Umbri est memorabile carmen.
Alphus Est (ut ais) sed non gratis, memorabile carmen.
quas referes grates? et quid mercedis habebo?
Iannus Accipe: promissis absolvo et spicula reddo.
Alphus Dum vado ad ventrem post haec carecta levandum,
Ianne, meum tu coge pecus, ne vitibus obsit.
Iannus O aries, aries, qui tortis cornibus atrum
daemona praesentas, semper vineta subintras.
non sapies donec fossa tibi lumina fronte
eruero. non sunt porrecta in iugera centum
pascua sat, nisi pampineos populeris et agros.
Alphus Ianne, recordatus redeo, sed plurima forsan
nondum nota tibi referam. cognoverat Umber
omnia quae fas est homini perdiscere, caelos,
sidera, tellurem, ventos, mare, flumina, fontes.
viderat et Rhodopen atque alta Ceraunia et Ossam,
Gallica regna, Ararim, Rhodanum Tiberimque Padumque.
Attica Romanis referebat carmina verbis
ore utroque potens et lingua primus utraque.
hunc unum nobis invidit Graecia et ipsi
Arcades et Thracum saltus et Thessala Tempe.
si quid erit quod forte velis tibi notius esse,
Candidus illius semper documenta secutus
non procul hinc; haec ille tenet, nos ille docebit.
sed iam septiforem flatu experiamur avenam.
ante tamen Nymphae precor ut Libethrides adsint,
praesertim quae plus meminisse Polymnia fertur.
"Femineum servile genus, crudele, superbum,
lege, modo, ratione caret. confinia recti
neglegit, extremis gaudet, facit omnia voto
praecipiti, vel lenta iacet vel concita currit;

her mouth and breasts and walked with her eyes turned cunningly towards the ground. She conducted herself with the simplicity of a fox. [70] These cares, these snares—these are the weapons of women. Hoping to win his Galatea at some time or other, the lad pursued his love, caring little for his wages. Thus I have returned to shepherd's toil, my cart, plow, and oxen left behind. This frivolity of youth, when ruled by love's rage, is upsetting the whole countryside!

Alphus What ingenuity can't accomplish, chance can. Oh, dullness! oh, clever chance! oh, tale that two months' laughter will go to celebrate! Jannus, my promise must be kept: for you the nightingale now labors. But what you recount so skillfully concerning the girl's cunning brings to mind a song about woman's guile that Umber often used to sing long ago.

Jannus [82] If you have any song of Umber's, pray sing it. For a little while rehearse both its words and measures. A song of Umber's is worthy of being remembered.

Alphus It is (as you say) a song memorable, but not free. What thanks will you give me? What reward will I have?

Jannus Take these things: I free you from your promises and give back your arrows.

Alphus While I go to relieve my bowels behind that sedge there, drive together my flock, Jannus, lest they harm the vines. [He departs]

Jannus Ah, ram—you who with your twisted horns bring to mind a black devil—you are forever stealing into our vineyards! Until I have plucked your eyes out, you won't know any better! A hundred acres of pasture aren't enough unless you have ravaged the vineyards and fields.

Alphus [94] I'm back, Jannus, and have recalled Umber's song. But let me also tell you of many things perhaps not yet known among men. Umber knew all that a man is permitted to learn thoroughly: the skies, stars, earth, winds, sea, rivers, and springs. He had viewed Rhodope, yes and the lofty Ceraunian peaks and Ossa, the Gallic kingdom with its Saône and Rhône rivers, and both the Tiber and Po. [100] With a Roman's words he rehearsed an Attic song, fluent in either tongue, most excellent in either language. Him alone Greece, the Arcadians themselves, the Thracian grove, and Thessalian Tempe envied us. If perchance you would like to know anything more about him, Candidus (who has always followed his example) dwells not far from here. He keeps Umber's wisdom, he will teach it to us. But now let me try with my breath my oaten pipe of seven holes. Yet first I pray that the nymphs of Libethra be present, and chiefly Polyhymnia who men say remembers many things.

[110] "Servile, cruel, and proud, a woman lacks law, measure and reason. She ignores the bounds of right, delights in extremes, does everything by whim. She lolls about or runs around excitedly; she is winter and fierce cold,

femina semper hiems atque intractabile frigus,
aut Canis ardentes contristat sidere terras.
temperiem numquam, numquam mediocria curat;
vel te ardenter amat vel te capitaliter odit.
si gravis est, maeret torvo nimis hernica vultu;
si studeat comis fieri gravitate remissa,
fit levis, erumpit blando lascivia risu
et lepor in molli radiat meretricus ore.
flet, ridet, sapit, insanit, formidat et audet,
vult, non vult, secumque sibi contraria pugnat
mobilis, inconstans, vaga, garrula, vana, bilinguis,
imperiosa, minax, indignabunda, cruenta,
improba, avara, rapax, querula, invida, credula, mendax,
impatiens, onerosa, bibax, temeraria, mordax,
ambitiosa, levis, maga, lena, superstitiosa,
desidiosa, vorax, ganeae studiosa, palatum
docta, salax, petulans et dedita mollitiei,
dedita blanditiis, curandae dedita formae.
irae odiique tenax in idonea tempora differt
ulciscendi animos infida, ingrata, maligna,
impetuosa, audax, fera, litigiosa, rebellis.
exprobrat, excusat tragica sua crimina voce,
murmurat, accendit rixas, nil foedera pendit,
ridet amicitias, curat sua commoda tantum.
ludit, adulatur, defert, sale mordet amaro,
seminat in vulgus nugas, auditaque lingua
auget et ex humili tumulo producet Olympum.
dissimulat, simulat doctissima fingere causas
ordirique dolos fraudique accomodat ora,
ora omnes facili casus imitantia motu.
non potes insidias evadere, non potes astum
vincere; tantae artes, sollertia tanta nocendi.
et quamquam videas oculis praesentibus, audet
excusare nefas. potis est eludere sensus
sedulitate animi; nihil est quod credere possis
et nihil est quod non, si vult, te credere cogat.
His facient exempla fidem. quae crimina non sunt
feminea temptata manu? dedit hostibus arcem
decepta ornatu bracchi Tarpeia sinistri,
saeviit in natos manibus Medea cruentis,
Tyndaris Aegaeas oneravit navibus undas,
Scylla hostem sequitur patri furata capillum.
fratrem Byblis amat, subicit se Myrrha parenti,
concubitus nati longaeva Semiramis ardet.
causa necis vati coniunx fuit Amphiarao,
occidere viros nocturnis Belides armis,

or with the Dog Star she torments the burning earth. A woman never cares for moderation or the mean: she either loves you ardently or hates you mortally. If she is sad, she grieves, wild–eyed, stony and stern. But if, her sadness abated, she should try to become loving, she becomes waggish; her wantonness breaks forth in seductive laughter, and a harlot–like submissiveness beams in her soft features. [122] She weeps, laughs, is judicious or mad, fears or is bold. She wants or doesn't want something, quarrels with herself. She is changeable, inconstant, wandering, prattling, vain, deceitful, domineering, threatening, indignant, bloodthirsty, wicked, greedy, grasping, complaining, envious, credulous, untruthful, impatient, burdensome, drunken, rash, carping, ambitious, frivolous, a witch, a bawd, superstitious, lazy, gluttonous, eager to stuff herself, overdelicate in her tastes, lecherous, impudent, given over to licentiousness, flattery, and pandering to her beauty. [132] Unyielding in her anger and hatred, she puts off her vengeful thoughts until the right moment. She is faithless, ungrateful, spiteful, impetuous, bold, savage, quarrelsome, and rebellious. She accuses others but with a tragic voice excuses her own misdeeds. She grumbles, inflames quarrels, disregards her bond, laughs at friendship, and cares only for her own advantage. She deceives, flatters, denounces, and nips at others with her caustic wit. She sows trifles among her neighbors, enlarges with her prattle tales she has heard, and makes a mountain out of a molehill. [141] Skilled in inventing motives, she conceals the truth and feigns falsehoods; she suits her looks to embarking on trickery and to deceiving, those looks readily suitable to all occasions. You cannot escape her schemes or defeat her cunning: so many are her arts, so great is her skill in doing harm. And though you might witness some crime of hers with your own eyes, she will nonetheless dare to justify it. Through the diligence of her mind she can delude your senses: there is nothing you can believe in and nothing in which, if she wishes, she would not lead you to believe.

[150] "Examples will bear these things out. What crimes have not been attempted by the hand of woman? Beguiled by an ornament for her left arm, Tarpeia betrayed her city to its enemies. Medea raged with gory hands against her children. Tyndareus' daughter burdened the Aegean waves with ships. Scylla followed the enemy, having stolen a lock of her father's hair. Byblis loved her brother, Myrrha gave herself to her father, Semiramis yearned in old age to lie with her son. The seer Amphiaraus' wife was the cause of his death, Danaus' daughters slew their husbands with weapons at night, and the

Orphea membratim Cicones secuere poetam.
cognita luxuriae petulantia Pasiphaaeae,
Phaedra pudicitiam contra crudeliter ausa est.
decepit Iudaea virum Rebecca suamque
progeniem velans hircino guttura tergo,
porrigit Alcidae coniunx fatale venenum,
decipit Hippodame patrem. Lavinia Troes
implicat ancipiti bello, Briseis Achillem
depulit e castris, demens Chryseide factus
fulminat Atrides et sentit Apollinis iras.
Eva genus nostrum felicibus expulit arvis.
credite, pastores (per rustica numina iuro)
pascua si gregibus vestris innoxia vultis,
si vobis ovium cura est, si denique vobis
grata quies, pax, vita, leves prohibete puellas
pellanturque procul vestris ab ovilibus omnes,
Thestylis et Phyllis, Galatea, Neaera, Lycoris.
dicite, quae tristem mulier descendit ad Orcum
et rediit? potuit, si non male sana fuisset,
Eurydice revehi per quas descenderat umbras;
rapta sequi renuit fessam Proserpina matrem.
at pius Aeneas rediit, remeavit et Orpheus,
maximum Alcides et Theseus et duo fratres,
unus equis, alter pugnis bonus atque palaestra,
et noster Deus, unde salus et vita resurgit.
haec sunt, pastores, haec sunt mysteria vobis
advertenda: animi fugiunt obscena viriles,
femineas loca delectant infamia mentes."

Ut semel in scopulos vento contortus et unda
nauta scit incautis monstrare pericula nautis,
sic senior longo factus prudentior usu
praeteritos meminit casus aperitque futuri
temporis eventus vitaeque pericula monstrat.

"Si fugiunt aquilam fulicae, si retia cervi,
si agna lupum, si damma canem, muliebria cur non
blandimenta fugis tantum tibi noxia, pastor?
est in eis pietas crocodili, astutia hyaenae;
cum flet et appellat te blandius, insidiatur.
femineos, pastor, fugito (sunt retia) vultus;
non animis, non virtuti, non viribus ullis
fidito, non clipeo cuius munimine Perseus
vidit saxificae colubros impune Medusae.
monstra peremerunt multi, domuere gigantes,
evertere urbes, legem imposuere marinis
fluctibus, impetui fluviorum et montibus aspris,
sacra coronarunt multos certamina; sed qui

Thracian women cut up the poet Orpheus limb by limb. [161] The wantonness of Pasiphae's lust is well-known; and Phaedra cruelly ventured against Hippolytus' chastity. Rebecca of the Jews tricked her husband and his son when she covered Jacob's neck with goatskins; Hercules' wife offered him the fatal poison; and Hippodamia beguiled her father. Lavinia involved the Trojans in a dubious war, Briseis drove Achilles from the camps, and maddened by Chryseis Agamemnon flashed lightning and felt Apollo's wrath. Indeed, Eve drove our race from those happy fields. [171] Believe me, you shepherds, (by the gods of the countryside I swear it!) if you want the fields safe for your flocks, if you care for your sheep, finally if quiet, peace, and life itself are dear to you, keep away those capricious girls; let all of them—Thestylis and Phyllis, Galatea, Neaera, and Lycoris—be driven far from your sheepfolds. Tell me, what woman ever descended into gloomy Orcus' realm and returned? Had she not been foolish, Eurydice could have been brought back from those shades among which she had descended. And Persephone, when she had been carried off, refused to follow her weary mother. [181] But pious Aeneas returned, yes and Orpheus came back, as did mighty Achilles and Theseus and the two brothers (the one skilled in riding, the other in boxing and wrestling) and in truth our Lord God, whence springs again our salvation and life. These, shepherds, these are mysteries you ought to consider: men's thoughts flee obscene matters while the minds of women choose shameful things."

—Just as a sailor, having been once hurled against the rocks by wind and waves, knows how to show the dangers to unsuspecting sailors, so an older man, made more prudent by great experience, remembers past misfortunes, lays bare their future consequences, and points out the dangers in life.—

[193] "If coots flee the eagle, deer the hunters' nets, if the lamb flees the wolf and the doe the hound, why, shepherd, don't you flee women's enticements, so harmful to you? In women there are the crocodile's compassion and the hyena's cunning: when they weep and call seductively, they are lying in ambush for you. Flee, shepherd—for they are snares—flee women's looks. Trust not to your reason, ability, or strength, or to that shield by whose protection Perseus safely viewed the serpents of Medusa, who turned men to stone. [202] Many men have slain monsters, conquered giants, overthrown cities, and imposed law on the seawaves, river currents, and craggy mountains; sacred contests have crowned many; but even those

cuncta subegerunt sunt a muliere subacti.
rex qui pastor erat funda spolioque leonis
inclutus, et natus qui templa Sionia fecit
primus, et excellens invicto robore Samson
femineum subiere iugum; minus officit ignis,
saxa minus, rhomphaea minus, minus hasta, minus mors.
nex formae contenta suae splendore decorem
auget mille modis mulier: frontem ligat auro,
purpurat arte genas et collocat arte capillos,
arte regit gressus et lumina temperat arte.
currit, ut in latebras ludens perducat amantem;
vult dare, sed cupiens simplex et honesta videri
denegat et pugnat; sed vult super omnia vinci.
femina Caeciaco (res mira) simillima vento est
qui trahit expellens mendaci nubila flatu.
quisquis es (expertus moneo) temptare recusa,
dum licet, hic fragilis quot habet fastidia sexus.
immundum natura animal, sed quaeritur arte
mundities; id luce opus est, ea somnia nocte.
deglabrat, lavat et pingit, striat, unguit et ornat
tota dolus, tota ars, tota histrio, tota venenum.
consilio speculi gerit omnia; labra movere
discit et inspecto vultum componere vitro,
discit blandiri, discit ridere, iocari,
incedens umeros discit vibrare natesque.
quid sibi vult nudum pectus? quid aperta superne
rimula quae bifidam deducit in ubera vallem?
nempe nihil, nisi quo virus penetrabile sensum
plus premat et Stygiae rapiant praecordia flammae.
hi iuvenum scopuli, Syrtes, Scyllae atque Charybdes;
hae immundae Phinei volucres quae ventre soluto
proluvie foeda thalamos, cenacula, mensas,
compita, templa, vias, agros, mare, flumina, montes
incestare solent; hae sunt Phorcynides ore
monstrifico extremis Libyae quae in finibus olim
aspectu mutare homines in saxa solebant."

Carmina doctiloqui cursim recitavimus Umbri.
quae si visa tibi nimium prolixa, memento
ipsius id rei vitium, non carminis esse.
non longum est carmen, mulierum amentia longa est.
Iannus O memorande senex, quo se vetus Umbria tantum
iactat et ipse tuae Tiberis conterminus urbi,
Martia non ab re tantum te Roma vocabat.
ipsa tuas artes et non trivialia norat
carmina. te vita functum flevere Latinae
Naiades et Graiae. tua molliter ossa quiescant

who have conquered all obstacles have themselves been conquered by women. That king, famous for his sling and lion's skin, who once was a shepherd, and his son who first erected Sion's temple, and Samson, distinguished for his unconquered strength—all these men submitted to a woman's yoke. Fire, stones, spears, arrows, death itself all are less harmful! [212] And not content with her beauty's radiance, a woman increases it by a thousand means. She binds her forehead with gold, artfully makes her cheeks rosy and arranges her hair, artfully governs her walk and controls the movements of her eyes. She runs away so as to lead her lover deceptively to her hideaway. She wants to surrender yet, wishing to seem simple and honorable, denies and struggles against him; but above all she wants to be conquered. Woman is like the wind named *caecias* that (a wondrous matter!) draws the clouds while it drives them away with its deceptive breezes.

[221] "Whoever you are—from experience I warn you—while you are able, don't put to the test how much fastidiousness this brittle sex possesses. By nature a filthy creature, woman nonetheless seeks through her art to be clean. That is her toil by day, her dream by night. She smooths her skin, washes and paints her face, wrinkles her brow, rubs her face with creams, and adorns herself—but all of her is trickery, artifice, mimicry, and poison! She does everything by the counsel of her mirror. Having gazed into a glass, she learns how to move her lips and compose her features, to flatter a man, to laugh and jest, and to wiggle her shoulders and hips as she walks. [231] What means that naked bosom? That uncovered cleft which cleaves a valley between her breasts? Doubtless for no other reason than for her piercing venom to oppress your senses further and for her Stygian flames to seize your heart. These are the rocks and sands, the Scylla and Charybdis of youth. These creatures are the foul–winged monsters known to Phineus that, loosening their bowels, are wont to defile with their filthy flood bedchambers, dining rooms, banqueting tables, crossroads, churches, highways, fields, seas, rivers, and mountains. These are Phorcus' daughters of monstrous visage who once in far–off Lybian lands were wont by their looks to transform men into stone."

[242] I have repeated in haste these verses of wise–spoken Umber. If they seem long to you, remember that it is the fault of the subject, not the song. The verses aren't long; the folly of women is unending.

Jannus Ah, memorable old man! Ancient Umbria and the Tiber itself that borders your city so boast of you; and to its advantage Rome, sacred to Mars, so often used to call upon your attendance. Rome itself had come to know of your achievements and rare verses. When you died, the Naiads of Rome and Greece wept for you. May your bones forever rest softly and may your

semper et in summo mens aurea vivat Olympo.

ECLOGA V
CANDIDUS
De consuetudine divitum erga poetas
Silvanus Candidus

Sil. Candide, nobiscum pecudes aliquando solebas
pascere et his gelidis calamos inflare sub umbris
et miscere sales simul et certare palaestra;
nunc autem quasi pastores et rura perosus
pascua sopita fugis et trahis otia cantu.
Can. Vos quibus est res ampla domi, quibus ubera vaccae
plena ferunt, quibus alba greges mulctraria complent,
cymbia lacte nivent et pinguia prandia fumant,
carmina laudatis; si quid concinnius exit,
plauditis ac laeti placidas extenditis aures.
pro numeris vanas laudes et inania verba
redditis; interea pastor sitit, esurit, alget.
Sil. Nonne potes curare greges et dicere versus,
cum vacat, et positis vitam traducere curis?
Can. Omnem operam gregibus pastorem impendere oportet,
ire, redire, lupos arcere, mapalia saepe
cingere, mercari paleas et pabula, victum
quaerere; nil superest oti. laudabile carmen
omnem operam totumque caput, Silvane, requirit.
grande utrumque opus est et nostris viribus impar.
cum cecini, sitio; sitienti pocula nemo
porrigit. irrident alii: "tibi paenula," dicunt,
"Candide, trita, genu nudum, riget hispida barba."
iam silvae implumes et hiems in montibus albet;
irascor, doleo, indignor. fert omnia victus,
lanitium fetusque mares; non vendimus agnas,
sed, quia lac pascunt, premitur nihil; ubera siccant.
paenitet ingenii, si quid mihi, paenitet artis,
paenitet et vitae, postquam mihi nulla secundant
ex tot sideribus quot sunt in nocte serena.
hactenus (ut nosti) gratis cantavimus; aetas
indiga paucorum merces fuit; altera longe
condicio senii quod nunc subit: omnium egenos
reddit et exstinctis lucri spem viribus aufert.
mox erit utendum partis, modo quaerere tempus.
en formica, brevis sed provida bestia, condit

resplendent soul dwell forever on the heights of Olympus.

ECLOGUE V
CANDIDUS
The Treatment of Poets by Rich Men
Silvanus Candidus

Sil. Candidus, once you were accustomed to graze your sheep with ours, to play your pipe beneath this cool shade, exchange jests, and take part in our wrestling matches. But now, as if detesting shepherds and fields, you flee our pastures and draw out your idleness, having put your song to sleep.
Can. You whose household goods abound, whose cows' udders are swollen, whose herds fill creamy milkpails, whose cups are snow–white with milk, and whose rich midday meals give off their steam—you it is who praise my songs, and if any of them turns out more neatly than the rest, you praise it and happily extend it an ear freed from stress. But in exchange for my verses you pay me with empty praise and meaningless words, and in the meantime as a shepherd I thirst, suffer hunger, and endure the cold weather.
Sil. [13] But can't you care for your flocks and sing your verses when there is time? Having laid aside your cares, can't you change your life?
Can. A shepherd must devote all his labor to his flocks. He must keep coming and going, chasing away the wolves, surrounding his sheds with a fence, buying straw and winter feed, and seeking food for himself. No leisure is left to him. A praiseworthy song, Silvanus, requires all my toil and thought. Both labors, singing and tending a flock, are great ones and unequal to my strength. When I sing, I grow thirsty, yet no man extends me a cup in my thirst. Some mock me and say, "your cloak is worn, Candidus, your knees are bare, your beard stiff with bristles." [24] Now the woods are unplumed and in the mountains winter seems white with snow; and now I am angry, I grieve and complain. For the way that we live now is taking all we have, our wool and young rams. We aren't selling the ewe lambs. And on the contrary, since they are being suckled, none of the ewes can be milked. The lambs dry up their udders. I rue my talents (if I have any), my trade, even my life, since none of the many stars that are in the clear sky has guided it favorably. [31] Up to now I sang (as you know) without payment. My youth, which needed little, was my reward. Far otherwise are the circumstances of advancing old age. It makes me needful of all things and, my strength extinguished, takes away all my hope of gain. Soon I must put to use what I have acquired, now is the time to seek it. Behold how the ant, a small but foresighted creature,

in brumam nova farra cavis aestate latebris,
neve renascantur fruges secat ore sepultas.
Sil. Scire genethliacos fatalia sidera dicunt.
hi sub Mercurio vates et sub Iove reges
magnatesque locant; istis dat Iuppiter aurum
atque magistratus, dat Maiae filius illis
ingenium, linguam, citharas et carminis artem.
haec tua sors; quid quaeris opes? Deus omnia in omnes
dividit, ut melius nobis videt esse futurum.
sorte tua contentus abi, sine cetera nobis.
Can. Sunt tibi divitiae, mihi carmina; quid petis ergo
carmen et invadis partes, Silvane, alienas?
Sil. Non tibi surripio carmen nec Apollinis arma,
sed dare dulcisonis aures concentibus opto.
Can. Si gaudere meis igitur concentibus optas,
nos gaudere tuis opibus, Silvane, decorum est.
Sil. Ille meis opibus gaudet qui diligit; odit
invidus atque animo bona fert aliena molesto.
Can. Sic quoque tu nostris absens gaudere Camenis
sat potes; haec artis sat sint tibi gaudia nostrae.
carmina sunt auris convivia, caseus oris;
si cupis auditu, fac nos gaudere palato.
hoc amor, hoc pietas, hoc vult Deus; omnia non dat
omnibus, ut nemo sibi sit satis indigeatque
alter ope alterius, quae res coniungit in unum
omne genus, Gallos, Mauros, Italos et Iberos.
sidera iungamus: facito mihi Iuppiter adsit,
et tibi Mercurius noster dabit omnia faxo,
pilleolum, virgam, citharas, nodum Herculis, alas.
Sil. Vana supervacuis inculcas plurima verbis.
Can. Vana inquis quae damna tuis inferre videntur
divitiis. si vis nostras audire Camenas,
erue sopitam de sollicitudine mentem;
vult hilares animos tranquillaque pectora carmen.
torpeo, ut esuriem patiens et frigora milvus,
iamdudum squarrosa cutis, situs occupat ora,
nec pecus in stabulis, nec in agro farra, nec aurum
in loculis; et vis positis me vivere curis?
non facit ad nostros talis medicina dolores.
fac alacrem, tege, pasce, gravi succurre senectae;
invenies promptum versu et cantare paratum.
plena domus curas abigit, cellaria plena,
plena penus plenique cadi plenaeque lagenae,
horrea plena, greges laeti, gravis aere crumena.
tunc iuvat hibernos noctu vigilare Decembres
ante focum et cineri ludos inarare bacillo,

lays up against the cold of winter fresh grain in his hollow storerooms during the summertime and, lest the grains sprout, cuts them in two with his jaws when he has stored them.

Sil. [39] Astrologers are said to understand the stars, those beacons of Fate. These men place poets under Mercury and put kings and other powerful men under Jupiter. To the latter Jupiter grants wealth and office. To the former the son of Maia gives genius, speech, the lyre, and the art of song. This is your lot. Why do you seek for riches? God divides all things among everyone, since He can see the future better than we. Remain content with your lot, then, without seeking ours.

Can. You have your riches, I my songs. Why then, Silvanus, do you seek to obtain poetry and usurp another man's portion?

Sil. [49] I'm not stealing Apollo's songs and instruments from you. On the contrary, I wish to lend an ear to their sweet–sounding harmonies.

Can. If then you wish to rejoice in my harmonies, Silvanus, it is fit for me to rejoice in your riches.

Sil. The man rejoices in my riches who loves them. The envious man hates them and endures another man's prosperity with troublesome thoughts.

Can. [55] So also you can rejoice in my songs in absence. Let these joys be enough of my art for you. Songs are a feast for the ears but food for the mouth. If you want to listen to them, you must please my palate. Love, piety, and God all desire this. For God grants diverse gifts to different folk in such a way that no man is wholly self–sufficient but each needs some aid from another. Just this circumstance joins together every race: Frenchmen and Moors, Italians and Spaniards. Let us unite our stars then; make Jupiter be favorable to me and I will cause my Mercury to grant you all his gifts: his cap, rod, lyre, Herculean knot, and wings.

Sil. [66] You're preaching idle thoughts with too many words.

Can. You say those things are idle that seem to lessen your wealth. If you want to hear my songs, rescue a mind dulled by care. A song wants cheerful thoughts and a tranquil heart. Like a kite enduring hunger and cold I feel numbed. For a long time my skin has been rough, old age has ravaged my face. I haven't a herd in my stables, grain in my field, or gold in my coffer—and you want me to live, having laid aside my cares! Such a remedy doesn't suit my afflictions. Come, give me life, clothe and feed me, hasten to relieve my burdensome old age. Then you will find me prompt in my verses and prepared to sing. [78] Cares are driven away by a well–stocked house and cellar, an ample store of victuals, full jars and wine–flasks, a full granary, sleek herds, and a purse heavy with coins. Then I delight to keep watch before the fire at night through wintry Decembers and to play at plowing into

torrere et tepidis tostas operire favillis
castaneas plenoque sitim restinguere vitro
fabellasque inter nentes ridere puellas.
Tityrus (ut fama est) sub Maecenate vetusto
rura, boves et agros et Martia bella canebat
altius et magno pulsabat sidera cantu.
eloquium fortuna dabat; nos, debile vulgus,
pannosos, macie affectos, farragine pastos
Aoniae fugiunt Musae, contemnit Apollo.
Sil. Si sperata mihi dederit fortuna quod opto,
Candide, praesenti te sollicitudine solvam.
Can. O utinam, Silvane, foret tibi tanta voluntas
quanta est hac etiam tibi tempestate facultas.
non ego divitias Cosmi, non Serica posco
pallia, non Tyrias chlamydes, non prandia regum,
non patinam Aesopi fameo clipeumve Minervae;
nil opus est regis laribus cui ferrea nomen
tradidit aut, si mens non fallitur, aenea barba
(haec me iam pridem memini didicisse sub Umbro)
postulo vestitum, peto victum sub lare parvo
certior istud opis toti non defore vitae;
sint mihi Pythagorae mensae Codrique supellex.
saepe alios qui spem dederint invenimus ore
magnificos, sed re modicos; tibi fidimus uni.
tu mihi si fueris mendax, praeciditur omnis
spes, ut solstitio fiam philomena reverso
mutus et elinguis. suspendere postibus arma
tempus erit clausoque abigi spectacula circo.
Sil. Candide, vidisti Romam sanctique senatus
pontifices, ubi tot vates, ubi copia rerum
tantarum? facile est illis ditescere campis.
Can. Deciperis me velle putans ditescere. vesci
et lupus omne animal crudis existimat escis
tuque putas alios quo tu pede claudere passum.
non ego ditari cupio, sed vivere parvo.
fac habeam tenuem sine sollicitudine victum;
hoc contentus eam. Romana palatia vidi,
sed quid Roma, putas, mihi proderit? o Silvane,
occidit Augustus numquam rediturus ab Orco.
si quid Roma dabit, nugas dabit. accipit aurum,
verba dat. heu Romae nunc sola pecunia regnat;
exsilium virtu patitur. sperare iubemur
undique et in toto vates spe pascimur orbe.
Sil. Dic pugnas, dic gesta virum, dic proelia regum,
vertere ad hos qui sceptra tenent, qui regna gubernant;
invenies qui te de sordibus eruat istis.

the ashes with a stick. Then I love to roast chestnuts, covering them afterwards with the warm embers, to quench my thirst with a brimful glass, and to laugh at a merry tale among the spinning maids. Under Maecenas' care of old, Tityrus (so men say) sang more loftily of the countryside, of the oxen and fields, and of the wars of Mars; and with his mighty song he battered the heavens. Good fortune gave him eloquence. But the Aeonian Muses flee us and Apollo slights us, the feeble crowd of poets: ragged, weakened by hunger, fed on scraps.

Sil. [92] If the conditions I hope for grant me what I desire, I will release you, Candidus, from your present cares.

Can. Ah, Silvanus, may you have as much good will then as you have means at this moment! I ask not for Cosimo's riches, silk garments and Tyrian cloaks, or the meals of a king. I hunger not for the delicacies of Aesop's dish or Minerva's shield. I don't need the dwelling of that king whose iron–colored—nay, bronze–colored—beard (for I remember having learned these things long ago under Umber) gave him his name. I ask for clothing and food within a small dwelling, more certain that that aid will last throughout my life. Let me have Pythagoras' meals and Codrus' furnishings. [105] Often I have met others who gave me hope, who were lavish in words but sparing in their gifts. In you alone I put my trust. If even you were to be false to me, all my hopes would be cut off so that I would become like the nightingale when summer's heat has returned: silent and dumb. There will come a time to hang up my arms on the door and, with the Circus' closing, to cease my gladiator's trials by combat.

Sil. Candidus, have you seen Rome and the holy prelates of its court where there are so many poets, so much abundance? 'Tis easy to grow wealthy in those fields.

Can. [114] You are deceived in thinking I want to grow wealthy. The wolf thinks that all animals devour their food raw, and indeed you believe that other men frame their songs by the measure you have allowed. I don't desire to become rich but to live with little. Give me a slender diet without care, with this I will live content. I have seen Rome's palaces. But why do you suppose Rome will help me? Oh Silvanus, Augustus has perished, never will he return from Orcus. If Rome will give anything, it will give me baubles. It takes gold but gives only words. Alas, wealth alone now rules in Rome. Virtue is banished. We are bidden to be hopeful, and indeed all round the whole world poets are fed on hope.

Sil. [126] Sing of battles, sing of men's deeds, sing of the strife of kings. Turn your thoughts to those who wield the scepter and govern kingdoms. You will find someone to rescue you from your squalor.

Can. Inveniam qui me derideat et subsannet.
tempestate ista reverentia tanta poesi
quanta lupanari; quid me, Silvane, lacessis?
Sil. Non decet obscenis vatem prorumpere verbis.
Can. Non possum non vera loqui. si vera taceri
forte velis, levibus me parce lacessere dictis.
Sil. Utile consilium praestare lacessere non est.
Can. Consilii locuples ego, sed pauperrimus auri.
qui pugnas, qui gesta virum, qui proelia regum
dicet inops vates cui nec quo fistula possit
aptius incidi fierique foramina culter?
aspice ut excussis luxata manubria clavis,
ut dentata acies veterique simillima serrae.
hoc leve, sed mensae grave et intolerabile damnum.
utile consilium firmat, sed inutile mentem
frangit et extenuat vires animumque retundit.
magnates dare parva pudet, dare magna recusant.
adde quod et nostri curant ita carmina reges
ut frondes Aquilo, mare Libs, vineta pruinae.
ipsi ad delicias reges et ad otia versi
quod celebrant laudari optant; hinc carmina manant
perdita de studio Veneris, de scurrilitate,
de ganea, de signitie, de infamibus actis
quae castum capitale nefas celebrare poetam.
at qui dura manu gesserunt bella potenti
fortiter utentes ferro, non molliter auro,
dilexere graves Musas; heroica facta
qui faciunt reges heroica carmina laudant.
ut cesssere viri fortes et mascula virtus,
dicendum altiloqui nihil invenere poetae;
occidit ingenium vatum, ruit alta poesis.
at si forte aliquis regum gerit aspera bella
et decus armorum studiis belloque paravit,
nil genus externum venturaque saecula curat
laude suae gentis satur et praesentibus annis;
barbarus est neque carmen amat vel avarus in auro
mergitur atque Midae curis flagrantibus ardet.
est et apud reges rudis, invida, rustica turba,
mimus, adulator, leno, assentator, adulter,
histrio, scurra, quibus virtus odiosa; poetas
mille modis abigunt, ut quando cadavera corvi
invenere, fugant alias volucresque ferasque.
sunt etiam vates quidam sine lege petulci
qui sine lege aliti sine praeceptoribus audent
quidquid amant reges (et amant infamia solum)
scribere; nam vates etiam dementia vexat.

Can. Nay, I'll find only men to deride and mock me. In that tempest poetry has as much respect as a bawdyhouse. Silvanus, why do you provoke me like this?
Sil. A poet shouldn't burst out in obscene language.
Can. I am unable to utter lies. If you perhaps wish the truth to remain silent, stop provoking me with foolish maxims.
Sil. To offer useful counsel is not to provoke you.
Can. [136] I'm rich in counsel but most poor in gold. How will a poor poet sing of battles, men's deeds, and the strife of kings who hasn't a knife fit to carve his pipe aright or bore holes in it? Look how the hilt is crooked, the pins having fallen out, and how its edge is jagged like an old saw. 'Tis a trifling inconvenience but grievous and intolerable when I eat. Useful counsel fortifies the mind. Useless advice shatters it, lessens its vigor, and blunts it. Great men are ashamed to grant small rewards and refuse to give large gifts. [146] Moreover, kings respect our songs in the same way that the north wind cares for the leaves, the south wind for the sea, or hoarfrost for the vineyard. Kings, themselves inclined to passing fancies and idleness, desire what they honor to be praised. From this arise dissipated songs of the desperate pursuit of Venus and scurrility, of gluttony and sloth, and of shameful deeds that it is mortal sin for an honest poet to celebrate. But kings who with their mighty hands vigorously waged war and bravely reveled in arms, not spinelessly in gold—these men loved the grave muses. Kings who do heroic deeds praise heroic verses. [157] When brave and manly virtue passed away, poets found no exalted subjects to sing. Their inspiration died and lofty poetry was brought to ruin. But if by chance some king now wages war cruelly and has obtained glory by his zeal for arms in war, he cares not at all for the regard of foreign peoples and the ages to come; the praise of his own people and the present age is enough. Either he is a barbarian and loves not our song or, a greedy man, he is immersed in his gold and burns with Midas' fiery cares. So too among kings there is a rude, envious, coarse mob of players, sycophants, pimps, flatterers, adulterers, court jesters, and buffoons, all of whom hate excellence. In a thousand ways they drive poets away: just as, when ravens discover a carcass, they put to flight the other birds and beasts. [171] Moreover there are also certain wanton, lawless poets who, reared without discipline, dare without instruction to write whatever kings like (and they like only infamous tales): for madness vexes poets too. By

hi se nescio qua mentis levitate poetas
esse volunt. postquam trivialibus ora cicutis
applicuere, sibi applaudunt, sua carmina iactant
insulsi, illepidi, indociles, improvidi, inepti.
qui solet his vacuas praebere ambagibus aures
id vitium commune putat dictisque resistit
vatibus a vero indoctus discernere falsum.
Sil. Candide, per Superos, per Olympica numina iuro
me tibi, si venti veniant ad vela secundi,
laturum auxilium. meliora in tempora vive
nec paulisper adhuc mecum sperare recusa.
Can. Si mihi sic optas, tibi sit, Silvane, quod optas.
Sil. Opto equidem, dictumque fides non sera sequetur.
Can. Vade malis avibus numquam rediturus, avare,
et facias subito quidquid tractaveris aurum
more Midae, quando virtus tibi vilior auro.

ECLOGA VI
CORNIX
De disceptatione rusticorum et civium
Cornix Fulica

Can. Ningit hiems, mugit Boreas, a culmine pendet
stiria; depositis bobus requiescit arator,
dormit humus; clauso pastor tunicatus ovili
cessat iners, sedet ante focum fumosa Neaera
atque polenta coquit. prius intolerabilis aestas
nunc laudatur, hiems aestu laudata molesto
displicet; optatum damnat praesentia frigus.
Ful. Omne bonum praesens minus est; sperata videntur
magna, velut maius reddit distantia lumen.
Can. Delicias habet omne suas et gaudia tempus.
aspice ut impexi tritaque in veste ligati
caede suum pueri exsultant. inflatur in utrem
immissis vesica fabis; sonat et micat acta
nunc pede, nunc cubito, stricto nunc obvia pugno.
si cadit, attollunt; cursu labor atque recursu
brumam abigit; glaciale gelu pila rustica vincit.
nos tamen his melius tepido sub stramine foti
transigimus tempus, dum lac coit igne recoctum.
Ful. Pauperiem declarat hiems. improvida certe
turba sumus iuvenes; securi aestate vagamur
immemores hiemis, nostrum aes tibicinis omne est;

some sort of foolishness in their thoughts these men aspire to be true poets. After they have pressed their mouths to their puny Pan pipes, they applaud themselves and boast of their songs—these insipid, graceless, ignorant, unforeseeing, tasteless men! He who is accustomed to lend an ear freed from other preoccupations to these long-winded verses thinks their defects to be faults shared by all poets and, unlearned himself in discerning what is false from what is true, opposes poets who are truly learned.
Sil. [182] By the gods above, by the spirits of Heaven I swear, Candidus, that, if favorable winds fill my sails, I will bring help to you. Live for better times, and for a little while refuse not still to join your hopes with mine.
Can. If this is what you wish for me, Silvanus, may you have it!
Sil. It is, indeed—and my good faith will soon follow my promise.
Can. Greedy wretch, go under evil omens, never to return! And like Midas may you suddenly gild whatever you touch, since in your eyes excellence is cheaper than gold.

ECLOGUE VI
CORNIX
A Dispute Between Townsmen and Country Folk
Cornix Fulica

Cor. Winter's snows have come, the north wind is bellowing, and icicles hang from the roof. Having bedded his oxen the plowman is resting, and the ground lies asleep. His sheepfold shut up, the shepherd, snug in his cloak, idly beguiles the time, and seated before the hearth, sooty Neaera is cooking polenta. Now we commend the summer season, intolerable to us before; and wintertime, commended once in summer's irksome heat, we now find displeasing. The presence of winter's chill condemns the cold weather we once wished for.
Ful. Every good thing, when it comes, is less than it seemed. Things hoped for seem great, just as distance makes a reflected light seem greater than it is.
Cor. [10] And every season has its own delights and joys. See how unkempt and ragged boys rejoice in the slaughter of a pig. Putting beans in the bladder they blow it up to make a ball. Then it resounds and darts about, driven now by their feet, now with their elbows, struck now head on by their clenched fists. If it falls, they loft it in the air again. The effort of running back and forth drives winter away. A simple ball defeats the icy cold. We, however, kept warm beneath the straw, pass the time better here while our milk is curdling, heated on the fire again.
Ful. Still, winter reveals our poverty. A shortsighted lot, to be sure, are we young men! Carefree in summer we roam about forgetful of winter, and the

ut redit e Scythia Boreas nidosque volucrum
frondibus ostendit nudata cadentibus arbor,
frigemus nudi scapulas, dorsum, ilia, plantas.
stultitiam declarat hiems. sapientius urbes
congeriem nummum accumulant et ad ilia vulpes
melotasque trahunt maculosaque tergora lyncis.
Cor. Desipiunt omnes nec nos in crimine soli.
immo ipsos vexat gravior dementia cives,
verum illis mater nobis Fortuna noverca
nos premit. infelix sors est dementia. fac sim
fortunatus, ero locuples, ero primus in urbe,
audiar, assurgent omnes, me vertice nudo
vulgus adorabit, me plebs, me consulet omnis
turba, magistratus etiam populusque patresque.
Ful. O Cornix, Cornix, non est Fortuna sed ipse
quo sapiunt homines animus. Fortuna potentem
non facit, immo Deus; causam recitabat Amyntas.
Cor. Est Fortuna Deus. sed quid recitarit Amyntas
dic, precor; in causis erat ingeniosus et acer.
ante tamen paulum pecus et praesepia vise.
vade, redi; calor est post frigora dulcior; ito.
Ful. Attingit nix alta genu, vix tecta resistunt
tanto oneri; sublimis apex in vertice furni
pyramidem fecit metaque assurgit acuta.
Cor. Da pecori cordum stipulisque foramina claude,
si paries hiat, et rediens laetamine muni
limina; nulla gregi gravior quam frigora pestis.
iamne ades? oh quaenam haec solito properantia maior?
Ful. Sollicitum me reddit hiems; in frigore et igni
maxima strenuitas; faeno recubare calenti
abscondique cavo accubitu post frigora dulce est.
Cor. Incipe, et enarra discrimina ruris et urbis.
Ful. Hoc igitur tantum ruris discrimen et urbis
taliter exortum noster recitabat Amyntas.
    Principio rerum primaque ab origine mundi
cum muliere marem sociali foedere iungens
caeli Opifex (sic namque Deum appellabat Amyntas;
nomen adhuc teneo) natos producere iussit
atque modum docuit fieri quo pignora possent.
accinxere operi, mandata fideliter implent;
sicque utinam de pomi esu servata fuissent.
femina fit mater, puerum parit atque puellam,
atque puerperio simili fecunda quotannis
auxit in immensum generis primordia nostri.
post tria lustra Deus rediit. dum pignora pectit

piper has all our money. Then when the north wind returns from Scythia and the trees, stripped bare of their falling leaves, reveal the birds' nests within them, we freeze with cold, our shoulders, backs, sides, and the soles of our feet all bare. And winter reveals our folly. The city man more wisely heaps up his pile of coins and warms his sides with skins from the fox and sheep, and from the spotted back of the lynx.

Cor. [28] All men lack reason, we country folk aren't alone in being arraigned. Indeed, a graver madness vexes city men. Yet Fortune, a mother to them, a stepmother to us, oppresses us sorely. Madness is an unlucky lot. Grant that I might have good fortune and I will be wealthy and a well-known townsman. All men will rise and listen to me; with bared heads the crowd will revere me; the multitude, the whole mob will consult me, even the judges, both the citizens and the city fathers.

Ful. Ah, Cornix, Cornix, not Fortune but the mind itself makes a man wise. And God, not Fortune, gives man his power. Amyntas used to recount the reason.

Cor. [39] Nay, Fortune is God. But pray tell me what Amyntas recounted: in argument he was always clever and shrewd. But before you do, look briefly to the herd and stables. Go and return. Warmth is sweeter after cold. Go.

Ful. [Going outside] The snow is up to my knees. The roofs are scarcely supporting so much weight. The peak of the oven rises at its top in a pointed cone.

Cor. Give late–grown hay to the herd. If a wall gapes wide, close its chinks with stubble. And when you return, be sure to stop up the door sill with dung. Besides the cold, no other plague is more harmful to a herd. [Fulica departs but soon returns] What, already returned? Oh, why this unusual haste?

Ful. [50] Winter quickens my pace: in cold and heat I'm most nimble. [Settling down by the fire] And after being in the cold it is pleasant to lie down in the warm hay and bury myself in its hollowed–out bed.

Cor. Begin then and recount the difference between the country fellow and the city man.

Ful. Our Amyntas used to say that thus arose so great a difference between the country fellow and city man:

[56] In the beginning, when the world had first been created, the Framer of the heavens (for so Amyntas called God—I still remember the name!), joining man with woman in a bond of marriage, bade them be fruitful and taught them how to bring their offspring into being. They made ready for the task and faithfully fulfilled His commands—and would that, in eating the apple, His commandments had been observed! Eve became a mother and bore a boy and girl; and abounding yearly in like number of offspring, she vastly increased the beginnings of our race. [66] After thrice five years God returned. While Eve was combing her children's hair, she looked outside

femina prospiciens venientem a limine vidit.
Adam aberat, securus oves pascebat; adulter
nullus adhuc suspectus erat; sed multiplicatis
conubiis fraudata fides, sine cornibus hirci
facti, et zelotypo coniunx suspecta marito.
nam quae quisque facit fieri sibi furta veretur.
erubuit mater nimiaeque libidinis ingens
indicium rata tot natos abscondere quosdam
accelerat; faeno sepelit paleisque recondit.
iamque lares Deus ingressus salvere penates
iussit et "huc," dixit, "mulier, tua pignora profer."
femina maiores natu procedere mandat.
his Deus arrisit, velut arridere solemus
exiguis avium pullis parvisve catellis.
et primo laetatus ait, "cape regia sceptra;
rex eris." at ferrum et belli dedit arma secundo
et "dux," inquit, "eris." fasces populique secures
protulit et vites et pila insignia Romae.
iamque magistratus celebres partitus in omnem
progeniem humanos tacitus volvebat honores.
interea mater rebus gavisa secundis
evolat ad caulas et quos absconderat ultro
protulit "haec," dicens, "nostri quoque pignora ventris;
hos aliquo, Pater omnipotens, dignabere dono."
setosum albebat paleis caput, haeserat armis
stramen et antiquis quae pendet aranea tectis.
non arrisit eis, sed tristi turbidus ore
"vos faenum, terram et stipulas," Deus inquit, "oletis.
vester erit stimulus, vester ligo, pastina vestra;
vester erit vomer, iuga vestra, agrestia vestra
omnia; aratores eritis pecorumque magistri,
faenisecae, solifossores, nautae atque bubulci.
sed tamen ex vobis quosdam donabimus urbe
qui sint fartores, lanii, lixae artocopique
et genus hoc alii soliti sordescere. semper
sudate et toto servite prioribus aevo."
taliter Omnipotens fatus repetivit Olympum.
Sic factum est servile genus, sic ruris et urbis
inductum discrimen ait Mantous Amyntas.
Cor. Mirabar si quid recti dixisset Amyntas.
civis erat; semper nobis urbana iuventus
cui nihil est praeter stulta haec commenta negoti
ludit; in agrestes semper iaculantur, et urbis
talia garrulitas et vaniloquentia fingit.
at neque de Superis pudet has componere nugas.

from the doorway and saw Him coming. Adam was away. Free from care, he was pasturing his sheep. For as yet no one was mistrusted as an adulterer. But after the number of marriages increased, marital trust was betrayed, goats were made hornless, and wives were suspected by their jealous husbands. For whatever anyone does, he fears will be done secretly to him. Mother Eve blushed, and, having reckoned so many children a grave sign of too much desire, hastened to hide some of them. Among the hay she buried them and hid them in the chaff. Then, having entered the house, God blessed those within and said, "Woman, bring hither your children." She bade her eldest children come forth. God smiled on them just as we smile on a bird's tiny nestlings or on small puppies. [81] And having rejoiced in the first of them He said, "Take this regal scepter. You will be a king." But a sword and weapons of war he gave to the second child and said, "You will be a general." And then He brought forth the citizens' fasces and axes, centurions' staffs, and Rome's famous javelins. And when He had divided these distinguished offices among all her offspring, He stood in silence considering their mortal honors. Meanwhile Mother Eve, pleased by these favorable gifts, flew to the sheepcote and brought forth unbidden the children she had hidden there, saying, "These too are the dear pledges of my womb. You will deem them worthy, almighty Father, of some gift." Their bristly heads were white with chaff, straw clung to their shoulders, yes and even spider webs, the sort that hang down from ancient ceilings. [93] God smiled not on them, but troubled, with a sad countenance, He said, "You smell of hay, earth, and straw. Yours then will be the goad, mattock, and dibble, yours will be the plowshare and yoke, yours will be all things belonging to the fields. You will become plowmen and shepherds, yes and mowers, ditchers, rivermen, and herdsmen. But I will give some of you to the city to be poultry men, butchers, sutlers, bakers, and others of this kind accustomed to befoul their hands in toil. Sweat and serve your betters throughout your lives." And having spoken in such a way, the Almighty returned to Heaven.

[104] Thus, declared Mantoan Amyntas, was created the race of servants, thus began the difference between the country fellow and the city man.

Cor. I was always amazed if Amyntas spoke anything honest. He lived in the city, and city wags, whose only business is these foolish fables, are forever mocking us. They are always reviling country folk, for the city's babbling and idle chatter invents such tales. Indeed, they aren't ashamed to invent such

iste iocus manifesta gerit convicia secum,
sed tu tam rudis es, tam pleno inflatus omaso,
ut neque perpendas isto te scommate carpi.
nos quoque paulisper mentem extendamus ad urbis
stultitiam, ne forte putes sapientius illos
vivere qui splendent auro, qui murice fulgent.
His oculis vidi tunicis plerosque superbis
vestiri atque foro regali incedere gressu
quos secreta fames premit atque domestica egestas.
stultius his certe nihil est; opulentia ficta,
paupertas et segnities et inertia vitae
vera, quid est aliud quam desipientia vera?
vidi etiam patres (o rem indignam atque nefandam)
dum segnes dormire volunt et vivere laute,
prostituisse suas vulgo cum coniuge natas;
quid peius? quid perfidius? quid stultius umquam?
Ful. Quid si vitam alio nequeunt traducere pacto?
Cor. Cum totidem quot nos habeant animasque manusque,
dic cur vitam alio nequeant traducere pacto.
Est etiam cuius vecors industria vanas
quaerat opes, ubi nullus opes invenit ab aevo:
aes lavat herbarum sucis et vertere in aurum
aestimat ac nigra semper fuligine pallet.
est qui, dum tellure latens desiderat aurum,
dat magicis operam studiis et tempora perdit;
quid levius? quid futilius? quid inanius umquam?
omnia, ne veniant ad opus telluris et agri,
omnia pertemptant; ut agant nihil, omnia versant.
semper agunt, numquam peragunt. ex faenore victum
infamen extorquent; vi, fraude dolisque laborant.
mille viis opibus, mille insidiantur honori.
nos capras et oves armentaque pascimus, illi
accipitres, catulos et equos et cercopithecos.
rusticus est ovium pastor, volucrumque canumque
civis; utrum melius, te iudice, nobiliusque,
o Fulica, utilitas unde et opulentia maior?
Ful. Si venit ex nostris operis opulentia maior,
civibus unde igitur tantarum copia rerum?
Cor. Ex vi, fraude, dolis; vi, fraude dolisque laborant.
nonne vides, insane, ut nos crudeliter urgent,
quo capiunt astu? nos irretire loquendo
sacrum offerre putant et opus sublime piumque.
huc aures oculosque adigunt, huc ora manusque.
Ful. Unde urbanarum tibi tanta peritia rerum?
Cor. Haec didici quondam ductis in moenia capris,

trifles even about the gods above. This kind of joke carries its own reproof, and yet you are so naïve, your belly is so puffed out that you don't consider that you are being sniped at by their ridicule. But let us also turn our thoughts for a little while to the folly of the city lest by chance you think that they live more wisely who gleam with gold and are resplendent in purple.

[118] With my own eyes I have seen many men who proudly arrayed themselves and paced regally in the marketplace but whom hunger and poverty secretly oppressed in their homes. Certainly nothing is more foolish than that sort of people: feigned riches, but in their lives poverty, laziness, and sloth—what is this other than true folly? And I have even seen fathers (oh, shameful and unspeakable thing!) who, as long as they wished to laze about and live in splendor, prostituted their daughters with common husbands. What was ever more wicked? more treacherous? more foolish?

Ful. But what if they can live by no other means?

Cor. [129] Since they have as much spirit and strength as we, tell me why they can live by no other means!

Furthermore, there are men whose frenzied diligence seeks vain riches where no man has ever found them. With potions drawn from herbs they bathe their copper coins and judge them changed into gold; and they are always pale in the black soot. Further, there are men who, as long as they desire the gold that lies hidden in the earth, toil in the study of magic and waste their time. What was ever more trifling, futile, and empty? They explore all manner of things thoroughly so as not to work the earth in the fields. So that they might do nothing, they try everything. [140] They are always doing, they accomplish naught. Through usury city men extort an infamous living; they labor by force, fraud, and deception. In a thousand ways they scheme to seize wealth and honors. We pasture goats, sheep, and cattle. They feed hunting falcons and young hounds, fine horses and monkeys. The countryman is a pastor of sheep, the city man a keeper of birds and hounds. Which in your judgment is better and nobler? Which one, Fulica, is more useful? which produces greater wealth?

Ful. But if greater wealth comes from our toil, whence then comes the city man's great riches?

Cor. [150] From force, fraud, and deception. They labor by force, fraud, and deception. Madman! don't you see how they cruelly oppress us? with what cunning they enthrall us? To ensnare us with words they think a sacred, a lofty, pious act. To this they impel their ears and eyes, their mouths and hands.

Ful. Where did you gain so much expertise in the ways of the city?

Cor. I learned it once when, having led my goats within the city's walls, I

cum lac vociferans ibam venale per urbem.
mansi apud artocopum. sapiens et ad omnia promptus
furta erat et crudum ferro subradere panem.
ipse, ut erat mores urbis doctissimus, ista
tradidit affirmans nihil esse nocentius urbe;
se quoque furari didicisse aiebat ab urbe.

Sunt etiam qui parta ab avis patrimonia fundunt
in meretricum usus; quid foedius improbiusque?
dic, ubi moechandi ars, homicidia, seditiones?
nonne inter cives atque intra moenia regnant?
quid reges qui regna hominum per vulnera quaerunt
in mortemque suos adigunt? quid pectora miles
obiciens telis, per mille pericula vadens?
pro stipe dat vitam; nulla est insania maior.
gloria praefertur vitae; quid gloria? quid laus?
quid fama est? quid honor? voces et opinio vulgi.
omnia longa dies abolet; cum vivere cessas,
omnia sic abeunt, ut lux cum sole recedit.
qui mare sollicitant remis, cum vivere possint
in patria, stulti; vento qui credit et undis,
stultus; divitiae cui sunt et neglegit uti,
stultus, qui, ut natis cumulet patrimonia, partis
abstinet et genium fraudat, stultissimus, et qui
quae facere ipse potest natis faciunda relinquit.
qui numerant stellas et se comprendere fata
posse putant, stulti; verum dementior istis
naturam quicumque Dei scrutatur et audet
figere in immensam lumen tam debile lucem.
nostra fides melior. civis ratione coactus
difficile assentit; nudis nos omnia verbis
credimus et plures faculas accendimus aris.
civibus est infida fides; inquirere numquam
mente sinunt arcana Dei. si numina scire
esset opus, poterant nobis se ostendere; verum,
quando latere volunt, quid vestigare necesse est
quae nos scire negant ipsi qui cuncta guberant?
nostra etiam pietas pietate potentior urbis.
namque viri qui sacra canunt templisque ministrant
quanta legunt ruri paucis alimenta diebus?
vidi ego quaesitas ex rure in moenia plenis
puppibus inferri (pietas ea rustica) fruges.
stultorum est aliud genus immedicabile quoddam,
causidici latratores rabulaeque forenses
nummorum aucupium docti legumque tyranni.
aere patrocinium vendunt; producere causas

walked through it crying out "milk for sale." I stayed with a baker. Cunning he was, easily inclined to every kind of thievery and quick to pare the bottom off the unbaked bread with his knife. As he was well versed in the ways of the city, he himself betrayed its tricks to me, affirming that nothing was more wicked than the city. Indeed, he used to say that it had taught him how to steal.

[163] Nay, there are even city men who squander on whoring the patrimony procured by their forefathers. What is fouler and more wicked? Tell me, where do you find the arts of adultery, murder, and sedition? Don't they hold sway among city men and within city walls? Why are there kings who seek kingdoms through men's wounds and who drive their subjects to their deaths? Why are there soldiers who fling their breasts against enemy arrows and pass through a thousand perils? For a paltry fee they give their lives—no madness is greater! Men value glory above their lives. But what are glory and praise? what is fame? what is honor?—the words and opinion of the mob! [173] Time at length effaces all things; and when you have ceased living, all things vanish, just as light departs with the setting of the sun. Foolish are those men who vex the sea with their oars though they might live in the land of their fathers. Foolish is the man who trusts to the wind and waves; foolish he who has wealth but fails to spend it; most foolish the man who, to heap up a legacy for his children, holds himself back from spending what he has acquired, cheating his desires, and the man who leaves things to be done by his children that he himself could have done. Those who number the stars and think they are able to comprehend their fates, those men are fools. But, indeed, madder still than those is the man who pries into the nature of God and dares to train so feeble a glimmer on so immense a light. [185] The faith of us country folk is better than the townsman's. Constrained by reason, he gives his assent only with difficulty; but we believe in all things that are plainly expressed and light more tapers at our altars. The townsman has a faithless faith. God's secrets never allow our minds to inquire into them. Should we need to understand the gods, they have the power to reveal themselves to us. But in truth, since they choose to hide themselves, why is it necessary to search after knowledge that they themselves who govern all things deny us to know? Moreover we give our alms more readily than does the townsman. For how much food is gathered from our fields in a few days by those men who celebrate mass and keep watch over our churches? I myself have seen the fruits of the countryside sought out and carried by fully laden boats (for such is rural piety) from the countryside within the city's walls.

[198] There is another incurable race of fools: lawyers, brawlers, and court tub thumpers—skilled in catching at coins and tyrants over the law. For money these men peddle their pleading. Dragging out cases and hanging up

et lites pendere diu vindemia quaedam est.
sunt et equestre genus medici qui tangere venas
non numquam illicitas audent et ponere quaedam
non intellectis temeraria nomina morbis.
his, etsi tenebras palpant, est facta potestas
excruciandi aegros hominesque impune necandi.
qui vero in populis praesunt hominesque gubernant
quo plus iuris habent quantoque licentia maior
insanire solent tanto amplius. o ubi sancti
rectores et iustitiae et pietatis amici
quos patres sero ante focum memorare solebant?
omnia nunc abeunt pessum. spoliata queruntur
templa, gemunt inopes, viduae lacrimantur, et huius
quaenam causa mali? quia stat pro lege libido.
Ful. Ista tua, o Cornix, excandescentia fines
transit honestatis; scelus omnibus obicis omne.
innocuos habitare homines et in urbe memento.
Cor. Non habitant colubri quaedam Balearibus arva
proxima (non memini nomen) neque noctua Cretam,
nec nemus Egeriae sonipes, nec vir bonus urbem.
Ful. Vir bonus est animal rarum paucasque per urbes
et per rura locos habet; est rarissima virtus.
Cor. Insanis, Fulica, insanis; tot in urbibus hostes
sunt tibi quot cives. hi nos tondentque pilantque
non habita nostri capitis ratione; coartant
nos ad furta, ipsi mox ad suspendia mittunt.
fas igitur, si quid nostris sese unguibus offert,
radere et insidiis ac nostra indagine captos
deplumare levi tactu sensim et pedepressim.
si videt, excusa, si sunt secreta, negato
furta; quod occultum est non est iniuria furtum.
quidquid habent noster labor est, industria nostra est.
Ful. Iam longe egrederus metam rationis et aequi.
Cor. O Fulica, improbitas urbana coinquinat orbem.
unde tot in terras veniunt aestate procellae,
fulmina, venti, amnes, grando? vidisse recordor
tellurem tremere ac postes et tecta labare,
solem obscurari, noctu obtenebrescere lunam.
cur segeti lolium, messi dominantur avenae,
uva in capreolos transit, caligine verni
depereunt flores? mala parturit omnia nobis
haec civile nefas, pariet quoque plura deinceps.
unde venit furor armorum bellique tumultus
qui genus omne mali secum vehit? omnibus urbs est
fons et origo malis. descendit ab urbe Lycaon,

lawsuits for a long time is, so to speak, their harvest. And there is that equestrian race of doctors that often don't hesitate to touch forbidden veins and impose names by chance on sicknesses they don't understand. These men, although they grope in darkness, are empowered to torment the sick and kill men with impunity. And indeed, those among the people who have control over and govern men, the more rights and greater license they have, the more they are accustomed to unleash their madness. Oh, where are those holy rulers and friends of justice and piety whom our fathers used to talk about before the hearth late at night? Now everything is going to wrack and ruin. Our pillaged churches lament their fate, the poor groan, and widows weep—and what is the cause of all this evil? Because desire stands in the place of law!

Ful. [216] This eruption of your anger, Cornix, transgresses the limits of honesty. You are accusing everyone of each of these crimes. Remember that innocent men also live in the city.

Cor. Snakes live not in the land near Majorca (I forget its name) nor do owls dwell on Crete nor in Egeria's grove dwells the horse with his resounding hooves—and the good man lives not in the town!

Ful. A good man is a rare being and dwells in few places in the city and countryside. Virtue indeed is most rare.

Cor. [224] Fulica, you're a madman!—you have as many enemies in the town as there are townsmen. They shear us, they fleece us, careless of our lives. They compel us to steal, then they themselves send us to the gallows. Right it is then that, if a thing is offered to our claws, we pluck it and deplume gently and carefully whatever we have snared. If someone sees these deeds, excuse them. If they are hidden, deny that they are thefts: the theft that stays hidden isn't a wrong. Whatever the townsman possesses results from our labor and industry.

Ful. Now you far exceed the bounds of reason and fairness!

Cor. [235] Nay, Fulica, the city's wickedness is defiling the entire world! Whence come over the land all those storms in summer, all that lightning, wind, floods, and hail? I remember seeing the earth shake, doors and roofs collapse, the sun obscured, and the moon darkened at night. Why does the darnel lord over the crops and the wild oat over the harvest? why does the grape turn all to tendrils? and why do the flowers of springtime perish in darkness? The city man's wickedness is pregnant with all these evils, and it will in turn bring forth more. [244] Whence come that fury of weapons and tumult of war that bring with them every kind of wickedness? The city is the fount and source of all evil. Lycaon came from the city. Deucalion and his

Deucalion Pyrrha cum coniuge rusticus. ille
intulit illuviem terris, hic abstulit; ille
abstulit humanum terris genus, intulit iste.
si terra (ut perhibent) flammis abolebitur umquam,
istud grande nefas ulla descendet ab urbe.
Ful. O Cornix, iam pone modum sermonibus istis;
audio iamdudum pueros de pulte loquentes.
cetera, si quicquam superest, post prandia dices;
pulti indulgendum monet urbibus hora relictis.

ECLOGA VII
POLLUX

De conversione iuvenum ad religionem,
cum iam auctor ad religionem aspiraret

Alphus Galbula

Alphus Galbula, quid sentis? Pollux doctissimus olim
fistulicen subito quodam quasi numine tactus
destituit calamos, tunicas, armenta, sodales;
bardocucullatus caput ut campestris alauda
quattuor ante dies in religiosa recessit
claustra. ferunt illum, pecudes dum solus in agris
pasceret, effigiem quandam vidisse deorum.
cetera non memini, sed tu quid, Galbula, sentis?
Gal. Ut dixere patres, iaciens primordia rerum
(magna canam nobis quae quondam tradidit Umber)
instituit Deus agricolas pecorisque magistros.
primus agri cultor rudis, immansuetus et asper
qualis humus segnis, lapidosa, rebellis aratro.
ast ovium primus pastor, mitissima proles,
instar ovis quae bile caret, quae lacte redundat,
mitis erat, nullis umquam pastoribus asper.
de grege saepe suo sacrum ponebat ad aras;
nunc ove, nunc pingui vitulo faciebat, et agno
saepius, et magno divos ambibat honore.
sic profecit apud Superos, sic numina flexit,
ut fuerit primo mundi nascentis ab ortu
tempus ad hoc caelo pecoris gratissima cura.
Assyrios quosdam (sed nescio nomina; curae
diminuunt animum) Deus ex pastoribus olim
constituit reges qui postea murice et auro
conspicui gentes bello domuere superbas.
cum Paris Iliaca tria numina vidit in Ida

wife, Pyrrha, were countrybred. Lycaon brought a flood on the earth, Deucalion put an end to it. Lycaon put an end to the human race, Deucalion restored it. If (as men say) the earth is ever destroyed by fire, that horror will arise from the deeds of some city.
Ful. Limit now, oh Cornix, this discourse of yours. For a long time now I have been hearing the shepherd boys talking about porridge. If anything remains to be said, speak of it after the midday meal. The hour urges us, having put aside all talk about the city, to enjoy our porridge.

ECLOGUE VII
POLLUX

The Conversion of Young Men to the Religious Life

WHEN THE AUTHOR IS ALREADY ASPIRING TO ENTER RELIGIOUS ORDERS

Alphus Galbula

Alphus Galbula, what do you think? Pollux, once a most skilled piper, as if suddenly touched by some god, has forsaken his pipe, coat, herds, and companions. His head hooded like a field lark, four days ago he retired into the ascetic's cloisters. They say that while he pastured his sheep alone in the fields he saw some sort of divine apparition. I don't remember the rest—but you, Galbula, what do you think?
Gal. [9] As our forefathers declared, when God established the beginnings of things—I will sing now of great matters that Umber once related to me—He instituted farming and the keeping of flocks. The first tiller of the field was rude, savage, and harsh: like idle, rocky soil rebellious to the plow. But the first shepherd—a progeny most mild, like a ewe that lacks choler and that abounds in milk—kind he was, never harsh towards his fellows. Often from his own flock he laid a sacrifice on the altar. With a sheep or fatted calf but more often with a lamb he made his sacrifice and with great offerings solicited the favor of the gods. [20] He so advanced himself in their eyes, so bent their will that from the world's beginning to this day the tending of sheep has been most pleasing to Heaven. Certain Assyrians—ah, I've forgotten their names! care has shattered my thoughts—God once made from shepherds into kings who, splendid afterwards in purple and gold, conquered proud nations in war. When on Trojan Ida Paris viewed the three goddesses

(aut Paris aut alius puerum qui obtruncat ad aram)
pastor erat. quando caelesti exterritus igne
venit ad ostentum pedibus per pascua nudis,
pastor erat Moses, Moses a flumine tractus.
exul apud Graios Amphrysia pastor Apollo
rura peragravit posito deitatis honore.
caelestes animi Christo ad praesepia nato
in caulis cecinere Deum pastoribus ortum,
et nova divini partus miracula docti
pastores primi natum videre Tonantem,
et sua pastores infans Regnator Olympi
ante magos regesque dedit cunabula scire.
se quoque pastorem Deus appellavit, ovesque
mitibus ingeniis homines et mentibus aequis.
et, ne vana putes haec somnia, nuper ab urbe
rus veniens picto perlegi haec omnia templo.
sunt pecudes pictae, parvi sub matribus agni
in tellure cubant, ingens equitatus ab alto
monte venit, radiant auro diademata divum
et suspensa tenent vaga lumina praetereuntum.
non igitur mirum noster si numina Pollux
vidit; amant villas et oves et ovilia divi.
simplicibus praesens Deus est, offenditur astu.
Alphus Vera refers. pecori sic sint innoxia nostro
pascua, vidi asinum, vidi praesepe bovemque.
iam memini turbae venientis, et ora videre
Indica iam videor regum sua dona ferentum.
unum oro, quaenam Polluci occurrit imago?
Galbula, si nosti, ne sit labor omnia fari.
Gal. Et novi et memorare libet; res digna relatu,
res digna auditu, pia, sancta, imitabile factum.
    Durus et immitis pater atque superba noverca
Pollucem graviore iugo pressere iuventae
tempore cum dulces animos nova suggerit aetas;
et cum iam invalidae longo sub pondere vires
deficerent nullaque odium mansuesceret arte,
constituit temptare fugam. res una volentem
ire diu tenuit: nimis impatienter amabat;
error enim communis amor iuvenilibus annis.
res est fortis amor, violentia fortior; ivit.
et tales abiens (mihi namque solebat amores
enarrare suos) maesto dedit ore querellas:
    "O virgo, lacrimaene tuis solventur ocellis
cum te tam caro cernes ab amante relictam?
ullane discessu duces suspiria nostro?

—Paris or that other man who slew his boy before the altar—he was a shepherd. When Moses, terrified by the fire from heaven, came barefooted through the fields to reveal this miracle, Moses, plucked once from the river, was a shepherd. [32] An exile among the Greeks, Apollo traversed Amphrysus' fields as a shepherd, the honor of his godhead put aside. When Christ was born in a stable, heavenly spirits sang to shepherds in their sheepfolds of the birth of God the Son. And when they had learned of the recent miracle of his divine birth, they were the first to see the newborn God of Thunder, and, before wise men and kings, the infant King of Heaven allowed shepherds to behold His cradle. God called Himself too a shepherd, and He called sheep those men of mild disposition and tranquil mind. [42] And lest you reckon these things empty dreams, coming recently from the city into the countryside I scanned all these matters in the paintings within a church. Sheep were pictured there and small lambs lay on the ground by their mothers. A great band of horsemen descended a mountain's heights. Celestial diadems beamed with gold and held fixed the passing observer's wandering eye. No wonder then if Pollux, our fellow, saw a divine spirit: the gods love cottages, sheep, and sheepfolds. God is present to the simple of heart, is offended by cunning.

Alphus [51] You answer truly. As surely as I hope the pastures may not be harmful to my flock, I too have seen that ass, stable, and ox. Now I recall the coming of that retinue. Further, I seem to see the Indian features of those kings bearing their gifts. But one thing, pray: tell me what sort of apparition appeared to Pollux? If you know, Galbula, let it not be burdensome to speak of the whole matter.

Gal. I both know and am pleased to recount the story. It is a thing worthy to be told and heard, a pious, saintly act, a deed to be imitated.

[59] His stern, harsh father and domineering stepmother burdened Pollux sorely in his youth when that fresh time of life is wont to prompt sweet thoughts. And since his patience, weak from this longstanding burden, failed him and by no stratagem could he gentle their hatred, he resolved to attempt his escape. But one thing, though he wished to go, long held him: he loved too impetuously, for love is the universal error of youthful years. Love is a strong force, but cruelty a stronger. He went, and departing (for he used to recount his love to me) with a mournful look he lamented in words such as these:

[70] "Ah, my girl, will you allow tears to flow from your eyes when you see that you have been left behind by your lover, so dear to you? Will you sigh at

tune mei crudelis eris forte immemor umquam?
usqueadeone tuum poterit frigescere pectus,
pectus quod toties, quod lumina fletibus implet?
tune trahes crebros gemitus et pallida fies?
cerno oculos, cerno lacrimas, cerno anxia corda
virginis. heu tantum qua dissimulare dolorem
fas erit arte? dolor duplex mea pectora torquet,
illius atque meus. sed fas mihi flere, quod illi
non licet; occultus longe magis aestuat ignis.
incolumem mihi vos, divi, servabitis illam,
ut, quando exsilio repetam mea rura peracto,
fiat amor felix saltem semel ante senectam."
Talia pergebat memorans, voluitque reverti
(tantus amor iuvenem, vis tanta furoris agebat)
sed iam iacta fuga cunctis erat alea nota.
fronde sub Herculea fessus maerore sedebat;
ecce puellari virgo stipata corona
ora, manus, oculos habitumque simillima Nymphae,
et tali affata est puerum sermone dolentem:
"Care puer, quo tendis iter? vestigia verte.
nescis, heu nescis quo te via ducat et audes
ignotis errare locis nihil insidiarum
per campos ratus herbosos, nihil esse pericli.
omnia tuta putas et quod placet utile credis
more iuventutis stolidae. collectus in orbem
saepe latet molli coluber sub graminis umbra;
est facile incautos offendere. parvulus infans
innocuos rutilum digitos extendit in ignem
nec nisi iam laesus vires intellegit ignis.
haec regio intrantes aditu consuevit amoeno
fallere, delicias offert et gaudia; verum
ingressis, cum triste nihil superesse putatur,
mille parat laqueos et mille pericula profert.
trames hic, ut collem gressu superaveris illum,
ducit in umbrosam silvam, crudele ferarum
hospitium, loca taetra situ et caligine opaca.
quisquis eo deceptus abit remeare vetatur,
et piceis primum velatur lumina vittis,
deinde per omne nemus, dumeta per aspera tractus
transit in effigiem monstri. dum volvere linguam
atque loqui temptat, mugit; dum attollere sese
credit, humi graditur quadrupes neque suspicit astra.
ima tenebrosae vallis lacus aequore nigro
occupat et nigris mons plurimus imminet undis.
huc tracti in Stygios latices altumque barathrum

all at my leaving? By chance will you ever cruelly forget me? Will your heart be able to grow so cold—that heart that has so often filled my eyes with tears? Will you not often sigh and become pale? [77] Ah! I see her eyes, I see her tears and troubled heart. Alas, by what art will it be possible to hide so great a sorrow? A two-fold sorrow, hers and mine, is racking my heart. But I can weep, which she is forbidden to do; and a fire long hidden rages still greater. Oh, you gods, keep her safe and sound for me so that when, my exile ended, I shall return to my native fields, my love may be made happy at least once before my old age."

[85] Speaking such words he was carrying out his resolve to flee, yet he wished to turn back—so great a love, so great a rage stirred him—but, his flight known to all, the die had already been cast. Under Hercules' leafy boughs he sat wearied by mourning. And behold! a virgin crowned with a girl's coronet, her face, hands, eyes, and manner most like to a nymph. And thus she addressed the grieving lad:

[92] "Dear boy, where are you directing your course? Turn around! You know not, alas, you know not where this path is leading you; and you dare wander in unknown places, thinking that throughout these grassy plains there are no snares or danger. You consider everything safe and, in the customary way of dull-witted youth, believe that what pleases also profits. Often a serpent hides coiled deep in the grass within the gentle shade. It is easy for him to strike the unwary. A tiny child extends his innocent fingers into the glowing fire, nor, unless he has already been hurt, does he understand its strength. [102] This region has been wont to deceive those entering it with its pleasant approach. Pleasures it offers and delights. But for those who have entered, though nothing sad might be thought to remain, it supplies a thousand snares and displays a thousand perils. This path, when you have crossed that hill there, leads into a shady wood, the cruel hospice of wild beasts, a hideous place of decay and darkness. Whoever, deceived by this way, departs on it is forbidden to return. First his eyes are covered by a pitch-black band and then, dragged through all the grove, through thorny thickets, he is changed into the likeness of a monster. When he tries to roll his tongue and speak, he bellows. When he thinks to lift himself up, he walks four-footed on the ground and looks not up to the stars. [115] A sable-surfaced lake takes up the depths of this gloomy valley, and a mountain looms large over its black waves. Dragged hence, men are hurled headlong

praecipites dantur rapidaque voragine mersi
in Styga et aeternas Erebi rapiuntur in umbras.
heu quot pastores istis ambagibus acti
cum gregibus periere suis! ego sedula semper
monstro iter; hic ad opem vigilo indefessa ferendam.
tolle moras igitur, mortis fuge blanda propinquae
atria; secreti tutam pete littoris oram
qua contra Idalios fluctus mihi tollit in altum
aëra Carmelus viridi caput arbore cinctum.
primus hic antiquis patribus spelaea domosque
praebuit arboreas intra nemus ilice densum.
ex hoc in vestros deducta cacumine montes
religio venit, sicut de fonte perenni
flumina, et ex uno multi genitore nepotes.
illius in silvis abies ubi plurima surgit,
pinguis ubi piceae sudat liber et terebinthi,
innocuum postquam feliciter egeris aevum,
mox tua mutatis aetas renovabitur annis.
in loca te tollam melior virentia semper;
immortalis eris divum comes, ire per astra
inter Hamadryades et Oreadas atque Napaeas
flore coronatas caput et redolentibus herbis
fas erit ac super et subter cognoscere caelos."
Sic effata leves virgo discessit in auras.
tum sua iuravit Pollux mutata repente
pectora et extemplo victum exspirasse furorem
non aliter quam flamma cadet, si ardentibus agris
effluat et totas praeceps Padus evomat undas.
sic abiit crudelis Amor qui saepe pharetram
in iuvenem, dum principiis obstaret amandi,
dum tepet ac timide insanit, consumpserat omnem.
sic igitur Pollux in claustra silentia venit.
Alphus Sunt quibus aspirent etiam nolentibus ultro,
sunt quibus infensi sine causa et crimine di sint.
Gal. Quod nos in pecudes, in nos id iuris habent di;
hoc rus scire sat est, sapiant sublimius urbes.
sic docuit rediens aliquando ex urbe sacerdos
Iannus et in magno dixit sibi codice lectum.
Alphus Sol cadit et Baldi vix summa cacumina tangit;
nos quoque iam sero cum sole recedere tempus.
Galbula, sarcinulas ne sit tibi ferre molestum,
pera levis, levis est et cantharus; omnia parvus
ferre labor sero, grave mane sed utile pondus.
ipse pecus ducam, mihi pars erit ista laboris.

into the deep abyss of its Stygian waters. And plunged thus into the swift whirlpool, they are swept into the Lower World and Erebus' eternal shadows. Alas, how many shepherds, driven on through these winding ways, have perished with their flocks!

[121] "I myself, ever diligent, show the way. Here unwearied I stand watchful to bring aid. Therefore put an end to your delay. Flee the alluring palace of an imminent death. Seek a secure, secluded seacoast where, facing Idalian waves, in my honor Mount Carmel raises high in the air its head wreathed in green trees. To the patriarchs of old this place first provided caves and houses of trees within a grove thick with ilex. From this peak reverence for God comes, led off into your mountains, just as streams issue from an unceasing fount or many descendants from a single sire. [132] Within the woods of this peak where the silver fir rises high, where the bark of the rich pitch-pine and terebinth oozes with resin, after you have successfully led a life of innocence, your youth will soon be renewed with the change of years. To a better place forever green shall I raise you. You will be the gods' immortal companion. You will be allowed to move through Heaven among wood nymphs, mountain nymphs, and nymphs of the dells, nymphs decked with garlands of flowers and fragrant herbs; and you will be permitted to learn of the heavens both above and below."

[141] Having thus spoken, the girl departed into the insubstantial air. Pollux swore that at that moment his feelings suddenly changed and that the fury in his heart, straightway overcome, expired: just as a blaze will abate if the Po overflows and headlong spews all its waters into the burning fields. Thus cruel Love expired, who, so long as Pollux resisted the beginnings of love and was cool and timid in his desire, had often used up his whole quiver on the lad. And thus Pollux entered within the silent cloisters.

Alphus There are men whom the gods of their own accord favor even though they are unwilling to accept their gifts. And there are men towards whom the gods are hostile without cause or offense.

Gal. [152] The control we have over our sheep the gods have over us. It is enough for the countryside and its people to know this. Let the city be more loftily wise. Jannus, our priest, returning once from the city, taught this truth and said that he had read it in a large book.

Alphus The sun is setting and scarcely touches Baldo's top. It is time now for us too to retire with the tardy sun. Let it not grieve you, Galbula, to carry the packs. Light is my satchel, light too my wine bottle. In the evening it is small labor to carry all these things. At morn it is a heavy but a worthwhile burden. I myself will guide the flock. That will be my portion of the toil.

ECLOGA VIII
RELIGIO
De rusticorum religione
Candidus Alphus

Can. Horrida solstitio tellus sitit, Alphe, reverso;
ad solitos montes, ubi ros in gramine et aestas
mitior, haec armenta monet deducere tempus.
Alphus Aerios montes et summa cacumina longe
prospicio; quid sint montes (tibi vera fatebor)
nescio, semper enim campestria rura lacusque
incolui. montanus ager qua fruge redundat?
Can. O rude et illepidum ingenium. prope flumina semper
versatus fulicae in morem limosa per arva,
sunt ubi ranarum, culicum, pulicum cimicumque
lustra, inter salices, ulvas viridesque papyros,
irridere audes et nauci pendere montes.
unde fluunt amnes? templis ubi tanta locandis
marmora caeduntur? fulgens ubi nascitur aurum?
quae parit antemnas tellus? medicamen ab herbis,
dic, quibus est nisi montanis? de vertice Baldi
saepe melampodion legi; medicina capellis
nulla magis praesens. quondam Valsasinus Aegon
tradidit hoc, dum vere sues castraret et agnos;
tradidit et dixit, "solus medicamen habeto."
dic, ubi castanea plures? ubi copia maior
glandis? in excelsis fontes et pascua vidi
montibus, artocreas et pingue polenta comedi.
sunt populi fortes illic. robusta iuventus
lata pedes, callosa umeros, nervosa lacertos
hispida, dura manus, moli indefessa ferendae
vallibus ex illis, onera ut navalia curet,
confluit huc. nullum est hominum genus aptius urbi,
sive velis castrare pecus, seu scindere fagos,
sive fimum ferri e stabulis, haurire cloacas
latrinasque curare viamque aperire coactis
sordibus et scalis puteos descendere in altos;
ingenio callent et duro robore pollent.
sed quid opus multis? subeunt opus omne: popinis
inservire, focos lignis cumulare veruque
artifici versare manu, dare libera fumo
spiramenta, boum ventres ad flumina ferre,
verrere humum immundam scopis doctissima gens est;

ECLOGUE VIII
PIETY
The Piety of Country Folk
Candidus Alphus

Can. Summer's solstice having returned, Alphus, the rugged earth is parched by drought. The season counsels us to drive our herds as usual to the mountains where the dew is on the grass and the summer is more gentle.
Alphus Far away I see the airy mountains' topmost peaks. But (I'll confess the truth to you) what the mountains are like I know not, for I have always lived on the lowland plains and among lakes. With what crops do mountain fields abound?
Can. [8] Oh, rude and barbarous soul! Having always lived near rivers like a coot amid muddy lowlands where there are bogs filled with frogs, gnats, fleas, and bugs, having dwelt among willows, sedge, and green reeds you dare to ridicule the mountains and esteem them a trifle. Whence flow the rivers? Where is so much marble quarried to found our churches? Where is glittering gold begotten? What earth produces yardarms for our boats? From whose herbs but the mountains' come our medicines? From Baldo's peak I have often gathered black hellebore—no medicine is better for my goats. [18] Aegon from Val Sasina once gave me this herb when he was castrating swine and young sheep in the springtime. He gave it to me and said, "Keep this medicine as yours alone." Tell me, where are there more chestnuts? where a greater store of acorns? In the high mountains I have beheld founts and pastureland, I have seen meat pies and thick polenta consumed. People are hardy there. Strong young men with big feet, shoulders toughened by toil, and sinewy arms, a shaggy, rugged band unwearied from carrying heavy loads—from mountain vales these men come together here to see to the cargos of our ships. [28] No kind of man is fitter for the town. If you want to castrate bulls or split beech trees, if you want dung carried from your stables or wish to clean sewers or toilets or open gutters clogged with refuse or descend a deep well on a ladder, these men have both seasoned skills and hardy vigor. But why say more? They endure all kinds of work. For serving food in taverns, building fires, turning spits with a skilled hand and cleaning chimneys, for lugging cattle guts to the river and sweeping up unsightly dirt

quodque magis miror, semper sub pondere currunt.
cotibus in duris oriuntur et ardua vivunt
per iuga; cum capreis habitant spelaea ferarum.
adde quod in caelum brevis est e montibus altis
transitus; erectum caput usque ad nubila tollunt.
nubila transcendunt aliqui, puto sidera tangant.
esse locum memorant, ubi surgit ab aequore Titan,
qui (nisi dedidici) contingit vertice lunam,
et vixisse illic hominem, sed postea abactum
improbitate gulae, quod scilicet omnia poma
manderet et magno servaret nulla Tonanti.
hinc divi sanctique patres in montibus altis
delegere domos tacitas; Carthusia testis,
Carmelus, Garganus, Athos, Laureta, Laverna
et Sina et Soractis apex Umbrosaque Vallis
et iuga Nursini fato senis incluta et altis
abietibus turrita caput Camaldula sanctum.
cetera praetereo, nec enim sermonibus istis
omnia complecti statuo. montana frequentant
culmina caelicolae, sed anas et mergus et anser,
ibis, onocrotalus, milvi fulicaeque paludes.
Alphus Inter montanae tantos regionis honores
cur de messe nihil, nihil est de palmite dictum?
haec tamen humanae duo sustentacula vitae
maxima. monticolae veniunt e rupibus ad nos
hordea mercatum torvi, fuligine tincti,
saetosi, macie affecti, laceri ac situosi;
indigenae ostendunt quae sit natura locorum.
sed quod montanis de religionibus inquis
rettulit in mentem quae de Polluce feruntur.
quae dea, si nosti, visa est, quae, Candide, Nympha?
dic, age, nam coeptum certamen inutile nobis;
utilior sermo de religione tenendus.
Can. Galbula qui solitus pecudes in pascua tecum
ducere te satis hoc potuit docuisse quod optas.
Alphus Plura quidem Polluce super narrata, sed ipsam
nec docuit Nympham nec me quaesisse recordor.
nunc subiit mentem, cum religionis oborta est
mentio, et illarum visa est mihi maxima laudum.
Can. Non erat illa Dryas neque Libethris nec Oreas;
venerat e caelo Superum Regina, Tonantis
Mater, anhelanti pacem latura iuventae.
huic Tethys, huic alma Ceres famulantur, et ipse
Aeolus aequoreis ventos qui frenat in antris.
hanc Deus astrorum flammas super atque volantes

with a broom they are a most able race. And—what I greatly wonder at—under their heavy burdens they always bustle lightly about. They are born among hard flints and live along the steep mountain ridges. With their goats they dwell in the caves of wild beasts.

[43] Moreover, the passage to heaven is brief from the mountains' heights. They raise their uplifted tops into the clouds. Some peaks rise above the clouds, I think they touch the stars! Men state that there is a place, where Titan rises from the sea, whose top (unless I have forgotten their tale) touches the moon. Moreover, a man lived there but he was banished afterwards for the wickedness of his gluttony, since he bit into every kind of fruit there and reserved none for the mighty God of Thunder.

[50] Hence the gods and blessed patriarchs chose quiet dwellings in the high mountains: witness the Grande Chartreuse, Carmel, Gargano, Athos, Loreto, and Alverno; Sinai, Soracte's peak, and Vallombrosa; the peaks renowned for the destiny of that aged Nursian, and Camaldoli, its blessed top castled by lofty firs. Others I omit, for it is not my intent to include every peak. Heaven's dwellers oft resort to mountain peaks, but the swampy lowlands are frequented by duck, diver, and goose, by ibis, pelican, kite, and coot.

Alphus [60] In praising the mountain regions so greatly why was nothing said about the crop and vine? All the same, these are the two greatest stays of human life. From their crags mountain people come to us to buy their barley. Grim of look they are and sooty, shaggy and lean, ragged and decrepit—the natives show the nature of a place! But what you said about religious devotion in the mountains brings to mind what men are saying about Pollux. What goddess (if you know), what nymph, Candidus, appeared to him? Tell me, for this quarrel we've begun is useless; more useful is a discussion kept to pious matters.

Can. [72] Galbula, who along with you used to drive the sheep to pasture, could have told you enough of what you want to know.

Alphus Indeed, many things were recounted about Pollux; but of the Nymph herself he said nothing, nor do I remember to have asked. Now she entered my thoughts when piety was mentioned. And in truth, piety seems to me the greatest of her glories.

Can. [78] She was neither wood nymph, mountain nymph, nor nymph of the fount. From Heaven she came, queen of the gods above, mother of the God of Thunder, destined to bring peace to young men panting with emotion. She is waited upon by Tethys and life-giving Ceres, by Aeolus himself, who bridles the winds in his sea caves. God has lifted her above the fires of the

Solis equos, supra fulgentem Cassiopeiam
extulit et sacram bis seno sidere frontem
cinxit et adiecit subter vestigia lunam.
Alphus Candide, mira canis nullis pastoribus umquam
cognita. quid Tethys? quid fulgens Cassiopeia?
Aeolus aequoreis ventos quis frenat in antris?
qui sunt Solis equi? magna atque ignota recenses.
Can. Sidera sunt partim, partim sunt numina prisca.
omnia quae Pollux mihi cum narrasset, in aedem
duxit et "ista sacer paries," ait, "omnia monstrat."
pictus erat paries signis et imagine multa.
omnia non memini (mens est mihi debilis) ista
vix tenui dum saepe animo volvo atque revolvo;
saepe recordari medicamine fortius omni.
ista potest nigro depellere nubila caelo,
ista potest siccis fluvios dare frugibus imbres.
cum volet, ista novos duris emittere campis,
cum volet, emissos poterit restringere fontes.
qui modo sunt steriles et nudi gramine campi,
si volet, in pingues poterit convertere glaebas.
frigida Saturni cum sidera suscipit atro
Scorpius hospitio, non auferet hordea grando
nec domus ardebit (nam tunc haec omnia caelum
dicitur iratis in terram effundere ab astris)
si volet, haec nobis custodiet omnia virgo.
si favet haec nobis, complebunt horrea messes
adicietque gregi semper fetura gemellos.
si pecus infelix erit et sine vellere, solo
ipsa potest nutu dare lac, dare vellera et agnos
et curare greges omnemque avertere morbum.
nil opus est modo Pana sequi neque cetera ruris
numina quae veteres frustra coluisse feruntur.
vidi ego circum aram Nymphae pendere capellas,
plaustra, boves et oves. hic Ianni vidimus hircum
et memini inscriptam versu hoc legisse tabellam:
VOTUM PRO SALVO IANNUS BREVE REDDIDIT HIRCO.
Dumque ea perlegerem, Pollux haec carmina supplex
ante aram genibus positis in marmore dixit:
"O Dea, quae servas urbes et rura, precamur
ne Padus exundet nec strix nocturna per umbras
hauriat infantes nec eant per compita larvae.
Diva, fave agricolis; talpas occide malignam
aggeribus pestem; gelidis sata laeta pruinis,
quando bruma venit, conspergere, Diva, memento,
ne tineae erodent anno frumenta sequenti.

stars and the Sun's winged horses and beyond glittering Cassiopeia. He has bound her sacred forehead with twice six stars and has cast the moon under her feet.

Alphus Candidus, you speak of wonders unknown ever to any shepherd. What's Tethys? What's glittering Cassiopeia? Who's Aeolus, who bridles the winds in his sea caves? Who are the horses of the sun? Great and unknown matters you recount.

Can. [91] Some are constellations, some gods of old. After Pollux had told me of them, he led me into a church and said, "That hallowed wall there will make everything known to you." The wall was painted with many symbols and pictures. I do not remember all of them (for my memory is weak). I understood what follows only with difficulty while I turned it over again and again in my mind. Repeating a thing over and over is stronger than any other remedy.

[98] She has the power to drive the clouds from the dark sky. She can bestow streams of rain on the dry crops. When she wishes, she can release fresh springs into the hardened fields; when she wishes, she can seal up those founts she has released. Fields that are now infertile and bare of grass she can, if she wishes, change into rich land. When Scorpio receives Saturn's chill star within his dismal house, if she wishes, hail will not destroy your barley nor will your house catch fire (since the sky is said to pour forth all these misfortunes at that time unto the earth from the raging stars). If she wishes, that maid will keep all these things safe for us. [109] If she looks with favor on us, harvests will fill our granaries and breeding will always add twin lambs to our flock. If a sheep is barren and without fleece, with only a nod she can give it milk, fleece, and lambs. Indeed, she has the power to watch over our flocks and avert every sickness. There is no need now to follow Pan and the other gods of the fields whom men of old are said to have worshipped in vain. Around the Nymph's altar I myself have seen hanging images of goats, carts, cattle, and sheep. Here I saw Jannus' goat and recall reading a votive tablet inscribed with this verse: "This small offering Jannus rendered in return for his unharmed goat." And while I was scanning the inscriptions, Pollux, his knees bent in prayer on the marble before the altar, sang this hymn:

[122] "Oh, Goddess who watches over the cities and fields, we pray you that the Po not overflow, that the screech owl not drain the blood of babes among the shades of night, and that evil spirits haunt not the crossroads. Goddess, smile on the farmer. Destroy the mole, that wicked pest with his molehills. When winter comes, remember, oh Goddess, to strew hoarfrost on the fertile crops lest the following year insect larvae gnaw at the grain. [129] Guard his

a Boreae flatu pingues defende mariscas,
a gruis ore fabas et ab ansere farra palustri,
a serpente boves, a vulpe et fure cohortem,
a brucho erucas, a bruma et grandine vites,
a vi et fraude lupi pecus, a robigine fruges,
a rabie catulos, a flamma et fulmine villas,
a murum insidiis petasonem, a milite pernas,
a campe et pigris—pigris" (heu cetera nescit
mens oblita sequi. numerus me in verba reduxit
saepius; ad numerum rediens oblivia forsan
mente abigam. retrogradior numerumque recurro)
"a murum insidiis petasonem, a milite pernas,
a campe et pigris virides limacibus hortos"
(Alphe, viden quae vis numeri? iam cetera cerno)
"a tonitru reboante cados, a frigore fetas,
a gravibus vitulos oestris, a gutture porcos
anginoso, operas pubes ne rustica perdat.
adsis, o Dea, nec laedant examina fuci
neu milium furentur aves neu vellera sentes
sucida neu lappas apprendat lana sequentes.
Diva gubernatrix hominum, custodia vatum,
Diva laborantum requies, medicina dolentum
et tutela gregum, nostris, precor, annue votis."
    Talibus orabat Pollux; ego postibus haerens
in baculum pede porrecto recitata notabam
altius ac memori condebam singula mente.
Alphus Candide, Polluci pro sollicitudine tanta,
pro precis officio, pro religione putasne
dandum aliquid nobis? pietate peculia crescunt.
Can. Quid ni aliquid dandum est? opus est persolvere crates.
Alphus Rusticus es, "crates" etenim pro "gratibus" inquis.
Can. "Crates" et "grates" parvo discrimine distant.
dandum aliquid; neu bis detur, sine Pascha reverti,
quando sacerdotes commissa piacula solvunt.
Alphus Quid dabimus? vituli gravis est iactura. vel agnum
vel leporem? pietas etiam laudabilis anser.
Can. Dona docet tempus. lepores brumalia dona,
quando nive hiberna currendi erepta facultas;
anser ad autumni finem nonasque Kalendas
pertinet; aestatis coryli, nova poma, racemi,
munera; lactentes haedi sunt veris et agni.
tunc si de cordis aliquem conspexeris aegrum
ac tenuem qui nec vendi nec vivere possit
(munus erit sollemne satis) donabimus agnum.
    Ipse mihi, cum iam regredi post prandia vellem,

rich fig trees from the North Wind's breath. Keep his beans from the crane's bill and his grain from the marsh–dwelling goose. Keep cattle from the serpent, the farmyard from the fox and thief, skirret from the locust, vines from snow and hail. Guard the herd from the wolf's strength and cunning. Protect crops from blight, puppies from rabies, our cottages from fire and lightning, bacon from theft by mice, ham from the soldier, green–growing gardens from caterpillars and sluggish—and sluggish . . ." [136] (Alas! forgetting to follow what's to be said, I can't think of the rest. Oft a measure has brought back the words. Returning to the melody, perhaps I will dispel this forgetfulness from my mind. I'll go back over the cadence.) ". . . bacon from theft by mice, ham from the soldier, green–growing gardens from caterpillars and sluggish snails . . ." (Alphus, see the power of melody? I recall the rest now!) [143] ". . . keep our wine jars from the reechoing thunder, the new mothers in the herd from the cold and their calves from oppressive horseflies, and guard the hogs from quinsy lest the lads of the countryside lose their labor. Be present, oh Goddess, so that the drones harm not the swarm nor birds steal the millet nor fresh fleece pick up brambles nor the wool collect clinging burrs. Divine ruler of men, guardian of poets, divine repose for those who toil, balm for the mournful, and safeguard of the flock, nod assent, I pray you, to our prayers."

[152] Thus Pollux prayed. Lingering by the door with my foot extended towards my staff, with exalted spirits I marked his orison and laid it up word by word in my memory.

Alphus Don't you think, Candidus, that we ought to give something equal to Pollux's great care for us, to the kindness of his prayer and his reverence for the gods? Herds grow by piety.

Can. Why shouldn't we offer something? We ought to give our harrows.

Alphus You're a rustic indeed: you said "harrows" [*crates*] instead of "thanks" [*grates*].

Can. [160] "Harrows" and "thanks"—small difference. Something ought to be given—but not twice until Easter returns when the priests absolve us of the penance we have incurred.

Alphus What shall we give? The sacrifice of a calf is a grievous thing. A lamb or a hare? Likewise, a goose is a praiseworthy offering.

Can. The season shows us the proper gift. Hares are the offering for winter, since they are unable to run in the snow. A goose suits the end of autumn at the beginning of November. Hazel nuts, fresh apples, and clusters of grapes are offerings for summertime. And suckling goats and lambs are the offerings right for spring. If at that time you spy among your late–born a sick and thin one that can't live or be sold, let us (for it is enough if the gift be solemnly offered) let us offer that lamb.

[173] Pollux himself, when I wished to return home after our meal, passed

carmina de Nymphae sollemnibus eruta fastis
tradidit et dixit, "si quando gravabere curis,
haec cane; pro mentis medicamine carmen habeto:
'Quando Molorchaeo Titan descendit ab astro
pronus et Astraeae iam limina virginis intrat,
Virgine laetetur pubes et cana senectus;
transiit ad Superos et Olympica regna petivit.
Ogdoas ut toto iam tertia fluxerit orbe,
festa dies iterum; natalia Virginis aras
ignibus illustrant, offert nova liba sacerdos.
Libra redit noctes properans aequare diebus,
exsultat Picenus ager, vehit Hadria puppes
Illyricas et Chaonias, cum mercibus adsunt
Tusci, Umbri, Veneti, Siculi; Lauretica templa
cum donis turmatim adeunt votisque solutis
in sublime iugum laeti ad commercia tendunt.
Et cum Thessalicas cursu breviore sagittas
sol subit et frigent urentibus arva pruinis,
clausa gynaecei sacris penetralibus hausit
corde Deum toto proprios oblita prarentes.
Et cum semiferi fugiens Chironis ab arcu
languet ad hiberni glacialia limina Capri,
induat ornatas et mas et femina vestes
laetitiaque diem celebrent quo semine sacro
coniugis annosus gravidam pater imbuit alvum.
illa dies etenim sanctae primordia Nymphae
fecit et in nostras vetuit descendere sordes.
Cum volat imbrifera lampas Phoebea sub urna
ad vernos reditura dies, iam proxima veri,
ite, nurus omnes, sacros altaribus ignes,
tura focis, faculas manibus date, ducite pompam;
attulit in templum nova dona puerpera virgo.
Quando gregis Princeps aurato vellere fulgens
incipiet Zephyris aperire tepentibus annum
et dare maiores luci quam noctibus horas,
aliger occultam redeat Paranymphus in aedem
et nova miranti referat mandata puellae.
festa dies Tuscis populos de collibus omnes
cogit et Arnicolas vocat ad Florentia templa.
tum quoque sed tenui virgo prius intervallo
nupsit, et haec teneris lux est celebranda puellis.
Quando sub extrema Cancri testudine Phoebus
volvitur et revehit vicina Canicula morbos,
ture piam celebrate diem; redit hospita mater
in proprios a matre lares. altaria circum

on to me a song on the Nymph's solemn feast days and said, "If ever you are burdened by cares, sing over these verses. Look on this song as a balm for your thoughts:

'When Titan sinks downward from Leo and is entering the threshold of Virgo, then youths and grey–bearded old men rejoice in the Virgin, then did she pass over to the gods above and direct her course towards heavenly realms.

[181] 'When throughout the world, thrice eight days have passed, once more it is a feast day. The feast of her birth lights up her altar with tapers, the priest offers new made cakes. Libra is returning, hastening to make night equal with day. The fields of Ancona leap for joy. The Adriatic bears Illyrian and Chaonian ships. With their wares appear Tuscans, Umbrians, Venetians, Sicilians and travel in bands with their offerings to visit that church at Loreto. And when on its lofty hill they have fulfilled their vows, they direct their course to the market places with joy in their hearts.

[190] 'And when in his briefer course the Sun enters Sagittarius and the fields are chilled by consuming hoarfrost, Mary, cloistered within the penetrable cell for women in the temple, took God into her heart, her own parents wholly forgotten.

'And when, fleeing the bow of Chiron the centaur, the Sun languishes near the wintry Goat's icy doorstep, let both men and women put on richly adorned apparel and joyfully celebrate that day when an aged father impregnated his wife's womb with consecrated seed. For indeed that day brought to pass the blessed Nymph's conception and forbade her to descend into our corruption.

[201] 'When the lamp of Phoebus flies under Aquarius' rainbearing urns and is about to return to vernal days, being nearest at this point to spring, go then, all you young wives, light sacred fires on the altars, furnish them with incense and tapers, lead forth your procession: for then the virgin–mother brought fresh offerings into the temple.

'When the Lord of the flock, shining in his golden, fleecy locks, begins to open the new year with warming west winds and to grant more hours to the day than to the night, let the winged Paranymph return to that room hidden from sight and deliver new instructions to the wondering girl. That feast day brings together all the people from the Tuscan hills, and to Florentine churches it calls folk dwelling on the banks of the Arno. Then too (but a short time before), a virgin, she was betrothed, and this day should be celebrated by delicate young girls.

[215] 'When Phoebus has been rolled forward under the edge of Cancer's shell and the neighboring Dog Star brings sickness back, celebrate with incense a day of piety: for then Christ's mother, a guest, returned from a mother to her own home. Around the altar hang the grainfields' first fruits

primitias Cereris geminae suspendite matri.' "
Ista dedit Pollux vigilans quae in montibus olim
fecerat ad pecudum caulas, dum nocte serena
militiam caeli sparsosque examinat ignes.
his quoque plura dedit; sed carmina plura referri
non sinit extremum deponens vespera solem.

ECLOGA IX
FALCO

De moribus curiae Romanae,
post religionis ingressum
Faustulus Candidus

Ful. Candide, quo casu patriis procul actus ab oris
haec in rura venis? hic pascua nulla nec amnes
nec liquidi fontes nec ovilia tuta nec umbrae,
et tamen assiduos gregis haec pascuntur in usus.
Can. Faustule, me noster Corydon (qui plurima quondam
his armenta locis habuit magnamque peculi
congeriem fecit) pecori me credere adegit
esse salutares istis in montibus herbas;
at postquam segnes agros et inertia saxa
vidimus et siccis arentem fontibus undam,
paenituit longaeque viae patriaeque relictae.
Ful. Postquam te incolumem saltus intrare Latinos
contigit, antiqui potes haec mea tecta subire
iure sodalitii. sunt hic mihi pauperis agri
iugera pauca meae vis sufficientia vitae;
quidquid id est commune puta. tibi forsitan ulla
prospera sors aderit; fortuna simillima vento est.
cariceae succede casae, dum praeterit aestus,
dum grex in gelida procumbens ruminat umbra.
pone pedum, discumbe parum, recreabere potu;
potu opus est, potu iste gravis compescitur aestus.
pocula prende; fluet melius post pocula sermo.
Can. Pocula quis tanta demens aestate recuset?
Ful. Vina sitim minuunt animique doloribus obstant,
vina ut amicitias vires ita corporis augent.
Can. Haec parit ora bonos (si patria vina) racemos.
Ful. Funde iterum; potare semel gustare, secundus
colluit os potus, calefacta refrigerat ora
tertius, arma siti bellumque indicere quartus

in honor of those two mothers.' "

Pollux gave me these verses that, guarding his flock once in the mountains, he composed near the sheepfold while he pondered the scattered fires of heaven's soldiery in the clear night. Concerning these matters too he gave me more verses, but Vesper, laying the sun at last to rest, allows me to sing no more.

ECLOGUE IX
FALCO
The Ways of the Curia at Rome

AFTER HIS ENTRY INTO RELIGIOUS ORDERS

Faustulus Candidus

Faust. By what misfortune, Candidus, driven far from your fathers' lands, have you come into these fields? Here are no pasturelands or rivers, no clear springs, secure sheepfolds, or shade. Yet flocks constantly pasture in these lands.
Can. Corydon, our fellow—who once kept many herds in this region and heaped up his savings—Corydon led me, Faustulus, to believe that the grass in those hills there would be wholesome for my flock. But after I saw the listless fields, lifeless stones, and dried-up springs, I regretted my long journey and leaving my homeland behind me.
Faust. [12] Since it has befallen you to enter safe and sound into these Latin groves, by the right of our fellowship of old, you may enter my house here. My few acres of poor land yield me barely enough for my living. Yet such as it is, consider it yours. Perhaps some favorable destiny will come to you. Dame Fortune is much like the wind. Enter my hut of reeds until the heat of the day has passed. While the cattle, sunk down within the cool shade, are chewing their cud, lay aside your sheephook, lie down for a little while, refresh yourself with a drink. Drink's a necessity: for by drink we subdue this burdensome heat. Take hold of the cup, then—after a draught our words will flow finer.
Can. [23] Crazed by so much heat, what man would refuse?
Faust. Wine lessens thirst and shields us from grievous thoughts. As it increases friendship, so wine fortifies our physical strength.
Can. This region—if this is local wine—grows good grapes.
Faust. Pour another cup! To drink once is to taste. A second drink rinses the mouth, the third cools a warm cheek, the fourth sets about disclosing

aggreditur, quintus pugnat, victoria sexti est,
septimus (Oenophili senis haec doctrina) triumphat.
Can. Res est consiliis secura fidelibus uti,
utile doctrinis praebere senilibus aures.
victa sitis, mens aegra manet curaeque supersunt.
Ful. Ut sedata sitis, sic mens sedabitur aegra.
funde merum, bibe; cardiaco medicina dolori haec,
utitur ad curas isto medicamine Roma.
Can. Omne opus atque labor vult intervalla; quiescat
obba parum, contra muscas impone tabellam.
Non madet imbre dies nec habet nox umida rorem
crescere nec duris possunt in cotibus herbae.
importuna fames, labor improbus, aëris ardor
confecere gregem macie; vix debile corpus
spiritus aeger agit, vacua cute porrigit ossa
clunis et exilis cava contrahit ilia venter.
hic aries qui fronte lupos cornuque petebat
nunc ove debilior pavidoque fugacior agno est.
haec mihi (sed nimium me ardentia vota ferebant)
omnia divino praedixerat omine cornix.
vix egressus eram limen, cum tristia portans
auguria a dextra venit tegetisque sinistrae
culmine consedit pressoque minaciter ore
vociferans iter auspicio prohibebat aperto.
heu pecus infelix, quod lacte et prole solebas
affluere, in nostris licuit dum pascere campis,
gramina dum quaeris, suci plus perdis eundo
quam referas pastu. simul hic tabescimus ambo,
tu tenui victu, curis ego victus amaris.
Ful. O nostrae regionis opes, o florida prata,
o campi virides, o pascua laeta feraxque
et numquam sine fruge solum, currentia passim
flumina per villas, rivi per rura, per hortos.
hinc pecus, hinc agri pingues; sub sidere Cancri,
cum tritura sonat passim, cum Iulius ardet,
arva virent, textae lento de vimine saepes
poma ferunt, redolent ipsis in vepribus herbae.
Can. O nemorum dulces umbrae mollesque susurri,
quos tecum memini gelidis carpsisse sub umbris
turturis ad gemitus, ad hirundinis ac philomenae
carmina, cum primis resonant arbusta cicadis.
aura strepens foliis nemorum veniebat ab Euro
et bacata super tendebat bracchia cornus.
ipse solo recubans pecudes gestire videbam
atque alacres teneris luctari cornibus agnos.

armed warfare against thirst, the fifth brings the fight, the sixth is victorious, and the seventh (this is aged Oenophilus' teaching) celebrates our triumph.
Can. [32] It is a deed free from care to accept trustworthy advice. It is useful to lend an ear to an old man's teaching. But though my thirst has been vanquished, my mind is still troubled and my cares remain.
Faust. Just as your thirst has been stilled, so too will be your troubled thoughts. Come, pour and drink the wine unmixed! This is the cure for your heartache, Rome uses this remedy for its cares.
Can. Each task and labor seeks a respite. Let the decanter repose for a little while, put on the stopper to keep out the flies.

[40] The days here are not drenched by rain, damp night has no dew, nor can grass grow among the hard stones. Relentless famine, ceaseless toil, and the heat of the air have all wasted my flock. Their diseased breath scarce causes their weakened frames to move. Their haunch bones stick out, and meager bellies contract their hollow entrails. Here's a ram that used to attack wolves with his forehead and horns. Now he is weaker than a ewe and more apt to flee than a fearful lamb. All this (but I was carried away too much by my burning desires) a crow foretold by a sign from the gods. [50] Scarce had I stepped from my door when, bearing its unhappy omen, the bird came from my right and settled on the left side of my cottage roof; and calling out threateningly in a subdued voice, by its clear sign it held me from my journey. Alas, you hapless flock that used to abound in milk and offspring when you were allowed to pasture in our native fields. While you are looking for grass, you lose more vigor in journeying than you gain in pasturage. Here we both are wasting away together: you by your lean diet and I overcome by bitter cares.
Faust. [59] Ah, the wealth of that land of ours! its flowery meadows and green fields! its pastures rich and fertile and its soil forever fruitful! its rivers everywhere running through farms and its brooks flowing through fields and gardens! On this side flocks, on that side fertile fields. Under the sign of Cancer when the sound of threshing everywhere fills the air and July burns with heat, the fields are green, hedges woven of pliant branches support their burden of fruit, and even among the brambles the wild herbs diffuse their fragrance.
Can. [67] Ah, the sweet shade and soft murmuring of the groves! I remember gathering the delights of these with you in the cool shade close by the turtledove's sighs and the songs of the swallow and nightingale when the orchards first begin to echo to the cicadas' notes. A breeze, rustling among the leaves in the groves, came from the east, and above us a cornel tree stretched out its branches laden with berries. Lying on the ground I myself used to watch the sheep exult and the lambs contend eagerly against one another

post somnos per gramen humi nunc ore supino
aut flatu implebam calamos aut voce canebam,
pectore nunc prono rutilantia fraga legebam.
Ful. Vivere tum felix poteras dicique beatus;
sed bona (quod nondum fueras expertus acerbam)
vilis erat tibi teque ideo fortuna reliquit.
quando iterum veniet (veniet si forsitan umquam)
sicut capreolis sursum nitentibus haerent
stipitibus vites stringuntque tenaciter ulmos,
sic illam tu prende manu neu desere prensam.
it, redit, effigiem mutat nec imagine constat
par lamiis quas nocte ferunt errare per umbras.
mobilis ut facies, ita mens; deludere gaudens
quod dederat tollit; pensi nihil, omnia casu;
qui nimium metuunt sapiuntve repellit et odit.
Can. Delicias patrii quotiens reminiscimur agri,
ferre tot aerumnas animo non possumus aequo.
sed quo mente feror? casu afflictatus acerbo
unde magis crucier felicia tempora volvo.
Maius adest: florent vites humilesque genistae,
iam spicata seges, malus iam Punica multo
flore rubet, redolent saepes albente sabuco
in patria, per rura Padi, per pascua Minci;
hic vero necdum incipiunt pubescere montes.
quod si vere solum torpet, quid frigora brumae
solstitiumque feret, gelidis cum terra pruinis
albicat et rapido cum caelum incanduit aestu?
sunt tamen hic armenta quibus cutis uvida, cervix
non signata iugis, gemino frons ardua cornu
luxuriansque toris pectus; nisi pabula carpant,
non erit hac tanta umectum pinguedine corpus.
Ful. Haec armenta quibus caput a tellure levatur
altius et cui sunt longa internodia crurum
cuncta vorant, herbas primum, mox ore supino
arboreas frondes summaeque cacumina silvae;
hoc imbelle pecus quod humi nascentia tantum
gramina decerpit vacuis ieiunat in arvis.
Can. Quid verbis opus est? cunctis animantibus una est
condicio: semper maiora minoribus obsunt.
agna lupo, mites aquilis sunt praeda columbae,
innocuos delphin venatur in aequore pisces.
unde fit hoc? (certe res prodigiosa videtur)
haec loca, si procul hinc videas e rupibus altis,
pingue solum et multo vestitum gramine dicas;
quo magis appropias tanto magis omnia sordent.

with their tender, new horns. After dreaming on the sward, sometimes, reclining on my back, I played my pipes or sang and sometimes, bent forward, I used to gather the gleaming red strawberries.

Faust. [78] At that time you were able to live as a fortunate man and could be called blessed. But when fortune was good, you valued her cheaply—because as yet you had not known her harshness—and therefore she abandoned you. When she comes again (if by chance she ever returns), as vines cling with their upward-striving tendrils to the trunks of elms and squeeze them tightly, just so catch hold of her with your hand and, once you have caught her, don't let her go. For she comes and goes, changes features, is inconstant in her image: like witches who men say wander among the shades of night. Like her looks, her intentions are changeable. Delighting in deception, she takes back what she's given. She weighs nothing, all goes by chance. She rejects and despises men who fear her too much or are too wise in her ways.

Can. [90] Whenever I remember the delights of my fathers' fields, I am unable to endure so many troubles with a composed mind. But where are my thoughts bearing me? Struck down by a cruel misfortune, why, to torment myself further, am I pondering the happy times of old! May has come. The vine and lowly broom are blooming there. The fields having already bristled with wheat, the pomegranates are red with flowers and the hedges are fragrant with blossoming elder in my native land, among the fields by the Po and the Mincio's pastures. But here the hills have not yet begun to put on their foliage. [99] If in spring the soil here is languid, what will winter's cold or the heat of summer's solstice bring, seasons when the earth is white with icy hoarfrost or when the sky glows with consuming heat? Yet here there are herds with sleek coats and necks unmarked by the yoke, cattle whose foreheads are lofty with twin horns and whose breasts ripple with muscle. If they didn't graze on good fodder, their bodies would not be sleek with so much fat.

Faust. [106] These cattle—their heads raised higher off the ground, their legs long—devour everything: first the grass, then, their mouths uplifted, the leaves and tops of the tallest trees. And this peace-loving herd here, who crop only the grasses growing on the ground, is left to fast in barren fields.

Can. [112] But why speak more of such things? For all living creatures the condition is the same: the larger ones always harm the smaller ones. Lambs are the wolf's prey, gentle doves are the eagles' booty. In the sea the dolphin hunts the harmless fishes. And how does this come about? (Indeed, it seems a monstrous thing.) If you viewed this place at a distance from some high cliff, you might call it rich land thickly arrayed in grass. But the nearer you approach it, the baser everything becomes.

Ful. Hoc est Roma viris avibus quod noctua: trunco
insidet et tamquam volucrum regina superbis
nutibus a longe plebem vocat. inscia fraudis
turba coit, grandes oculos mirantur et aures,
turpe caput rostrique minacis acumen aduncum;
dumque super virgulta agili levitate feruntur
nunc huc, nunc illuc, aliis vestigia filum
illaqueat, retinent alias lita vimina visco,
praedaque sunt omnes veribus torrenda salignis.
Can. O bellum hoc; poterit dici nihil aptius umquam.
sed procul en coluber tortos in pulvere gressus
flectit et exsertis sitiens ferit aëra linguis.
Ful. Candide, quae moneo memori sub pectore serva.
quando inter silvas graderis, defende galero
lumina, namque rubi praetendunt spicula longis
dentibus et curvus discerpit pallia mucro.
nec depone pedum multaque armare memento
cote sinum, ne te subito novus opprimat hostis.
et perone pedem tegito; spineta colubris
plena hominum vitae morsu insidiantur amaro,
et nunc longa dies aestu facit acre venenum.
mille lupi, totidem vulpes in vallibus istis
lustra tenent et, quod dirum ac mirabile dictu est,
ipse homines (huius tanta est violentia caeli)
saepe lupi effigiem moresque assumere vidi
inque suum saevire gregem multaque madere
caede sui pecoris; factum vicinia ridet
nec scelus exhorret nec talibus obviat ausis.
saepe etiam miris apparent monstra figuris
quae tellus affecta malis influxibus edit;
saepe canes tantam in rabiem vertuntur, ut ipsos
vincant caede lupos, et qui tutela fuerunt
hostiles ineunt animos et ovilia mactant.
fama est Aegyptum coluisse animalia quaedam
et pro numinibus multas habuisse ferarum;
ista superstitio minor est quam nostra. ferarum
hic aras habet omne genus, contraria certe
naturae res atque Deo qui dicitur olim
praeposuisse hominem cunctis animantibus unum.
saepe etiam morbosa aestas et pestifer annus
ingruit et passim languens pecus omne per arva
sternitur; exstinctae dum balat ad ubera matris,
agnus obit, moritur duro sub pondere taurus.
nec modus est morbo, non est medicina veneno,
sed vicina domus vicino a limine mortem

Faust. [120] Rome is among men what the owl is among birds. She sits on a tree trunk and, as if she were the queen of birds, summons the multitude from afar with her haughty commands. Ignorant of her deception, the crowd assembles. They wonder at her large eyes and ears, foul head, and the hooked point of her menacing beak. And while their nimble lightness bears them here and there on to the trees' twig growth, a string ensnares the feet of some, twigs smeared with birdlime hold fast others, and all become spoils to be roasted on willow spits.
Can. Oh, this is good! Nothing more apt could be said. But look! over there a serpent is making its winding way through the dust and in its thirst smites the air with its outstretched tongue.
Faust. [132] Candidus, keep the warnings I am giving you, holding them close within your thoughts. When you walk among the brushwood, protect your eyes with your hat: for the brambles stretch out long thorns, and their curved points tear a mantle to pieces. Don't put down your sheephook; and remember to arm your pockets with many stones lest a new enemy suddenly take you by surprise. Put boots on your feet: thorn hedges filled with serpents lie in ambush with their bitter sting for men's lives, and now the heat of the long days makes their venom keen. [141] A thousand wolves and as many foxes dwell in dens in those valleys there. And—what's dreadful and wondrous to tell—I myself have often seen men (so great is the violence of this region) assume the shape and ways of a wolf and rage among their own flocks, drenching themselves with the slaughter of their sheep. Their neighbors laugh at what is done, neither trembling at the crime nor preventing such bold acts. Moreover, often monsters of wondrous shape appear here which the earth, affected by evil influences, brings forth. And often dogs are transformed by so great a rage that they better even the wolves in slaughter, and those who were guardians take on a hostile intent and kill their own flock in the sheepfold. [153] Men say that the Egyptians worshipped certain animals and held as gods many of the wild beasts. That superstitious practice of theirs is less serious than ours. For here every kind of wild animal has his altar, a thing contrary indeed to the workings of nature and to God, who is said to have placed man once long ago above all living creatures. [159] Moreover, the heat of the year's pestilential season often strikes, and the entire flock is laid low, languishing in their sickness here and there throughout the fields. The lamb, while it bleats near the udders of its dead mother, is dying, and the bull perishes under its hard burden. Nor is there a limit to the disease nor an antidote against the poison, but a house

haurit et assidue sumunt contagia vires.
ista feras raro pestis rapit, utile semper
fert pecus; exstinctas caulas epulantur atroci
dente lupi nostraque ferae iactura opulescunt.
Can. Heu, heu quam praeceps miserum me insania traxit;
credere fallaci gravis est dementia famae.
Romuleos colles, Tiberim Romanaque tecta
audieram et studio mens est accensa videndi
ducendique bonis in tot praestantibus aevum.
accessi cum parte gregis, tentoria demens,
totum paene larem cum pastoralibus armis
trans iuga summa tuli, mulctraria, cymbia, aëna
et cacabos et quo formatur caseus orbem
fagineum; impensam atque operas amisimus omnes.
quid faciam? quo me vertam? sperata negantur
pabula; tot casus, tot ubique pericula. cogor
in veteres remeare casas et coepta fateri
consiliis egressa malis iterumque per aestus
et montana pati longos per saxa labores.
heu pecus infelix, o laevo sidere pastor
huc avecte. fuit multo praestantius istud
ignorasse solum patrioque in limine tutos
consumpsisse dies, gelidis senuisse sub antris
atque Padi circum ripas Athesisve per agros
aut ubi per virides campos et pascua nota
Mincius it vel qua vitreo natat Abdua cursu
consedisse, gregem pavisse salubribus herbis.
Ful. Te tua credulitas, et me mea fallit in horas.
vidi ego supremae qui prosperitatis habebant
culmina, dum laudata petunt, cecidisse nec umquam
emersisse malis; facit experientia cautos.
hi prius explorant et non laudata sequuntur
omnia; laude carent quae sunt meliora. fuerunt
(non nego) quae famam retinent ac nomina servant
(cuncta suis pollent vicibus) Luna, Hadrai, Troia,
Salvia (quas nobis memorabat saepius Umber)
nomine sunt solo, delevit cetera tempus.
si minor est patriae forsan modo gloria nostrae,
res tamen est melior. laudatae gloria Romae
quanta sit in toto non est qui nesciat orbe;
fama quidem manet, utilitas antiqua recessit.
illi prisca quibus maduerunt pascua fontes
nunc umore carent, venis aqua defuit haustis,
nulla pluit nubes, Tiberis non irrigat agros,
tempus aquaeductus veteres contrivit et arcus

takes in death from its neighbor, and the contagion continually assumes greater strength. That foul plague rarely snatches away wild beasts; it always carries off the farm animals useful to man. With their savage teeth wolves dine on the slaughter within the sheepfolds, and wild animals grow rich on our losses.

Can. [169] Alas, alas, with what haste my madness drew me into this misery! Grave madness it is to trust deceptive rumors. I had heard about Romulus' hills, about the Tiber and the roofs of Rome, and my mind burned with zeal to see and lead my life among things excellent in so many ways. I drew near with part of my flock. Over mountain ridges in my madness I bore my tents and almost all my household goods along with the tools of a shepherd's trade: my milk pails, cups, and bronze bowls, my cooking pots and that beechen ring that shapes our cheese—and this expense and all this labor I've lost! [179] What should I do? Where should I turn? I'm denied the pasturage I hoped for—so many misfortunes, so many dangers on every side! To my huts of old am I forced to return, confessing that my venture went astray because of bad counsel; and again in heat and among mountain rocks must I endure long hours of toil. Alas, unfortunate flock! Oh, shepherd borne hither by an unlucky star! More excellent far were it not to have known of this land, better to have passed my days securely in my father's house. Better to have grown old within the cool caves; and on the banks of the Po or in Adige's fields or where the Mincio glides among green plains and familiar pasturelands, or where the Adda floats along in its glassy course, better far to have settled down and pastured my flocks on wholesome grasses.

Faust. [192] Your credulity deceives you and mine deceives me from hour to hour. I myself have seen men who used to dwell on fortune's peak fall when they sought things of praise and never rise from their troubles. Experience makes these men cautious. They explore matters beforehand and follow everything that men don't extol: for those things that are better are wanting in praise. There are places—I don't deny it—that retain their reputation and watch over their famous names (for all things are strong in their turn): Luna, Hadria, Troy, Salvia—places Umber often used to speak of—these exist now in their names alone, time has destroyed the rest. [202] If only the renown of our homeland is perhaps less, in itself it is nonetheless better. In the whole world there is no one ignorant of how great is Rome's glory. Her fame indeed remains, her former usefulness has passed away. Those springs by which the ancient pasturelands used to be moistened now lack water, their channels drained dry. Clouds pour down none of their rain, the Tiber does not irrigate the fields, time has worn down the old aqueducts, and both arch and fortress

et castella ruunt; procul hinc, procul ite, capellae.
hic ieiuna fames et languida regnat egestas.
Hic tamen (ut fama est et nos quoque vidimus ipsi)
pastor adest quadam ducens ex alite nomen,
lanigeri pecoris dives, ditissimus agri,
carmine qui priscos vates atque Orphea vincat,
Orphea qui traxit silvas et saxa canendo.
hic alios omni tantum virtute Latinos
exsuperat quantum Tiberim Padus, Abdua Macram,
lenta salix iuncum, tribulos rosa, populus algam.
credimus hunc illi similem cui Tityris olim
bis senos fumare dies altaria fecit.
hic ovium custos ipse vigilantior Argo
Daphnide nec solum sed eo qui dicitur olim
Admeti pavisse greges per Thessala rura
doctior, omne pecus Solymi curare magistri
dignus et antiquo dignus succedere patri
qui fuit Assyrii pecoris post retia pastor.
iste potest servare gregem, depellere morbos,
umectare solum, dare pascua, solvere fontes,
conciliare Iovem, fures arcere luposque.
si favet iste, mane. quod si negat iste favorem,
Candide, coge pecus melioraque pascua quaere.

ECLOGA X
BEMBUS

De fratrum observantium et non observantium controversia, post religionis ingressum

Candidus Bembus Batrachus Myrmix

Can. Maxima pastores agitat discordia, Bembe,
qui Solymos colles Galilaeaque rura colebant;
Batrachus hinc, Myrmix illinc certare parati
iudice te paucis, si non audire recusas
et nisi te revocant maiora negotia, dicent.
tu pater es vatum, tu scis componere lites
iurgiaque et blandis convicia tollere verbis;
te quoque Pierios fama est potasse liquores
et vidisse deas quibus est custodia sacri
fontis et Eurotae campos ac Phocidis arva,
ipse ubi fronde sua tibi tempora cinxit Apollo,

are collapsing in ruins. Hence, you goats, get you hence! Here reign lean famine and dull poverty!

[212] And yet here—for such is the rumor, and I have seen him myself—there is present a shepherd to help us, a shepherd who takes his name from a certain bird, a man rich in woolbearing flocks, most rich in land, a man who might overcome in song the bards of old and even Orpheus—Orpheus who drew the trees and rocks when he sang. This man exceeds other Latians in every virtue as much as the Po exceeds the Tiber or the Adda the Magra, the pliant willow the rush, the rose the thistle, or the poplar seaweed in the ocean. I think this man to be like him in whose honor Tityrus once long ago caused an altar to smoke twice six days. [222] This guardian of the flock is more vigilant than Argus himself, more skilled not only than Daphnis but him who is said once to have pastured Admetus' flock in the fields of Thessaly; worthy to watch over the whole flock of that master from Jerusalem and to succeed that father of old who, forsaking his nets, was shepherd of the Assyrian flock. This man has the power to protect the flock, dispel sickness, moisten the ground, bestow pasturelands, release springs, appease Jupiter, and keep away thieves and wolves. If he smiles with favor, stay. But if he denies his favor, drive forth your flock, Candidus, and seek greener pastures.

ECLOGUE X
BEMBUS

A Controversy Between Observant and Nonobservant Brethren

AFTER HIS ENTRY INTO RELIGIOUS ORDERS

Candidus Bembus Batrachus Myrmix

Can. The greatest discord, Bembus, now stirs shepherds who used to dwell on Jerusalem's hills and in Galilee's fields. On one side Batrachus, on the other side Myrmix say they stand ready to contend briefly against one another for your judgment unless you refuse to hear them or greater business recalls you. You yourself are a father of prophets. You know how to lay quarrels to rest and banish disputes and insults with soothing words. [8] They say that you have even drunk of Pierian waters and have seen those goddesses who watch over that sacred fount, and those plains of Eurotas and Phocian fields where Apollo himself wreathed your temples with laurel and gave you as a

dona dedit citharam, nervos et eburnea plectra.
Bem. Dicite, quandoquidem tepidos admovit ad ignes
nos hiberna dies, dum non sinit ire per agros
bruma gregem, flatu Boreas dum saevit acuto,
dum riget omne solum, tectis dum plurima pendet
stiria, dum torpent sub aquis glacialibus amnes;
otia damnantur quae nulla negotia tractant.
Myr. Pastores, genus infelix, aestate vagamur
pro grege solliciti, sed cum nos frigidus imber
continet in stabulis, lites et iurgia surgunt.
Bat. Qui veteres audent ritus mutare suoque
arbitrio et nullis ducunt sub legibus aevum,
hi sunt, o Myrmix, qui bella domestica gignunt.
Bem. De veteri ritu, de consuetudine patrum
rixa agitur vobis? leges moresque parentum,
Batrache, dic. dic, cur nostrum venistis in orbem
ex Phoenice solo? nos pascua vidimus illa,
vidimus herbosos felici uligine campos.
vertice Carmeli vitreis uberrimus undis
fons cadit et rauco densum nemus irrigat amne.
vidimus et Iordanis aquas, ubi maximum olim
pastor oves mergens scabiem resecavit avitam.
amnis hic a Libano veniens Galilaea per arva
transit et ampla lacu consurgit in aequora magno;
unda coit rursum, rursum mare fundit apertum,
urbs ubi Romani de nomine dicta Tiberi;
unda coit rursum, tandem Iericunte relicta
intrat in infames Asphalti gurgitis undas.
hinc satis est nos oram omnem vidisse probatum;
dicite, et hinc tandem vestras demergite lites.
Myr. Batrachus audaci semper sese ingerit ore
et mihi se praefert magno temerarius ausu.
Bat. Non ego me ingessi, processi a iudice iussus.
Bem. Pone pedum, Myrmix, et tu quoque, Batrache; non est
orandum armatis manibus, sed mentibus aequis.
Batrache, dic; Myrmix, animi compesce furorem
interea, ut venias magis ad responsa paratus.
qui furit insanit; qui vero insanit amaro
impatiens animo nec corda nec ora gubernat;
quidquid ait vanum est, quidquid molitur ineptum.
Bat. Bembe, genus nostrum generisque exordia dicam.
venimus Assyriis (ut Candidus inquit) ab oris.
est pater Elias nobis qui sustulit armis
pastorum genus omne malum, quo traxit Olympo
flammigeros ignes, qui ascendit in aethera curru.

gift the cithara: its strings and ivory plectrum.

Bem. Speak, seeing that we are led to our warm fires by the winter's days, a time when the weather forbids the flock to roam the fields and the north wind rages with its keen breath, when the ground freezes solid, when icicles hang thick from the roof and the streams' icy waters flow sluggishly. Leisure is condemned when it has no tasks to perform.

Myr. [19] We shepherds, a hapless race, range about in the summertime, anxious for our flocks. But when the chilly rain keeps us among the sheepfolds, then quarrels and disputes arise.

Bat. Those who dare to change the old ways (moreover, at their own discretion) and who live under no rules—those, oh Myrmix, are the men who are causing these quarrels within our own house.

Bem. [25] So you are quarreling about the long–established rite, the customs of your forefathers? Tell me, Batrachus, of their rules and ways. Tell me, why from Phoenician soil have you both entered our part of the world? I myself have seen those pastures, I have seen those rich, grassy marshlands. From Carmel's heights a spring most rich in crystalline waters descends and with its noisy stream refreshes a thickset grove. And I have seen Jordan's waters, where once long ago a very great shepherd, dipping his sheep, checked their ancestral scab. [34] Coming here from Mount Lebanon, this river crosses Galilee's fields and rises to the ample surface of a big lake. Its waters meet again, and again they flow into an open sea where a city was named for Tiberius the Roman. Its waters meet again and finally, Jericho left behind, they enter the infamous waves of Asphaltites' flood. Whence is proof enough that I have seen your whole country. Speak and, after this, drown your strife at last.

Myr. With his bold words Batrachus is forever forcing himself on us. Recklessly and with great daring he even prefers himself to me.

Bat. [44] I've forced myself on no one! I've advanced at the bidding of a judge.

Bem. Put down your sheephook, Myrmix! Yes, and you too, Batrachus! You must plead not with arms but with tranquil thoughts. Speak, Batrachus. Meanwhile, Myrmix, restrain the rage in your mind to be more ready to answer. He who rages is a madman. And indeed, he who is a madman, impatient and embittered, rules neither his heart nor his words. What he says is hollow, what he attempts is foolish.

Bat. Bembus, I'll speak of our race and its beginnings. We came (as Candidus said) from Assyrian lands. Our father was Elijah, who with shepherds' weapons endured every kind of evil, who drew fiery flames down from Olympus and ascended into the sky in a chariot.

Bem. Nobile et antiquum genus hoc, et clara propago.
Bat. Pastores alii quotquot per rura vagantur
omnia sunt rivi nostris a fontibus orti;
nos dedimus leges, pascendi ostendimus artem.
quo magis hi peccant qui, cum sint ordine primi,
primatum amittunt studia inconsulta sequendo.
nos radix, alii rami; sed nos quoque rami
a veteri radice patrum iam aetate caduci.
tradidit Elias certam pastoribus artem
qua curare greges, qua noxia pabula fas est
discere et occultos imbres ventosque latentes
quive salutaris foret et qui pestifer annus;
signa dedit, nihil omisit quod ovilia tangat.
sed fons ille fluens Carmeli e rupibus altis
tam nitidus quondam, tam dulci limpidus unda,
tramite mutato (patet id) modo currit in Austrum.
sed prius (extat adhuc vetus alveus) ibat ad ortum.
hi cursus fecere novos, liquere priores
quos dederat rivo veterum prudentia patrum.
Myr. Quid tibi, sive novo currat seu tramite prisco,
dummodo fecundis umectet pascua lymphis?
et quid de caeli quereris regione? per Austrum
solis iter, melior vitis quae respicit Austrum,
et melior legitur Libycis de collibus uva.
Bat. Est melior taxus Boream quae respicit; ergo
in Boream melius poterat decurrere rivus.
pastor es, et cura pecoris male sane relicta
sermonem de vite facis quasi legibus isdem
grex et vitis eant, nec quod discrimen in undis
gramineque et ventis nosti et quam noxius Auster
sit pecori; disce a Roma si noxius Auster.
cur Mutinensis agri pecudes sunt vellere fusco?
cur Clitumnus habet niveas? cur Mantua molli
lanitio excellit Veronaque proxima Manto?
unde haec multiplici rerum variantia forma?
non aliunde nisi a caelis, a gramine et unda.
Bem. Candide, utrumque pedum procul hinc (rogo) protinus aufer;
inter eos hodie video bellum acre futurum.
clam cape et auferto; subter sarmenta reconde.
Bat. Bembe, mihi tecum sermo est. dum viximus una,
dum commune pecus nobis fuit, heu mihi quantum
dedecus, heu quot sunt pecudes incommoda passae.
nec mersare gregem fluvio nec vellera certis
temporibus (sicut mos est) tondere licebat.

Bem. [57] Noble and ancient stock this, and an illustrious progeny!
Bat. Other shepherds of whatever number, roaming through every field, are streams sprung from our fount. We bequeathed the rules, we revealed the art of pasturing. How greatly those men err who, though of highest rank, dismiss this preëminence by following uncounseled zeal. We are the roots, others the branches. But we too, branches of our forefathers' ancient roots, are decayed now by age. To shepherds Elijah left behind trustworthy rules which enable us to care for our flocks and know which pasturage is harmful, to discern invisible storms and lurking winds and to foresee wholesome and pestilent times. [69] He gave us the signposts, he omitted nothing that has to do with the sheepfold. But that stream that flows from Carmel's high cliffs—so shining once, its sweet waters so clear—its course changed (it's apparent), now flows towards the south. But before (for the old channel can still be seen) it flowed towards the east. These men have made new courses, have abandoned the previous ones that our ancient fathers' prudence gave to it.
Myr. [76] What is it to you if the stream runs in a new course or an old one, so long as it moistens the pastures with its life-giving waters? And why complain about the direction? The sun's course is through the south. Better is the vine that looks to the south, better the grape gathered from Libyan hills.
Bat. [81] And better the yew tree that looks to the north!—for this reason better it is that our stream was able to flow down towards the north. You are a shepherd, and yet, having rashly abandoned the flock's care, you speak of the vine as if the same rules governed the flocks and vineyards. You haven't learned the distinctions of waters, grass, and winds or how injurious the south is to sheep—learn from Rome whether the south wind is harmful. Why is the fleece of Modena's sheep dusky? and why are Clitumnus' sheep white as snow? Why do Mantua and nearby Verona excel in soft wool? Whence come these various differences? From nowhere else but the region, the grass, and the water.
Bem. [93] [aside] Candidus, take far hence (I beg you) both their sheephooks at once. I see that there is going to be keen warfare between them today. Take them in secret and carry them away. Hide them under the brushwood.
Bat. But Bembus, I must talk to you. While we lived together and shared the flock—alas! how much disgrace, how many vexations the sheep endured! I wasn't permitted to dip them in the river or (as is our custom) to shear off

nudabant spineta pecus, nudata secabant
terga rubi; scabie cutis aspera, tabidus umor
pestis, et in totum serpebant ulcera corpus.
multum igitur refert pecudes quae pabula carpant,
flumina quae potent et qua regione morentur.
Dic mihi, dic, Myrmix, priscum cur lana colorem
perdidit? haec gregibus quidnam nova vellera fecit?
cur pecus est nigrum quod erat melioribus annis
clarum? immutarunt mutati vellera mores.
Beme, ad te redeo. paucis absolvere nitar,
sed, quo digna omni tua sit sententia laude,
vera loquar. tu iura tenes, ego facta docebo;
iudicium reddit verum enarratio vera.
his animadversis aegre tot damna ferentes
venimus ad fontem, rivumque a vertice summo
scrutari mihi cura fuit; tu, provide Myrmix,
interea nidos avium vel dorcada pravam
venabare tuae quae dona darentur amatae.
Myr. Bembe, vides ut aperta in me convicia torquet?
auguror, ista manu lis est, non ore, agitanda;
mos mihi, non lingua, maledicta refellere dextra.
Can. Batrache, ne verum taceam, linguosior aequo es;
iurgia bilem acuunt, convicia pectus acerbant.
non tibi cum puero res est, nec homuncio Myrmix;
res male tuta viros lingua irritare proterva.
Bat. Da veniam, Myrmix; "amitam" proferre volenti
nescio quis mihi misit in os malus error "amatam."
Myr. Do veniam; cave ne rursum me voce lacessas.
Bat. Alveus excelsa saliens de rupe lacunam
foderat et clausis ripas aequaverat undis;
gurges erat textu silvarum umbrosus opaco
densaque saepierant tristem spineta lacunam.
mille venenorum species in gurgite vidi,
mille secus ripas in opaco margine, mille
per nemus ad lymphas sinuoso serpere gressu.
obstupui, et rapido rediens ad ovilia cursu
incipio paleas furca versare tricorni.
ecce caput tollit coluber linguaque trisulca
sibilat, inflantur fauces, nepa livida tendit
bracchia, ventrosus profert vestigia bufo,
vipera per stipulam gradiens strepit. "o loca," dixi,
"non pecori tantum verum et pastoribus ipsis
noxia." mox grege diviso de sedibus illis
pascua quaesitum tristis meliora recessi.
perque iter antiquum fontis nova flumina duxi

their fleece at the appointed times. Thorn hedges stripped the sheep and brambles cut their backs after they had been stripped. Their coats were rough with scab. Their bodies' moisture was dried up by sickness. Sores crept throughout their frames. Much it matters therefore what grass the sheep crop, from what rivers they drink, and in what region they tarry. [106] Tell me, Myrmix, why has the wool lost its ancient color? What has caused this new kind of fleece within the flock? Why are sheep black now that in happier years were gleaming white? Our customs, when changed, changed the color of their fleece!

But Bembus, I return to you. I'll strive to conclude briefly. But, so that your judgment will be praiseworthy, I'll speak the truth. You judge and I'll recount the facts. A true account yields a true judgment. Having pondered so many losses and enduring them with great difficulty, we came to that fount, and my task it was to explore the stream from its highest reaches. You meanwhile, prudent Myrmix, were hunting birds' nests or a small gazelle to give your beloved.

Myr. [119] See, Bembus, how he openly insults me? I foresee that this quarrel must be conducted with fists, not words. It is my custom to refute insults not with my tongue but my right hand.

Can. Truly, Batrachus, I cannot keep silent. You talk too much. Strife sharpens choler, and quarrels embitter the heart. You're not dealing with a boy, nor is Myrmix a puny fellow. It is scarce safe to incite a man with impudent words.

Bat. Pardon me, Myrmix. I wanted to say "aunt" [*amitam*] but some manner of mischievous error put "beloved" [*amatam*] on my tongue.

Myr. You're forgiven—but beware, lest your words provoke me again.

Bat. [129] Tumbling down from a high cliff, the stream's channel had dug out a pool and levelled the enclosed waters with its banks. A whirlpool was there, shaded by a dark tangle of trees, and thick thorn hedges encircled the gloomy pool. A thousand kinds of venomous things I saw in that watery abyss, a thousand sorts of creatures on the shady margins along its banks, a thousand things that wound sinuously through the woods towards its waters. I was struck with terror, and running back to the sheepfold I began to turn over the straw with my three–pronged pitchfork. [138] And, lo! a serpent raised its head, hissed with its three–forked tongue, and swelled open its jaws. A scorpion stretched out its spiteful claws. A big–bellied toad advanced towards me, and a viper rustled, moving through the straw. "Oh place," said I, "harmful not only to the flocks but to the shepherds themselves!" Directly, having divided the flock in two, I departed in sadness from that abode to seek out better pastures. And through the fount's old channel I led new streams

in campos ubi prima suos Aurora colores
explicat et croceos Phoebi redeuntis ad ortus.
hic mihi fecundae pecudes, hic pascua laeta
et sine labe liquor, dulces sine crimine lymphae.
haec loca primaevi sunt quae coluere parentes;
signa casae superant, puteus cariosaque ligna
fixa solo seiuncta pedum discrimine septem
et focus et lacera quae cingitur area saepe.
Myr. Cura viris levibus rerum solet esse novarum;
propterea certe nova pascua quaeris et amnes
fingis inauditos et vis novus auctor haberi.
Bat. Cura viris gravibus rerum solet esse suarum;
propterea, Myrmix, nimis a gravitate recedis.
haec novitas non est novitas, sed vera vetustas.
religio et pietas patrum instaurata resurgit
quam tua corrupit levitas et nota tuorum
segnities. igitur si quis labentia tecta
erigat et sterilem qui mansuefecerit agrum
iudice te damnandus erit? non ponitur arbor
altera, sed veteri inseritur bona virgula trunco;
segne prius lignum nostro fit fertile cultu.
Myr. Quamvis pingue tuo pecori sit gramen et unda
defaecata, tamen multae cum matribus agnae
interiere; lupi et pastae meminere volucres.
Bat. Hae (fateor) quae dira tuae contagia pestis
accepere. etiam procul aspicientibus obsunt;
tantum virus inest, vestri vis tanta veneni.
propterea magis atque magis discedere semper
est animus. patitur pecus haec incommoda nostrum
sola, quod in vastam nondum discessit eremum
nec satis a vobis procul in deserta recessit.
Myr. Batrache, de gregibus mentiris plurima nostris.
certe alienarum tibi cura superflua rerum,
et temere assumis partes censoris iniqui.
cur mihi qui pasco cuium pecus ista tueri
non licuit? solisne domus mea cognita vobis?
Bat. Aethiopes una quoniam nigredine sordent,
ille color nulli vitio datur; omnibus idem
vultus et alterius si quis reprenderet ora,
et sua damnaret. pecori pecorisque magistris
faex eadem, scabies eadem, cutis et color idem.
Bem. Parcite; iam satis est lis intellecta diesque
inclinata cadit, iam post iuga summa ruit sol.
audite, o magni generis longaeva propago
lite super vestra quae sit sententia nostra.

into fields where Aurora first unfurls her colors and towards sunrises gilded by returning Phoebus. [148] Here my sheep are fertile in fleece, and rich are the pasturelands. Here the waters are without taint, the sweet springs without fault. This is the place where our youthful forefathers dwelt. The traces of their cells still remain: the well, the decayed logs driven in the ground seven feet apart, the hearth, the torn–up plot surrounded by a hedge.

Myr. [154] Frivolous men are wont to busy themselves with newfangled things. Surely it is for this reason that you have sought out new pasturelands, invented unheard–of streams, and want to be thought our new founder.

Bat. Serious men are wont to busy themselves with their own interests. For this reason, Myrmix, you depart too much from seriousness. This newness isn't newness but true antiquity. [160] Our fathers' reverence and piety, tainted by your frivolity and the well–known sloth of your fellows, has been restored and now surges anew. If then a man is raising buildings that are falling down and has tamed unfruitful fields, judge you that he should be condemned? We aren't planting a second tree. Rather, a healthy slip is being engrafted on the trunk of the old one, wood dormant before is becoming productive again under our care.

Myr. Though the grass might be made luxuriant for your flock and the waters be cleansed, nonetheless many lambs have perished with their mothers. Wolves and birds gorged with prey remember them well.

Bat. [170] 'Tis true—of those sheep infected with your fearful pestilence! Even from afar it harms those who look upon it, so much poison is in it, so great is the power of your venom. For this reason I am minded to depart still further from you. My flock endures these afflictions only because it has not yet withdrawn into the vast wilderness or departed far enough from you into the desert.

Myr. You're lying grossly, Batrachus, about my flock! Assuredly, your care for the affairs of others is unnecessary. Indeed, you're rashly taking the side of an unjust censor. Why couldn't I, who pasture anyone's flock, look after these things? Is my house known only to you?

Bat. [182] Since Ethiopians are all soiled by blackness, that color is thought no blemish. It is the same among all of them, whether one visage condemns itself or another. Shepherd and sheep have the same impurity, the same scab, the same skin color.

Bem. Cease! Now I understand your quarrel well enough. Moreover, the day is ending and now the sun is hastening behind the highest mountain ridges. Hearken, oh aged offspring of a great race, to my judgment on your quarrel.

Myr. Batrache, me audaci totiens sermone lacessis.
Bat. Non ego, sed non aequa magis te causa lacessit
iudiciumque timet sibi mens male conscia iustum.
Can. Quando inimicitias tempus deponere, rursum
vestra novas lites vecordia suscitat. ergo
perpetuis haec rixa odiis aeterna manebit?
quae vos debilitas capitis, quae insania vexat?
non pudet his uti tanto sub iudice nugis?
ergo animis audite aequis odiisque sepultis
ultima doctiloqui quae sit sententia Bembi.
Bem. Ferte per antiquos patrum vestigia gressus
et veteres servate vias. revocate vagantes
per valles et saxa greges, per lustra ferarum.
figite in antiquis iterum magalia campis.

Myr. Batrachus, you provoke me so often with your bold talk!
Bat. [192] Not I but the unfairness of your case greatly provokes you. Moreover, your mind, scarcely conscious of what is just, fears to receive judgment.
Can. When it is time to lay aside your hatred, your madness is again stirring up new quarrels! Will this brawling, born of constant ill will, continue then forever? What madness, what weakness in your head thus afflicts you? Aren't you ashamed to indulge in this nonsense before so great a judge? Therefore with tranquil thoughts and hatred laid to rest listen to the final judgment of wise–spoken Bembus.
Bem. [201] Walk in the footsteps of your forefathers and keep up the old ways. Call back flocks wandering among the valleys and rocks, among the haunts of wild beasts. Build your huts again in the fields of old.

NOTES

Dedicatory Letter

For Paride Ceresara and the relation of this letter to the early history of Mantuan's collection, see "Introduction: Composition and Publication of the *Adulescentia*."

A portion of Mantuan's opening sentence is quoted, as Mustard notes (46), in *Lamentationes novae Obscurorum Reuchlinistarum* (*Ulrichi Hutteni . . . opera . . . omnia*, ed. Edvard Böcking [Leipzig: Teubner, 1859–70], VI, 375), and a bizarre echo appears in the prologue to Alexander Barclay's eclogues, where (in lines 65–82) Barclay couches the background and reasons for publishing his poems in the language of Mantuan's letter (**M** 49).

Eclogue I

One searches in vain in ancient pastoral or in the eclogues of Petrarch and Boccaccio for what the headnote of this eclogue describes as love's happy outcome (*felix exitus*). Indeed, Fortunatus' comments aside, Faustus himself suggests that not all aspects of his courtship of Galla have been "honorable (*honestus*),"[1] his dalliance with her in the fields (lines 63–113) being characterized in a darker mood (line 110) as a "crime (*scelus*)." Within the collection as a whole, Faustus' love is to be compared with Pollux's devotion to the Virgin Mary in the seventh and eighth eclogues. Badius has a lengthy introductory note on this eclogue, doubly interesting when we consider how widespread was the use of his commentary in Renaissance grammar schools:

> Not without reason is this first eclogue entitled "Honorable Love and Its Happy Outcome." For though Mantuan, having not as yet professed his vows, had already composed these poems, a prelude, as it were, to

[1] Essentially the epithet echoes the Church's distinction between an honorable sexual union (*honesta sexuum commixtio*) in marriage and the alternative, a sexual liaison not intended to lead to marriage: Philippe Ariès, "The Indissoluble Marriage," in *Western Sexuality: Practice and Precept in Past and Present Times*, eds. Philippe Ariès and André Béjin (Oxford: Blackwell, 1985), 145.

> his genius (having doubtless been born to be a poet), nonetheless because even in his youth he wished to conceive or circulate nothing in the least dishonorable, now in reviewing these eclogues again, he would certainly have rejected anything in them that might give offense. Accordingly, lest, if too severely religious a person, in the habit of reading the title "Love," should put this poem aside, he entitled it "Honorable Love," a kind of love indeed than which nothing is more appropriate to a man. Moreover, this love is defined as honorable because it originated in matrimonial affection. "And Its Happy Outcome" is added so that those who desire to fall in love might be incited to an honorable love, one in fact whose issue is a happy one.[2]

With details from the second, third, and fourth eclogues, "Eclogue I" was imitated in the first eclogue of Francis Sabie's *Pan's Pipe*.[3] As late as the eighteenth century it still found an English translator in William Bewick,[4] and numerous twentieth-century translations attest to renewed interest in what Leonard Grant has described as "the best-known Neo-Latin pastoral ever written in Europe."[5]

---

2 *Haec prima ægloga de honesto amore foelicique eius exitu inscribitur non sine ratione : nam licet nondum religionem professus haec veluti ingenii sui praeludia composuerat : ad poesim haud dubie natus auctor : tamen quia ne tunc quidem quicquam inhonestum aut concipere aut edere voluisset : & nunc cum recognosceret si offendisset nimirum reiecisset. Proinde ne si de amoribus titulum quispiam severus [severius?] religiosus lectitans aufugeret : inscipisit de amore honesto : quo revera nihil est homine dignius. Hic autem amor honestus describitur : quia affectione matrimomiali initus. Additur autem de foelici eius exitu : vt eos qui amare volent ad honestum amorem inuitet quippe cuius foelix est exitus.* (**Ad**, fol. 107)

3 Echoes first noted by Katarina Windscheid in *Die englische Hirtendichtung von 1570-1625* (Halle: n. p., 1895), 39-40. Sabie's eclogues are reprinted with a discussion of sources by Mustard and J. W. Bright in "*Pan's Pipe*, Three Pastoral Eclogues, With Other Verses, By Francis Sabie (1595),"*MP*, 7 (1910), 433-64. Mario Equicola summarizes the action of Mantuan's first three eclogues in his *Libro di natura d' amore* (Venice: Gabriel Giolito de Ferarra, 1554), 68-69 (**M** 48).

4 See "Introduction," note 73, for Bewick's and other translations in collections. Lines 48-52 were anonymously translated as "Eclogue the First Baptistae Mantuani. Love Described," in MS. *Rawl. poet. 197, fol. 10v, Bodleian Library, Oxford.

5 *Neo-Latin Literature and the Pastoral*, (Chapel Hill: Univ. of North Carolina Press, 1965), 129. In addition to Grant (129-34), the following have also translated this eclogue in this century:

- Lucia Gualdo Rosa, in *Poeti latini del quattrocento*, eds. Francesco Arnaldi, Lucia Gualdo Rosa, and Liliana Monti Sabia, (Milan/Naples: Ricciardi, 1964), 888-99.
- Pierre Laurens, in *Musae reduces: anthologie de la poésie latine de la renaissance*, (Leiden: Brill, 1975), 84-87.
- Thomas A. Ryan, "The First Eclogue of Mantuan," *Allegorica*, 1 (1976), 117-25. (Ryan also includes a translation of Mantuan's dedicatory letter.)
- Fred J. Nichols, in *An Anthology of Neo-Latin Poetry* (New Haven: Yale Univ. Press, 1979), 203-11.

1–5 As J. W. Bright and W. P. Mustard point out (437), these lines are paraphrased in lines 27–32 of Francis Sabie's first eclogue. Mustard (54, 53) finds echoes of the first line in Euricius Cordus *Ecl.* III, 34 and of the first two lines in the first (72) and sixth idyls (19) of Helius Eobanus Hessus.
5 melior vigilantia somno is echoed in Euricius Cordus, *Ecl.* X, 6 (**M** 55) and is quoted in William Martyn's *Youth's Instruction*, printed in 1612: *English Writers on Education 1480–1603*, ed. Foster Watson (1903–06; rpt. Gainesville, Fla.: Scholars' Facsimiles and Reprints, 1967), 116 (**M** 44).
6–8 Adapted, as Harry Vredeveld points out, in Eobanus Hessus' *Bucolicon* III, 67–69 ("A Neo–Latin Satire on Love–Madness: The Third Eclogue of Eobanus Hessus *Bucolicon* of 1509," *Daphnis*, 14 [1985], 700).
9–10 Quoted as the motto at the end of William Basse's *Three Pastoral Elegies*, printed in 1598 (**M** 43).
14–18 Quoted in Robert Burton's *Anatomy of Melancholy*, ed. Holbrook Jackson (London: Dent, 1932), III, 151 (**M** 45). (Burton's copy of the *Adulescentia*, in the collection of pastoral verse printed by Oporinus [C399], is preserved in the Bodleian Library, Oxford.)
19–25 An expanded version of a detail found in descriptions of the Cyclops in love (e.g., Ovid, *Met.* XIII, 763).
24 sortiri digitis, i.e., to compete at *morra*, an ancient and modern game in which a player tries to guess the number of fingers simultaneously held up by the other player. This bit of rustic realism is perhaps borrowed from Calp., *Ecl.* II, 25–26.
27–31 An echo of Virgil's famous image in *G.* IV, 511–12. Noting this, Mustard also cites Statius' version in *Theb.* V, 601–3.
32–35 Mustard cites Stat., *Theb.* VI, 189–92, but cf. also Lucretius II, 355–66, Ovid, *Fast.* IV, 359–60, and centrally Virgil, *Ecl.* VIII, 85–88.
38 Quoted by Burton in his *Anatomy of Melancholy*, III, 145 (**M** 45).
40 syrtes: from the name of two areas of sandy flats on the coast between Carthage and Cyrene, proverbially dangerous to shipping (*OLD* s. v. "Syrtis"). Whence, as Badius observes, they came to signify figuratively the inextricable bonds of love ("*hic . . . pro inextricabilibus amorum nexibus*"). Cf. Propertius' delight at having finally escaped them (III, 24, 15–16).
42 Galla: A non–Virgilian name, echoing ironically the beautiful, faithless Galla of Boccaccio's first eclogue.
45 Badius notes here that "Venus too is said to have squinted slightly (*et Venus paeta dicitur*)." The rustic realism of lines 44–47 nonetheless offended the French writer and critic Fontenelle (see "Introduction: Themes, Style, and Organization"). Grant (*op. cit.*, 170) notes that Galla's coarseness supplied a precedent for the portrait of Phyllis in Euricus Cordus' eighth eclogue.
47 Like lines 14–18 and 38, quoted in Burton's chapter on love melancholy (*Anatomy of Melancholy*, III, 156) (**M** 45).
48–51 Quoted in Burton's chapter on beauty as a cause of love melancholy (*Anatomy of Melancholy*, III, 85). Line 48 appears in Abraham Fraunce's Latin comedy *Victoria*, ed. G. C. Moore–Smith, in *Materialien zur Kunde des älteren Englischen Dramas*, 14 (Louvain: A. Uystpruyst, 1906), 66 (**M** 51).
52 Mustard notes (40–41) that this line is quoted in one of Gabriel Harvey's letters to Spenser (*Works*, ed. A. B. Grosart [London: n. p., 1884–85], I, 25) and appears as the motto on the title page of *Alcilia: Parthenophil's Loving Folly*, published in 1595.
53 Quoted in part in *Wily Beguiled*, published in 1602 (**M** 43).
61 Citing Jerome and Aeneas Sylvius, Mustard notes that the expression was proverbial.
62 Mustard notes that this line appears in the Cambridge Latin play *Laelia*, ed., G. C. Moore–Smith (Cambridge Univ. Press, 1910), 16: "*quas nulla premit sitis / sunt illae asperiores semper sitientibus.*"

68–69 Love–gifts are a familiar convention of pastoral (e.g., Theocritus, *Id.* III, 33–34), but the rabbit and doves here most likely derive from Calp. III, 76–78 and Nemes. II, 67–68.
73 Quoted in Burton's *Anatomy of Melancholy*, III, 103 (**M** 45).
83 Roman senators were distinguished by a broad purple stripe worn on their clothing.
97 potum . . . amnen: varied as a half–line in the eclogues of Eobanus Hessus (for this and other such adaptations of half–lines by Eobanus Hessus, see **V** 472).
100 Quoted in Burton's *Anatomy of Melancholy*, III, 145 (**M** 45).
104 Like 73, quoted by Burton in his chapter on artificial allurements in love (*Anatomy of Melancholy*, III, 91, 103) (**M** 45).
108 Quoted in Burton's *Anatomy of Melancholy*, III, 174 (**M** 45).
113 Cf. the lovesick Gallus' words in Virgil, *Ecl.* X, 49 (**B**).
115–16 As Mustard notes, a common motif in Roman amatory poetry: cf. e.g., Tibullus II, 3, 79-80; Ovid, *Her.* VI, 97.
114–15 Like lines 100 and 108, quoted in Burton's chapter on love melancholy in his *Anatomy of Melancholy*, III, 153, 145, 174 (**M** 45). Lines 114–16 are also paraphrased in the seventh idyl (line 135) of Helius Eobanus Hessus (**M** 53).
118 semel insanivimus omnes (We have all been crazy once) echoes through subsequent English and Continental literature, eventually becoming, in Boswell's words, one of those sayings "which everyone repeats, but nobody knows where to find" (in a costly lapse of memory, Johnson himself once missed winning ten guineas by failing to identify its source): *The Life of Samuel Johnson*, ed., G. B. Hill, rev., L. F. Powell (Oxford: Clarendon Press, 1934), IV, 181–82. The title of two poems in *Witt's Recreations* (*Facetiae* [London: J. C. Hotten, 1874], 196, 220) (**M** 44) and the motto for Samuel Nicholson's *Acolastus his After–witte* (**M** 43) and one of the satires (VI, 1) in Joseph Hall's *Virgidemiae* (**M** 42), it is quoted in the following: Stephen Gosson's *Schoole of Abuse*, ed. Edward Arber (London: A. Murray and Son, 1869), 41 (**M** 40); Robert Greene's "Epistle to the Gentlemen Schollers of both Universities," prefixed to his *Mourning Garment* (*Life and Complete Works*, ed. A. B. Grosart [London: n.p., 1881–6], IX, 124) (**M** 41); Thomas Nashe's *Have with you to Saffron–Walden*, and the prologue to *Summer's Last Will and Testament* (*Works*, ed. R. B. McKerrow [London: Sidgwick and Jackson, 1910], III, 79, 225) (**M** 41–42); Robert Ward(?), *Fucus histriomastix*, G. C. Moore–Smith (Cambridge Univ. Press, 1909), 27 (**M** 51); and *The Three Parnassus Plays*, ed. J. B. Leishman (London: Nicolson and Watson, 1949), 326 (**M** 43). With a portion of line 52 ("*amor est amaror*") Johannes Murmellius cites it in 1513 as being a trite proverb (*protrita proverbia*): *Ausgewählte Werke*, ed. A Bömer (Münster: Regensberg, 1892–95), IV, 34 (**M** 46).
121 in nonam horam, i.e., **meridie** See "Introduction," note 88. Despite the comic confusion, "noon" is in fact the correct translation, as Harry Vredeveld points out, of "*in nonam . . . horam*," the canonical hour of "nones" having been shifted by the fourteenth century from the ninth to the sixth hour after sunrise: "'*In Nonam Horam*': A Misunderstood Phrase in Baptista Mantuanus' First Eclogue," *Aevum*, 3 (1985), 460. Vredeveld notes that Eobanus Hessus adapts this time–expression in *Bucolicon* VIII, 31 (**V** 473).
129 infelix puer: a line beginning also used by Eobanus Hessus (for this and other such borrowings at the beginnings of hexameters, see **V** 471-72).
135 potum . . . amnem: a line ending slightly varied in seventh eclogue of Eobanus Hessus' *Bucolicon* (for this and other such borrowings at the end of hexameters, see **V** 472).
148 semel = aliquando (see "Introduction," note 88).
161 Oenophilus (i.e., "wine lover"), for "Onophryus" (see "Introduction," note 88).
163–69 The bagpipe is unknown in ancient pastoral. Helen Cooper (*Pastoral: Medieval*

Into Renaissance, 54–55) points out that the instrument is one of the conventional items in the literature of *bergerie*, noting that it even appears in an illustration at the beginning of an Italian Renaissance manuscript of Virgil's *Eclogues* (B. L. King's MS. 24, fol. 1). In *L'Églogue en France au XVIe siècle* (Paris: E. Droz, 1938), 430–31, Alice Hulubei discusses the influence of Mantuan's description of Tonius on the "Chant pastoral" of Pierre de Ronsard.
163 multifori buxo Cf. Helius Eobanus Hessus, *Id.*, XI, 18 (M 53).
167 multotiens: Badius notes that this is a comparatively low form of speech ("*satis humile aduerbium quo idonei abstinere dicuntur*")—an indication of Mantuan's attempt here and there throughout the eclogues to imitate the diction of his speakers.
174 Quoted in Heinrich Bebel's *Adagia Germanica*, reprinted in *Proverbia Germanica*, ed. W. H. D. Suringar (Leiden: Brill, 1879), 69 (M 46).
175–76 An interruption similarly concludes the singing match in the tenth eclogue of Eobanus Hessus' *Bucolicon* (V 475).

Eclogue II

The first of two eclogues in which Fortunatus modifies the original proposal to speak of "our old loves" (line 27; see I, 2) in order to recount the unhappy outcome of Amyntas' extravagant and unrequited love. Geographically accurate, his wanderings can still be followed on a map of the region north of Mantua. At the same time, Amyntas' ramblings foreshadow, as the wordplay on "Solferino" and "Goito" suggests (see lines 37, 60, and notes), the destiny that awaits him. His remarks on honor and free love (lines 157–67) introduced this important topic into pastoral poetry (see "Introduction: Themes, Style, and Organization"). The allusion to Narcissus in lines 84 f. looks to a self-involved quality in Amyntas' love that will be more fully displayed in the third eclogue (III, 128 f.). Fortunatus' denunciation of the fruitlessness of erotic love in these two eclogues echoes a theme dominant in Mantuan's later poetry (cf., e.g., *Contra amorem elegia*) and evident even in his early verse (see lines 115–19n). The first eclogue in Sabie's *Pan's Pipe*, as Mustard and J. W. Bright point out (*op. cit.*, 437–39), draws on this and the next two eclogues. As Mustard notes (49), Alexander Barclay, whose eclogues are similarly indebted to the *Adulescentia*, begins his second eclogue with a paraphrase of the first sixteen lines of Mantuan's poem and echoes Faustus' attack on rustic impiety (lines 66–78) towards the conclusion of his fifth eclogue (lines 803–30).

1 For pastoral tardiness Mustard cites Calp., *Ecl.* VI, 1 and VII, 1.
8–9 Vaurentius notes the echo of *G.* I, 481–83 in which Virgil makes the Po's overflowing one of the portents foreshadowing the civil wars after Julius Caesar's death. Mantuan follows a practice, well established in antiquity (Mustard cites Calp. IV, 62 and Nemes. II, 84), of identifying Virgil with the Tityrus of his first eclogue.
18–19 noster lacus: the Lago Superiore, Lago di Mezzo, and Lago Inferiore, linked bodies of water formed by the river Mincio at Mantua.
25–26 These lines, as Mustard documents (41), are paraphrased in Robert Greene's *Tritameron of Love* (*Life and Complete Works*, III, 100–1).

27 Eridanus: the Po, as in, e.g., Virg., *G.* I., 482 (**M**).
28–30 A pastoral motif, as in, e.g., Virg., *Ecl.* III, 55–57 (**M**). Unlike Faustus, Palaemon in Virgil's eclogue establishes the association of human sexuality and nature's revival solely by implication (see **Col** 116).
37–38 Fortunatus is referring to Goito, a town approximately ten miles upstream on the Mincio from Mantua. The substitution of *coitus* is, of course, intentional on Mantuan's part, if not on Fortunatus' (see "Introduction," note 88).
58 Benace: the Lago di Garda, north of Mantua.
60 sulphuris arcem (tower of sulphur): Mantuan is playing on the name of Solferino, a town approximately twenty miles NNW of Mantua. Raised above the Po river valley, it is crowned by an eleventh–century tower. For sulphur and brimstone, see Gen. 19:24; Isa. 34:9; Luke 17:29; Rev. 21:8; et passim.
63 August 1, the feast day of Saint Peter in Chains. It became a sort of early harvest festival—see *Butler's Lives of the Saints*, eds. Herbert Thurston and Donald Attwater (London: Burns and Oates, 1956), III, 237—a detail also noted by Mantuan in his treatment of the feast in *De sacris diebus* (*Opera*, II, 326r–v).
63–65 Echoed in Euricius Cordus, *Ecl.* III, 148–49 (**M** 54).
85 Vaurentinus notes the verbal echo of Ovid, *Met.* III, 415 (of Narcissus): "*dumque sitim sedare cupit, sitis altera crevit.*"
101–2 On these lines Badius cites Horace, *Sat.* I, 2, 28–29, to which Zabughin (**Z_2** I, 270) adds Ovid, *Ars am.* I, 32. In Roman poetry this flounce, which makes a skirt hang down to the feet, marked wives and women of good character.
103–8 Badius notes the clear echo of Virgil, *Ecl.* VIII, 41 ("*ut vidi, ut perii*"). As Mustard documents, lines 103–5 and 107–8 repeatedly echo the images and diction of Roman amatory poetry: e.g., Virgil, *Aen.* IV, 2 ("*et caeco carpitur igni*"); Ovid, *Her.* V, 142 ("*me miseram, quod amor non est medicabilis herbis*"); *Met.* I, 523 ("*hei mihi, quod nullis amor est sanabilis herbis*"); *Her.* XVII, 190 ("*flamma recens parva sparsa resedit aqua*"); *Met.* XIII, 762–63 ("*validaque cupidine captus / uritur oblitus pecorum antrorumque suorum*").
115–25 Cf. Mantuan's early *Ad Brognolum sodalem*: "If any reward at all followed from this kind of love, I would praise and give myself as a devotee to it. But since nothing except immense shame follows it, better by far it is to have walked on. (*ex hoc si quisquam fructus sequeretur amore, / laudarem hunc, isti me comitemque darem. / Sed quoniam nihil hinc sequitur nisi dedecus ingens, / est satius multo continuisse pedes.*)" (**Gir** 87)
124–26 These lines are echoed in the conclusion of Teofilo Folengo's "Alphabetum" (A. Momigliano, "Le quattro redazioni della 'Zanitonella'," *GSLI*, 73 [1919], 196–97).
140–42 Badius cites Acts 15:10: "Now therefore, why tempt you God to put a yoke upon the necks of the disciples, which neither our fathers nor we have been able to bear?" But see also the conclusion of Peter's words: "But by the grace of the Lord Jesus Christ we believe to be saved, in the like manner as they also."
145–46 Cf. Vulg. Ps. 54:7 and Paul. Nol., *Carm. XVII, 89–92*: "Oh, who would give me wings like a dove that I might swiftly take part in that choir which, hymning (at your bidding) Christ as God the Son, beat their wings against the stars? (*Quis mihi pennas daret ut columbae; / ut choris illis citus interessem, / qui deum Christum duce te canentes / sidera pulsant?*)"
151–52 Adapted in Eobanus Hessus' *Bucolicon* III, 111–13 (Vredeveld, *op. cit.*, 708).
154 In "Marius and Carbo: A Ciceronian Allusion in Mantuan's *Ægloga Secunda*," Anthony L. Pellegrini, ed., *The Early Renaissance: Virgil and the Classical Tradition*, *Acta*, vol. IX, (Binghamton: State University of New York, 1985), 67–68, John B. Dillon suggests that the two are orators mentioned by Cicero in *Brutus*, 223.
172 Fortunatus is punning on two meanings of *livens*: "bluish, darkening; envious."

Mount Baldo lies to the east of the Lago di Garda.

Eclogue III

Fortunatus' sequel to the story begun in the second eclogue. Amyntas' plaint at lines 90–144 provided schoolboys with an early introduction to the commonplaces of the literature of love (see lines 103–8, 130 and notes), some of the echoes recalling Mantuan's early interest in the elegies of Tibullus. Though Amyntas comes to a predictably bad end, his death calls forth lines strongly reminiscent (see esp. lines 182–85 and notes) of the lament for Daphnis in Virgil's fifth eclogue. Along with the fourth eclogue "Eclogue III" was translated into German at the end of the sixteenth century.[6] As Oswald Reissert points out,[7] the six speeches that open Barclay's first eclogue are based on the first thirty seven lines of this eclogue, and a portion of the preliminary discussion (lines 17–27, 32–33) in Mantuan's eclogue echoes, as Mustard notes (127), a similar debate on the uses of adversity in the ninth eclogue of Petrarch's *Bucolicum carmen*, Mantuan's most extensive single borrowing from his Italian predecessor.

1 The storm whose approach cuts off the second eclogue.
2–3 For the sake of the ensuing discussion I have retained the classical meaning of *divi*. Badius glosses *divi* as "saints (*sancti*)," the meaning Mustard notes that the word regularly carries in *De sacris diebus*, Mantuan's series of poems on feast days in the Church.
4 Harcules: see "Introduction," note 88.
17–27 Fortunatus' complaint and Faustus' initial response to it (32-33) echo, as Mustard points out, a similar debate in the ninth eclogue of Petrarch's *Bucolicum carmen* (6–28; 82–83).
17–24 These lines are paraphrased in lines 18–24 of Francis Sabie's first eclogue (Bright and Mustard, "*Pan's Pipe*," 437).
29 Probably the same waxen images that Candidus alludes to in the eighth eclogue (116–17).
81 Freely quoted, as Mustard documents (**M** 44), by Priscian, a "poor Scholar," in Beaumont and Fletcher's *Wit at Several Weapons*, in *The Works of Francis Beaumont and Sir John Fletcher*, eds. Arnold Glover and A. R. Waller (Cambridge Univ. Press, 1905–12), IX, 77.
83–85 Badius notes echoes of the love gifts in Virgil, *Ecl.* II, 45–55; III, 71, 68–69.
85–86 Imitated in Euricius Cordus, *Ecl.* III, 115 (**M** 54).
86 Mustard points out that Ovid similarly deprecates love gifts in *A.A.*, II, 267–68, 277–78.
87 regia res amor est: quoted as the motto on the title page of Richard Brome's *The Queenes Exchange* (**M** 43).
100–2 The notion that when a lover sees his beloved, "his eyes snatch that image and carrie it to the hart" (Baldassare Castiglione, *The Book of the Courtier*, trans. Thomas Hoby [London: Dent, 1928], 313) is a commonplace of literature and Renaissance

---

6 Anon., *Mantuani Æglogae tertia and quarta. . . .*, Teucrides Annaeus Privatus [i.e., Johann Adam Lonicer], 1601 (C447).

7 "Die Eklogen des Alexander Barclay," *Neuphilologische Beiträge*, I (1886), 27.

psychology: see M. B. Ogle, "The Classical Origin and Tradition of Literary Conceits," *American Journal of Philology*, 34 (1913), 135–39. Discussing lines 101–2 Badius cites 1 Cor. 6:16: "for (they say) they shall be two in one flesh"; but the cloud of commonplaces swirling about neoplatonic love theory in the late *quattrocento* would seem to provide an apter context: e.g., "O wondrous exchange in which each gives himself up for the other, and has the other, yet does not cease to have himself." (Marsilio Ficino, *Commentary on the 'Symposium,'* trans. Sears Jayne, Univ. of Missouri Studies, vol. 19, no. 1 [Columbia: Univ. of Missouri Press, 1944], 145).

103–7 Lines 103–7 echo, as Mustard notes, Tibullus' famous lines (I, 1, 59–62): "May I look on thee when my last hour comes; may I hold thy hand, as I sink, in my dying clasp. Thou wilt weep for me, Delia, when I am laid on the bed that is to burn; thou wilt give me kisses mingled with bitter tears (*te spectem, suprema mihi cum venerit hora, / et teneam moriens deficiente manu. / flebis et arsuro positum me, Delia, lecto, / tristibus et lacrimis oscula mixta dabis*)": J. P. Postgate's translation, in *Catullus, Tibullus and 'Pervigilium Veneris,'* rev. ed. (London: Heinemann, 1924), 197, 196. A common motif in Roman elegiac poetry (see, e.g., Prop. I, 17, 19–24; II, 13, 27–30; Ovid, *Am.* III, 9, 51–58), Mantuan's version would nonetheless seem, like lines 108–9 below (see note), to be an interesting relic of a period when, as he remarks in one of his unpublished elegies, "I eagerly followed the fashion and numbers of terse Tibullus (*sectabar tersi mores numerosque Tibulli*)" (**Gir** 91).

108 Again, as Mustard notes, a Tibullan echo, here of I, 3, 57–66—though without Tibullus' certainty that after death he will be born off to Elysian fields.

117–24 Badius first noted the echo of Virgil, *Ecl.* V, 40–44, the ultimate source for the combined gestures of strewing flowers and composing funerary verses.

119–20 puellæ Pierides (Pierian maidens): the Muses.

126–27 See lines 230–31 of Francis Sabie's second eclogue (Bright and Mustard, "*Pan's Pipe*," 439).

130 A commonplace in Roman amatory poetry, of course, but one found, as Mustard notes, in Tibullus' elegies (I, 1, 63–64).

161 Cf. I, 52.

174 Tityrus: i.e., Virgil, as in II, 9. Virgil's second eclogue is addressed to Alexis whom, as Mustard notes, a tradition recorded by Servius had early identified with Octavian.

182 Orphea (Orpheus), whose death, as Badius notes, is lamented in Virgil's fourth georgic.

183 Daphnim (Daphnis): the Sicilian shepherd whose death is mourned in Theocritus' first idyll and Virgil's fifth eclogue.

182–85 Mustard records the dense cluster of echoes of Virgil's fifth eclogue here: the languishing herds (cf. Virgil, *Ecl.* V, 24–25), fields, and pastures (cf. V, 35) and the strewing of flowers (cf. V, 40).

188 Cf. Heb. 11:16: "They desire a better, that is to say, a heavenly country." (**M**)

188–89 Late classical Elysium is subterranean (e.g., *Aen.* VI, 637 f.), but for Mantuan, as for other Christian poets (e.g., Dante, *Par.* XV, 25–30), Elysium was "high (*altum*)," imaginatively correlated with a Christian abode of the blessed. Lines 188–89 bothered Badius; but given what Fortunatus previously said about Amyntas, Faustus' description here of his fate would seem more a pious wish than a statement of fact. See *Ecl.* VII, 132–40 and notes.

192–94 In the coming of the evening star, Badius notes an echo of the concluding lines (85–86) of Virgil's sixth eclogue, where "Vesper gave the word to fold the flocks and tell their tale, as he set forth over an unwilling sky (*cogere . . . ovis stabulis numerumque referre / iussit et invito processit Vesper Olympo*)," *Virgil*, trans. H. Rushton Fairclough, rev. ed. (London: Heinemann, 1932), 47. Mustard documents how common a device the evening star's advent became for closing up pastoral poems: see, e.g., Calp. II, 93–94;

Nemes. II, 89–90; Boccaccio, *Ecl.* II, 158-59. None of these endings (to which one should add Virgil, *Ecl.* X, 77) has Mantuan's stress, seen also in the conclusion of his second eclogue, on impending bad weather. Alexander Barclay's first eclogue, as Oswald Reissert has pointed out (*op. cit.*, 28), has a similarly threatening conclusion, as do the concluding lines of Barnabe Googe's eighth eclogue (Mustard 50).

Eclogue IV

The earliest instance in Latin pastoral of sustained misogynistic satire, Umber's tirade in this eclogue (lines 110–241) remained controversial throughout the Renaissance. Turberville and Harvey both tried to qualify it in their translations; Robert Greene and Thomas Nashe clearly thought the attack too extreme;[8] and an anonymous paraphrase of lines 110–60 printed in 1679 (C480) immediately drew *An answer to the Mantuan, or False Character, lately wrote against Womankind.*[9] Nonetheless, this eclogue has been the most widely translated of Mantuan's pastorals, with versions in Italian, French, German, Dutch as well as English.[10] Its antifeminism set a

[8] Like Nashe, Greene contends that Mantuan inferred "a generall by a particular" (*Mamillia*, in *Life and Complete Works*, II, 100-1), failing to recognize, as Nashe puts it, that among women "as amongst men, [there be] some good, some badde. . . ." (*Anatomy of Absurditie*, in *Works*, III, 225). Besides these references (M 41-42), Mustard notes (41) that Greene twice returned to the topic in *Mamillia*, stressing in the second part that Mantuan's railing is "more of course then cause, and rather inforced by rage than inferred by reason" (*Life and Complete Works*, II, 107, 226). In "Julia," one of John Donne's elegies, Mantuan's name has become virtually synonymous with misogyny: "Would to God [Julia] were / But halfe so loath to act vice, as to heare / My milde reproofe. Liv'd *Mantuan* now againe, / That fœmall Mastix, to limme with his penne / This she *Chymera*. . . ." (*The Elegies and The Songs and Sonnets*, ed. Helen Gardner [Oxford Univ. Press, 1965], 100-1).

[9] As Mustard points out (44), Umber's attack is alluded to contemptuously by Jane Shore in a passage in *England's Heroicall Epistles* that Drayton notes he would annotate with quotations from Mantuan's eclogue "were it not, that [fantasticke and insolent women] are growne wiser, then to amend for such an idle poets speech" (*Works*, II, 255, 259). Nonetheless, Lord Bonavida threatens to throw Mantuan's words back at the "proud Queen" Isabel in Thomas Heywood's *Challange for Beautie* (*The Dramatic Works*, ed. R. H. Shepherd [London: J. Pearson, 1874], V, 6) (M 44).

[10] Besides versions in the collections recorded in the "Introduction" (see note 73), the following translate or paraphrase large portions or the whole of this eclogue:

Hermann von Sachsenheim, *Die mörin. . . .*, Strasbourg: J. Grüninger, 1512. (C212)

Anon., "Pastorale in dispregio delle donne," appended to *Consiglio Matrimoniale fatto a dì . . . 1553*, in MS. Cod. Ferrajolus 723, pp. 962-68, Bibl. Apostolica Vaticana, Rome. (A translation of lines 110-245)

Anon., *Mantuani Æglogae tertia and quarta. . . .*, Teucrides Annaeus Privatus [i.e., Johann Adam Lonicer], 1601 (C447). (A translation into German)

William Parsons, "Woman, the cause of all our joys and pains," in MS. *Don. d. 123, p. 211, Bodleian Library, Oxford. (A paraphrase of lines 110-49)

N. N. *Vrouwen-lof . . . , in Nederduytschen Rijm gesteldt. . . .*, n. p., 1678. (ref. C483) (A translation of lines 110-241)

Pierre Laurens, in *Musae reduces: anthologie de la poésie latine de la renaissance*, Leiden:

gloomy and enduring precedent:[11] besides a passage in Teofilo Folengo's *Zanitonella*,[12] a condemnation of women in the fourth eclogue of Petrus Pontanus of Bruges is modelled on Umber's tirade, as is the fifth eclogue of Paolo Belmisseri.[13] Matteo Bandello has an amusing, probably fictional account (quoted in **LR** 66) of the genesis of Mantuan's eclogue in a fit of spleen directed at a young lady who had spurned his advances. Just why Mantuan put his attack on women into the mouth of Gregorio Tifernate (see below, line 81n.) puzzled Mustard since, as he observes (130), nothing in Gregorio's published poems suggests a distinctive strain of misogyny. Rhetorically, however, the strategy distances Mantuan from full responsibility for Umber's tirade (a strategy he uses to similar effect with Batrachus in "Eclogue X"), while the veneration accorded Umber in the eclogue serves to lend his words unusual authority.

3–4 Details of the goat's sickness derive from Virgil, *Ecl.* V, 25–26 and *G.* III, 465–66 (**M**).
11–12 Rewards for singing are conventional in pastoral: e.g., Theocritus, *Id.* I, 25–26 and Virgil, *Ecl.* V, 81 f.
17 Badius notes the echo of Aeneas' invocation (*Aen.* II, 13)—here, of course, with a mock heroic effect.
19 philomenaeos nidos (nests of Philomel): i.e., of the nightingale.
22–23 Echoed in Euricius Cordus, *Ecl.* X, 22 f. (**M** 55).
34 As love–gifts: see I, 68–69 and note. It is a gently learned irony that Jannus' song will be rewarded with the same gift and in diction (line 13) meant to recall, as Mustard notes, Damoetas' love–gift in Virgil, *Ecl.* III, 69.
35–36 Cf. III, 93–96.
43 tertia hora (the third hour of the day), i.e., it was midmorning. The ancients divided the time between sunrise and sunset, however short or long, into twelve equal hours.
60–61 Cf. III, 144; VII, 107–8; X, 203.
71 Mantuan probably has in mind the Galatea who drains Tityrus of his money in Virgil, *Ecl.* I, 31–35.
81 Umber: Mustard quotes part of a letter, first printed in the 1503 Strasbourg edition of the *Adulescentia*, in which the Northern humanist Thomas Wolf Jr. states that, when visiting Mantuan in 1500, the Italian poet had told him that the figure of Umber denoted Gregorio Tifernate, his teacher at Mantua ("*Aiebat ipse a se notari Gregorium tiphernum praeceptorem suum* . . . ."), for whom see lines 95–97 with notes and "Introduction: Life."
82–83 Mustard notes an especially dense tissue of echoes here from Virgil's eclogues:

Brill, 1975, pp. 86-93. (A translation of lines 110-245)

11 Culturally as well as in literature: in *Table Talk* Martin Luther quotes a portion of Umber's attack (lines 110-50), apparently from memory: *D. Martin Luthers Werke. Tischreden* (Weimer: Hermann Böhlau, 1912-21), III, 376. (At another point [*ibid.*, I, 107] he remarks that the enforced study of scholastic philosophy in the schools confined his study of poetry to the works of Mantuan, Virgil, and Ovid [the *Heroides*]).

12 A string of epithets attacking women in Folengo's fourth eclogue, according to A. Momigliano in "Le quattro redazioni della 'Zanitonella,'" *GSLI*, 73 (1919), 196-97.

13 Grant, *op. cit.*, 397, 396. Mustard (56) also finds a clear echo of Umber's attack in Luigi Pasqualigo's influential comedy *Il Fedele* (see line 124n.).

III, 52 ("*quin age, si quid habes*"); IX, 45 ("*numeros memini, si verba tenerem*"); IX, 38 ("*neque est ignobile carmen*").
87–88 Mustard notes the echo of Virgil, *Ecl.* III, 20 ("'*Tytyre, coge pecus,' tu post carecta latebas*") in an earthy adaptation that offended Fontenelle (see I, 44–47 and note). Alphus' language is echoed, as Mustard points out (55, 46), in Euricius Cordus, *Ecl.* VIII, 64–65 and Johannes Murmellius' *Pappa puerorum*, in *Ausgewählte Werke*, IV, 16.
91 Echoed in Euricius Cordus, *Ecl.* IV, 33 (**M** 54).
95–97 In an early, unprinted elegy, *De morte Tiphernatis eius praeceptoris*, Mantuan mourns the death of his old teacher in similar terms (**Gir** p. 87). Under the patronage of Nicholas V, Gregorio Tifernate translated a variety of Greek prose works into Latin, including books 11–17 of Strabo's *Geography* (*De situ orbis*), short essays by Theophrastus on fish and fire, and the Pythagorean *De mundi* of Timaeus of Locris (see Mustard, 131–32).
98–99 Gregorio may have looked on Rhodope and the Ceraunian peaks, but it seems equally likely that, as Mustard suggests, Mantuan merely appropriated part of a line from Virgil's *Georgics*: "*aut Rhodopen aut alta Ceraunia*" (I, 332). Discussing these lines, Mustard goes on to quote a passage from Gregorio's poetry in which he speaks of his travels: "As a younger man I drank from Eurotas' waters. Grown older, I drink from the Loire. I have looked on the Western Ocean and the Hellespont—for thus God has wished that I should travel in long drawn out ways. (*Iunior Eurotae potavi fluminis undam, / de Ligeri factus grandior amne bibo. / vidimus Oceanum mare, vidimus Hellespontum: / sic voluit longas nos Deus ire vias.*)" (*Gregorii Tipherni . . . Opuscula* [Venice: Bernardinus Venetus, 1498], sig. c3).
105 Candidus here is to be connected with Mantuan, as in the ninth and tenth eclogues. (Headnotes introducing the unprinted versions of these two eclogues make this connection explicit: **P1** 646, 655.) Within the overall design of Mantuan's collection, Candidus' name (adj. " white; morally pure") alludes to the dispute in the tenth eclogue concerning the color of the Carmelite habit.
108 Badius notes the echo of Corydon's invocation in Virgil, *Ecl.* VII, 21.
110–241 An elaborate example of the "*quid est mulier*" *topos*, a convention that, reduced even in antiquity to compilations and variations of established commonplaces, is, as Anthony K. Cassell observes, conspicuously lacking in originality (Giovanni Boccaccio, *The Corbaccio*, trans. and ed. A. K. Cassell [Urbana/Chicago: Univ. of Illinois Press, 1975], xix). For its sources and tradition, see, *inter alia*, Carlo Pascal, "Antifemminismo medievale," *Poesia latina medievale, saggi e note critiche* (Catania: F. Battiato, 1907), 151–84 and "Misoginia medievale," *Studi medievali*, 2 (1906–7), 242–48; August Wulf, *Die frauenfeindlichen Dichtungen in den romanischen Literaturen des Mittlealters bis zum Ende des XIIIen Jahrhunderts* (Halle a. S.: M. Niemeyer, 1914); Francis Lee Utley, *The Crooked Rib* (Columbus: Ohio State Univ. Press, 1944), 39–52; A. K. Cassell, "*Il Corbaccio* and the Secundus Tradition," *CL*, 25 (1973), 352–360.
110 Citing passages from Boccaccio, Aeneas Silvius, and Martinez de Toledo, Mustard points out that strings of uncomplimentary epithets were common in misogynistic literature (see 110–241*n*). Robert Greene, as he notes (41), quotes this line in his *Historie of Orlando Furioso* (*Life and Complete Works*, XIII, 149). Along with lines 111, 112, 116, 163, and 170, it is also quoted to be refuted in an epigram in *Crepundia poetica* (n.p., 1648), 54 (**M** 47).
118 hernica: A learned medievalism for "stony": John B. Dillon, "Some Passages in the *Carmina* of James Foullis of Edinburgh," *SSL*, 14 (1979), 192.
123 This line appears in part in Abraham Fraunce's Latin comedy *Victoria*, 19 (**M** 51).
124 f. These lines are imitated, as Mustard points out (56), in a long speech of invective in Luigi Pasqualigo's Italian comedy *Il Fedele*. From here the passage found its way into Pierre de Larivey's *Le Fidèle* and the English *Fidele and Fortunio* (ibid., 56, 132).
150 f. Quoting a passage from the *Epistola adversus Jovinianum*, St. Jerome's famous

attack on marriage, Mustard notes that the examples cited here and in lines 207 f. had long been staple items in medieval attacks on women. See 110–241n.
166 Boccaccio (*Genealogiae deorum*, bk. IX, chap. 7) recounts how Hippodamia bribed Myrtilus, Oenamaus' charioteer, to insure that he would lose the race to Pelops.
176 As Mustard points out, the names all appear in Virgil's *Eclogues*. Oswald Reissert (*op. cit.*, 30) notes that they reappear in Barclay's second eclogue (lines 385–86).
178 A puzzling remark, at variance with ancient sources as well as Boccaccio's account (*op. cit.*, bk. V, chap. 12) of the story. An undocumented version recorded by Mustard that Eurydice was lost for tasting a pomegranate would seem more appropriate to Persephone. Robert Greene's version in *Orpharion*, in which Eurydice purposely returns to Pluto, whom she has chosen over Orpheus, may, as Mustard suggests (51), derive from this passage or ultimately from some source also known to Mantuan.
180 As Badius first noted, Mantuan follows Virgil's version of the story (*G.* I, 39) in which Persephone, having been reclaimed by Demeter, chooses not to follow her mother out of the underworld ("*nec repetita sequi curet Proserpina matrem*").
181–83 The two brothers are Castor and Pollux. Mustard notes that Umber's choice of examples in these lines echoes Aeneas' catalogue in *Aen.* VI, 119–23.
193–95 A rustic analogy: see **Col** 9.
194–95 Cf. III, 65–66.
196–97 Hyenas were thought to learn a shepherd's name and call it to attack him. Similarly, crocodiles were believed to weep in order to attract their victims. Mustard cites passages from a variety of texts to document these bits of curiosa.
207–9 rex et natus (that king and his son): David and Solomon.
216 Badius notes the echo of Damoeta's description of Galatea's behavior in Virgil, *Ecl.* III, 64–65.
218 Quoted in Robert Burton's discussion of artificial allurements in love (*Anatomy of Melancholy*, III, 113) (**M** 45).
219–20 For *caecias*, see Aulus Gellius' *Noctes Atticae* II, 22, 24 (**M**).
230 This line is repeated in part in Edward Forsett's Latin play *Pedantius*, ed. G. C. Moore–Smith, in *Materialien zur Kunde des älteren Englischen Dramas*, 8 (Louvain: A. Uystpruyst, 1905), 2 (**M** 51).
235 Syrtes: see I, 40 and note.
236 immundæ volucres (foul winged monsters): the Harpies, who tormented Phineus by defiling his food.
239–40 Phorcynides (Phorcus' daughters): the three Gorgons.
247 urbi (city): Città di Castello, on the upper course of the Tiber.
251 An echo of Gallus' wish to be laid in Arcadia (Virgil, *Ecl.* X, 33) (**M**).
250–52 In his unprinted elegy on Gregorio Tifernate (**Gir** 85) Mantuan similarly describes the soul of his teacher rising to seek Jupiter's palace and bids Gregorio's fellow poets already in heaven to mourn his death (". . . *tecta Iovis petiit. / Illum autem vos, qui super estis, flete, poetae: / namque decus vestri nominis ille fuit.*").
252 Olympo (Olympus): an ancient metonymy: see Virgil, *Ecl.* V, 56 and **Col** 166.

Eclogue V

Complaints against the niggardliness of patrons had a long literary history in pastoral when Mantuan turned to the topic. Theocritus, Petrarch, and Boccaccio all dealt with the subject, but Mantuan's main literary model for this eclogue lies outside pastoral, in Juvenal whose seventh satire, as Badius first noted, is several times clearly echoed in "Eclogue V" (see lines 11–12, 33–34, 90–91 with notes). The penultimate elegy in Mantuan's contemporaneous collection of verse similarly offers literary fame in exchange for financial support (see **Gir** 91–94), and his concluding elegy, a farewell to poetry, echoes Candidus' gloomy observations on the place of the poet in society (see lines 166–81 and note). The attack on Rome (lines 120–24) appealed to Thomas, Lord Fairfax (among other Protestant writers), who used a portion of it in his condemnation of corruption with the Papal Court (**P**$_2$ 117). Mantuan's focus in this eclogue is, unlike his ninth, not exclusively ecclesiastical, however, its inspiration deriving in all likelihood more from literature (see line 123n) than life. Along with "Eclogue X," it supplied matter for a quarrelsome amoebean contest in the eleventh idyl of Eobanus Hessus (**V** 483–84). Alexander Barclay's fourth eclogue paraphrases "Eclogue V,"[14] which also supplied the framework for Edmund Spenser's great "October" eclogue in *The Shepheardes Calendar.*[15]

1–3 These lines are echoed in the first four lines of Francis Sabie's first eclogue (Bright and Mustard, "*Pan's Pipe*," 437) as well as in the opening lines of the fifth idyl of Eobanus Hessus (**M** 53).
11–12 An echo, as Badius notes, of Juvenal's complaint against miserly patrons (VII, 30–32).
12 Echoed in Euricius Cordus, *Ecl.* VI, 142 (**M** 55).
23 Cf. Euricius Cordus, *Ecl.* II, 91 (**M** 54).
24 Cf. a similar wintry setting ("*Vitrea iam rapidos glacies astringet aquarum / cursus, iamque gelu tota rigebit humus*") in Mantuan's unprinted appeal for support written while he was a student at Padua (**Gir** 93).
26 Badius explains that the ewe lambs have been kept for future propagation.
33–34 Mustard notes the echo of Juvenal VII, 32–33.
38 A bit of natural history recorded, as Mustard notes, in the *Physiologus* and repeated (among other places) in Niccolò Perotti's *Cornucopiae.*
46 sorte tua contentus is twice used, as Mustard notes (44), as titles in *Witt's Recreations* (*Facetiae*, 47, 98).
63–64 Quoted as the motto on the title page of Thomas Middleton's *Familie of Love*, printed in 1607 (**M** 43).
65 nodum Herculis (Herculean knot): made, according to Macrobius (*Sat.* I, 19, 16), by the coiled serpents on his caduceus (**M**).
82 Badius notes that country folk plow furrows in the ashes in order to predict their fortunes.
85 Echoed in Euricius Cordus, *Ecl.* X, 28 (**M** 55).
86–91 Tityrus: Virgil, as in II, 9. For lines 90–91 Mustard notes the echo of Juvenal's link (VII, 59–61) between eloquence and creature comforts.
88 Tityrus (i.e., Virgil) is similarly praised in Eobanus Hessus' *Bucolicon* III, 15–16 (**V** 474).

14 Oswald Reissert, *op. cit.*, 23-26.

15 For Spenser's use of Mantuan's eclogue, see **Var** VII (1), 372-73, 378-87, 389-90. In *L'Eglogue en France*, Alice Hulubei discusses the influence of "Eclogue V" on Clément Marot's "Eglogue au Roy soubz les noms de Pan et Robin" (pp. 218-20). Mantuan's eclogue has been translated in the twentieth century by William Porter in "Eclogue Five of Mantuan (1448-1516): Candidus: On the Treatment of Poets by the Wealthy," *Allegorica*, 6 (1981), 7-20.

96 Cosmi: Cosimo de' Medici (1389–1464), whose wealth was, as Mustard documents, proverbial in Mantuan's time.
98 patinam Aesopi (Aesop's dish): Mustard cites a passage from Pliny's *Natural History* in which he describes this as a dish of great value in which Clodius Aesopus served birds able to talk or sing a particular song.
98 clypeum Minervæ (Minerva's shield): Vitellius, a notorious glutton, ordered a platter fashioned that was so big he called it the shield of Minerva (see Suet. *Vit.* XIII.2). (Glossing this phrase, Mustard notes that, like "*patinam Aesopi*," it is explained by Joannes Murmellis in his *Scoparius*.)
100 aenea barba (bronze–colored beard): playing, as Badius points out, on "*Aenobarbi*," a family name of the Domitian *gens* which claimed Nero, whose Golden House (as Mustard notes) is referred to in line 99 (*regis laribus*).
101 Shepherds must not seem too erudite (see, e.g., Virg., *Ecl.* III, 40–42). Hence, Candidus' explanation. For Umber, see the note on IV, 81; for Candidus, the note on IV, 105.
104 Codrus is, as Badius notes, a poor poet in Juvenal *Sat.* III, 203–11. In the same satire (229), as Mustard points out, Juvenal alludes to Pythagoras' well known austerity of diet (see also *Sat.* XV, 171–74 [**M**]).
105–6 Echoed in Euricius Cordus, *Ecl.* II, 118–9 (**M** 54).
109 As Mustard notes, the image of gladiatorial combat is used in the same way in Horace, *Ep.* I, 1, 1–6.
123 Following Badius, Mustard cites Horace, *Ep.* I, 6, 37 (*regina Pecunia*) and Juvenal I, 112–13 (*inter nos sanctissima divitiarum / maiestas* [among us no god is held in such reverence as is wealth]), to which Howard Easton adds Petronius, *Sat.* 14 (*quid faciunt leges, ubi sola pecunia regnat?* [what can laws do where riches alone reign?]).
146–47 A rustic analogy: see the note to IV, 193–95.
166–81 Bidding farewell to the muses in the concluding elegy in his unprinted collection of verse, Mantuan similarly complains about the unjustness in patrons' distribution of their gifts to good and bad poets (**Gir** 95). Mustard notes a possible echo in Palingenius' *Zodiacus vitae* II, 549–51.
190 Badius notes a probable echo of Horace, *Ep.* I, 1, 52: "*vilius argentum est auro, virtutibus aurum* (cheaper than gold is silver, than virtue gold)."

Eclogue VI

Along with the fifth and tenth eclogues, Mantuan's "Eclogue VI" shows the formal influence of medieval debate poetry. The comparative merits of the city and countryside, a standard topic in ancient rhetoric (e.g., Quintilian, *Inst.* II, 4, 24), is not, however, a subject treated in surviving medieval debate literature.[16] The wry delicacy in Amyntas' account of the origin of townsmen and country folk, a version of the folk motif of "the various children of Eve,"[17] is virtually buried under Cornix's attack on city ways in the latter half of the eclogue. The intensity of Cornix's invective is foreign to ancient pastoral, though at one point (see line 175 and note) the language recalls a similar attack on worldly ambition in the second book of Virgil's

[16] H. Walther, *Das Streitgedicht in der lateinischen Literatur des Mittelalters*, esp., for contrast, p. 154.

[17] A. 1650. 1, in Stith Thompson, *Motif-Index of Folk-Literature*, rev. and enlarged ed. (Bloomington: Indiana Univ. Press, 1955-58), I, 245.

Georgics. Among other critics, Zabughin (Z_1 148) has admired the social realism depicted in Cornix's attitude towards the city (lines 224–33). Alexander Barclay paraphrased Mantuan's "Eclogue VI" in his "Fifth Eclogue,"[18] and the opening lines, as Mustard points out, can be seen transmuted in Winter's song at the end of Shakespeare's *Love's Labor's Lost.*

1–5 Mustard compares the winter picture in Shakespeare's *Love's Labor's Lost* V, ii, 912–20: "When icicles hang by the wall . . . . While greasy Joan doth keel the pot" (*The Riverside Shakespeare*, eds. G. Blakemore Evans et al., [Boston: Houghton Mifflin, 1974], 212).
2–3 Echoed in Euricius Cordus, *Ecl.* VII, 32 (**M** 55).
5 polenta: a porridge still commonly prepared (now usually with corn meal) in the country kitchens of northern Italy.
19–25 Cf. "February" lines 33–50 in Spenser's *Shepheardes Calendar* (**Var** VII[1], 257–58). Lines 19–20 are echoed in Euricius Cordus, *Ecl.* IV, 69 (**M** 54–55).
41–48 A similar interruption occurs in *Bucolicon* III, 60–62 of Eobanus Hessus (**V** 475).
84 pila (javelins): i.e., high military offices.
105 Mantous Amyntas (Mantoan Amyntas): i.e., a descendent of Manto, an Italian nymph and mother of Ocnus, who founded Mantua. As Mustard notes, this is the same Amyntas who appears in Mantuan's second eclogue: see esp. II, 132.
113 As Shakespeare's Longaville puts it, "Fat paunches have lean pates" (*Love's Labor's Lost* I, i, 26, in *op. cit.*, 179) (**M**).
155–57: a motif varied by Eobanus Hessus in *Bucolicon* X, 104 f. (**V** 475).
175 Mustard cites *Georgics* II, 503 in an echo of Virgil's dispraise of deviation from the life of the countryman.
203 equestre genus (equestrian race) A sarcastic remark since, as Baduis notes, doctors usually rode on she–mules.
219–20 quaedam Balearibus arva proxima (the land near Majorca): Ibiza, an island off the coast of Spain. For Cornix's ignorance, see V, 101n.
220 Mustard cites Pliny's *Natural History* and Niccolò Perotti's *Cornucopiae* as authorities for the absence of owls on Crete, *Aeneid* VII, 778–79 as the source for keeping horses away from sacred groves (here conflated with Egeria's grove in Virgil's story).
238–39 Candidus' language here echoes Virgil's account of the consequences of Caesar's death in *G.* I, esp. 475 and 466–68.
240 lolium (darnel): Badius cites Virgil, *G.* I, 153–54 and Matt. 13:24–30, passages that suggest the symbolic power this weed carried in antiquity.
246–47 An odd detail, absent from both Ovid's version of the two related stories (*Met.* I, 163–415) and Boccaccio's account of Lycaon and Deucalion in *Genealogiae deorum*, bk. IV, chs. 66 and 47.

Eclogue VII

Badius' general note on this eclogue is the most comprehensive in his commentary:

If it might not seem foolish, let me say that with reason Mantuan

[18] Oswald Reissert, *op. cit.*, 15-16, 17-23.

writes of the conversion of young men in his seventh eclogue. For the number seven, produced as a sum of the first uneven number and the nearest even number following it, is well known to have something mysterious about it not only in Scripture but also among the poets: whence "Oh thrice and four times blest . . ." [*Aen.* I, 94]; "for now it is the seventh summer that bears thee a wanderer over every land and sea" [*Aen.* I, 755–56]. Moreover, men say that every seven years the period of our life changes: so that for our first seven years we are babes, children for the next seven, youths for the third seven, and young men for our fourth seven years, at which time the character of our lives—who, of what condition, and how we want to live—is all established. Rightly then, (for I pass over in silence the other seasons of our lives, each of which succeeds in equal order) in this seventh eclogue youth's conversion to the religious life is at stake, a conversion concerning which I believe that up to now Mantuan has sung of his youth (for so he entitled his work [i.e., *Adulescentia*]) and that in turn he will sing of his young manhood and adult years, namely in the last two poems which he composed in religious orders.[19]

Although Mantuan doubtless knew Boccaccio's fourteenth and fifteenth eclogues (the first a famous account of Boccaccio's conversion by a female visitor from Paradise, the second an allegorical presentation of his painful religious conversion under the tutelage of Petrarch), this seventh eclogue, as Mantuan's title indicates, is clearly a poetic refraction of the choice he saw facing him during his years at Padua and Mantua.[20] Galbula's disquisition on the select status of shepherds (lines 9–50) became a favorite passage among poets, with echoes in Spenser's *Shepheardes Calendar* ("July" lines 129–58) (**Var** VII[1], 331–33) as well as in Barclay's "Fifth Eclogue" (lines 435–534),[21] Euricius Cordus' third pastoral (**M** 54), and the third eclogue of Sabie's *Pan's Pipe* (lines 90–138).[22]

1 Pollux: for Pollux, see "Introduction: Themes, Style and Organization," note 88.

[19] *Si friuolum non sit dicam non sine ratione in hac septima aegloga agi de conuersione iuvenum. Nam septenarium numerum qui ex primo impari & proxime illum subsequente pari consicitur constat habere nescio quid mysterii : non solum in sanctis literis sed etiam apud poetas. Vnde est illud. O terque quaterque beati. Et Nam te iam septima portat Omnibus errantem terris & fluctibus aestas. Dicunt praeterea septimo quoque anno immutari nobis aetatem. Vt primis septem annis simus infantes. Proximis pueri. tertiis adolescentes. quartis iuuenes: qua aetate constituendum est nobis genus vitae: quos & quales nos esse velimus: & in quo genere vitae. Bene ergo (vt de caeteris aetatibus quae pari ordine subsequuntur : taceam) in hac septima aegloga agitur de iuuenum ad religionem conuersione. Vnde hactenus adolescentiam suam (sic enim inscripsit opus) poeta cecinisse putatur : deinceps canturus iuuentam : & virilem aetatem : in duobus videlicet vltimis carminibus quae in religione composuit.* (**Ad**, fol. 125v)

[20] See line 88n. and "Introduction: Composition and Publication of the *Adulescentia.*"

[21] Oswald Reissert, *op. cit.*, 16-17.

[22] Katarina Windscheid, *op. cit.*, 41.

10 Umber: see IV, 81n.
11 Cf. VI, 97.
14 ast: as Mustard notes, an archaic form—no doubt in imitation of Virgil's use of similar forms in his *Eclogues* (e.g., III, 1): see "Introduction: Themes, Style and Organization," note 88.
19 divos (gods): see III, 2–3n.
23 Assyrios (Assyrians): Badius adduces Abraham, Lot, Jacob, and other patriarchs. Helen Cooper (*op. cit.*, 71) points to the development of this theme in the literature of *bergerie*.
27–29 See Virg. *Ecl.* II, 61, where Paris is similarly enrolled among the shepherds.
27 This line appears in Abraham Fraunce's Latin comedy *Victoria*, 9 (**M** 51).
28 Probably Abraham, who (as Badius explains) offered to sacrifice his son.
29 caelesti igne (fire from heaven): as Badius notes, the fire from the burning bush.
37 Tonantem (God of Thunder): against denunciations of Mantuan's use of Graeco–Roman diction here, Mustard rightly adduces the use of this term by a long line of Christian poets: e.g., Paul. Nol. (whom Mantuan admired from early youth) XXII, 149; Juvenc. II, 795; Prud. *Apotheosis* 171; *Cathemerion* XII, 83.
40 The *locus classicus* for Galbula's assertion is, as Badius notes, John 10:14.
52 Like Galbula, Alphus too (as Badius suggests) has seen these things, in pictures.
59 Given Mantuan's contemporaneous letter to his father (see "Introduction: Composition and Publication of the *Adulescentia*"), the echo of Virgil, *Ecl.* III, 33 cited by Mustard does not eliminate the biographical foundation Badius found in these lines. With Pollux's shrewish stepmother, cf. "March" 40–43 in Spenser's *Shepheardes Calendar* (**Var** VII[1], 270).
70 virgo: cf. line 89 and I, 72.
75 Translation of this line follows the pointing of the 1498 edition, which places virgules after *pectus* and *totiens*.
79–80 See III, 101–2 and note.
88 fronde sub Herculea (Under Hercules' leafy boughs): a deceptively simple detail. In *Ecl.* VII, 61 Virgil describes the poplar tree as being "most pleasing to Hercules (*Alcidae gratissima*)"; but, as Badius first pointed out, Mantuan also has in mind the story of Hercules at the crossroads. Alluding to Cicero's account in *De officiis* (I.118), Badius goes on to indicate more specifically the significance which the story would have had for Mantuan's audience (Badius' elaboration is drawn verbatim from a widely printed commentary on *De officiis* by Mantuan's friend [**M** 24], Pietro Marsi):

> It is said that while [Hercules] stood in doubt, two noble women, Virtue and Pleasure, came to him. Pleasure, who entered in front, was adorned with the greatest care and drew behind her every kind of worldly delight. Looking back now and then, haughtily displaying many things to his view, and promising him much more, she attempted to draw Hercules away with her. Virtue, on the other hand, was stern and hard, and regarding him gravely face to face she said, "I promise you neither pleasure nor repose. Rather, I offer you toil, danger, and countless labors to be endured on land and sea. The reward of them will be, however, that you will become a god." When Hercules had heard this, he rejected Pleasure with harsh words and followed after Virtue. *(Aiunt . . . inter dubitandum duas accessisse Matronas virtutem & voluptatem. Quarum voluptas prior ingressa : accuratissime erat ornata & omnes delicias post se trahebat : respectans aliquando cum fastuque omnia ostentans et multo etiam plura pollicens secum trahere Herculem tentavit. At virtus aspera & dura, sevuereque intuens contra. Non polliceor inquit aliquam voluptatem aut quietem : sed laborem / pericula / sudores infinitos / terra marique tolerandos : sed horum praemium erit te deum fieri. Quod*

> *audiens hercules gravibus verbis voluptatem repellens virtutem secutus est.)* (**Ad**, fol. 127)

In his letter to his father Mantuan describes his decision to enter the Carmelite order in similar terms: "This then is my life on which I have firmly fixed my step. In this is all my care and all my comfort. For so long a time I stood at the crossroads; now indeed standing on the right horn of Pythagoras' letter . . . . (*Haec mea vita est in qua pedem firmiter fixi. In hac omnis mea cura. In hac omne meum solatium. Tamdiu in bivio steti, jam vero dexterum cornu pythagoricæ litteræ stando* . . . .) [the sentence is unfinished]" (**MHC** 489). In Pythagorean lore the letter Y symbolizes the moral choice between a life of virtue or vice which a young man must make on reaching manhood. Pythagoras' letter, the subject of an ancient anonymous poem long attributed to Virgil beginning "*Littera Pythagorae, discrimine secta bicorni* (Pythagoras' letter, divided by the space separating the two horns)," was frequently connected with the tale of Hercules at the crossroad (see S. K. Heninger, *Touches of Sweet Harmony: Pythagorean Cosmology and Renaissance Poetics* [San Marino: Huntington Library, 1974], 269–72, and Erwin Panofsky, *Hercules am Scheidewege* [Leipzig: Teubner, 1930], esp. 64–68 and *tafel* XXXV). Mantuan's conjunction of the choice of Hercules with the *umbrosam silvam* described in lines 107 f. is perhaps based on a similar fusion made by Servius, in a note on *Aen.* VI, 136, of Pythagoras' letter with the forest Aeneas must penetrate to find the golden bough (see below, 109–19n).

90 Badius notes an echo of *Aen.* IV, 558–59, Mercury's appearance in a dream to Aeneas: "*omnia Mercurio similis, vocemque coloremque / et crinis flavos et membra decora iuventa.* (in all points like to Mercury: in voice and hue, in golden hair and handsome, youthful limbs.)" But Mantuan's audience would also be apt to recall Venus' famous appearance to her son in *Aen.* I, e.g., 327–28: ". . . *quam te memorem, virgo? namque haud tibi voltus / mortalis, nec vox hominem sonat; o dea certe!* (. . . by what name should I call thee, O maiden? for thy face is not mortal nor has thy voice a human ring; O goddess surely!)."

92 quo tendis iter? (where are you directing your course?): Cf. Fortunatus' warning to Amyntas in III, 63: "*prospice quo tendas* (look where you're heading)."

102–19 A passage with a rich literary background. Zabughin (**Z1** 149) has pointed out its links with various descriptions of the Other World popular in the Middle Ages (for which, see *inter alia* Howard Rollin Patch, *The Other World According to Descriptions in Medieval Literature* [Cambridge: Harvard Univ. Press, 1950]). A number of images are (like medieval accounts of the Other World) ultimately rooted in the language of the Bible and recur throughout Mantuan's poetry and prose. Finally, various details along with much of the diction are found in Graeco–Roman accounts of the underworld (see lines 107–19n).

102–4 Cf. the Bible's two paths, the strait and narrow and the broad and pleasant one (Matthew 7:13–14), the biblical counterpart of Hercules' two choices discussed in line 88n. Often elaborated in medieval literature (H. R. Patch, *op. cit.*, 228), Mantuan's fair–seeming path resembles, as Mustard points out (141), Boccaccio's labyrinth of love in the *Corbaccio.*

107–19 Here as in a similar passage in his tenth eclogue (lines 129–32) Mantuan is in part drawing details and diction from Graeco–Roman accounts of the underworld, notably (as Badius points out) from *Aen.* VI. In post–classical pastoral this technique had already been used in Radbert's *Ecloga duarum sanctimonialium* (line 100) and Boccaccio's tenth eclogue (lines 76–80). Virgil's account was, of course, understood in light of a vast body of allegorical commentary stretching from Servius and Bernardus Silvestris to (in Mantuan's time) Cristoforo Landino, for which, see *inter alia* Domenico Comparetti, *Vergil in the Middle Ages*, trans. E. F. M. Benecke (London: Swan Sonnenschein, 1908),

104–18; Don Cameron Allen, *Mysteriously Meant: The Rediscovery of Pagan Symbolism and Allegorical Interpretation in the Renaissance* (Baltimore: Johns Hopkins Univ. Press, 1970), 135–54.

107–8 ferarum hospitium (hospice of wild beasts): A common feature in medieval accounts of the Other World (H. R. Patch, *op. cit.*, 92, 93). Noting the suitability of the phrase, Badius rightly recalls a similar description of the forest in *Aen.* VI as being filled with "*stabula alta ferarum* (the deep lairs of beasts)" (179). See lines 110–14n.

108 loca . . . opaca (a hideous place . . . darkness): see Patch, *op. cit.*, 130, who notes links of medieval descriptions of the Other World with the image of "the valley of the shadow of death" of the twenty third psalm and the biblical associations of the region (e.g., Isaiah 9:2). For Mantuan's diction, cf. Ovid, *Met.*, X, 53–54 (**M**) and Dido's fate in *Aen.* VI, 462 to pass through "lands squalid and forsaken (*per loca senta situ*)" in the underworld.

109 remeare vetatur (is forbidden to return): Badius quotes the Sybil's famous warning to Aeneas before he enters the underworld: ". . . easy is the descent to Avernus: night and day the door of gloomy Dis stands open; but to recall thy steps and pass out to the upper air, this is the task, this the toil! (. . . *facilis descensus Averno: / noctes atque dies patet atri ianua Ditis; / sed revocare gradum superasque evadere ad auras, / hoc opus, hic labor est.*)" (*Aen.* VI, 126–29).

110 piceis vittis (by a pitch–black band): "that is, by the darkness of ignorance and despair (*i.e. caligine ignorantiae et desperationis*)" (**B**).

110–14 Badius notes the presence of the Circe myth here (cf. *Odyssey* X). In his contemporaneous elegy *Ad Brognolum* Mantuan describes the effects of erotic love in similar terms ("*cur tamen hoc* [sc. *vere*] *plures alio quam tempore semper / insaniant iuvenes, me modo causa latet, / ni forte haec: tauros et oves imitantur amando.*" [**Gir** 87]), and, more strongly, in his *Contra amorem elegia* (ca. 1498), a work sometimes appended to editions of the eclogues, he accuses love of bestializing and drawing lovers into a concealed hell ("*Sic amor ante oculos animi velamina tendit, / et trahit in cæcum pectora nostra chaos . . . . Quisquis . . . uivit sine lumine mentis & usu, / Fert hominis vultus ingeniumque feræ*": *Opera* I, 176). But the Virgin's warning is more general, beginning in upheavals occasioned by erotic love (Mary in "Eclogue VIII" supplying "young men panting with emotion [*anhelanti iuventae*] "[80] with an alternative in devotion to her) but ultimately having to do (as Bernardus Silvestris interprets the temptations of Virgil's *antiquam silvam* [*Aen.* VI, 179–89]) with the ravaging effects of dwelling on temporal goods, effects that (as Badius also points out) figuratively transform men into beasts: "**Ferarum**: men transformed by vice into bestial nature. For philosophy calls lecherous men swine, fraudulent men foxes, babbling men dogs, truculent men lions, wrathful men boars, rapacious men wolves, and sluggish men asses. All of these dwell in temporal goods, just as in contrast 'the conversion of the good is in Heaven.' [Phil. 3:20] (*FERARUM* [*Aen.* VI, 179]*: id est hominum in ferinam naturam vitio transformatorum. Vocat enim philosophia luxuriosos sues, fraudulentos vulpes, garrulos canes, truculentos leones, iracundos apros, rapaces lupos, torpentes asinos. Hii omnes temporalia bona inhabitant sicut econtra 'bonorum conversatio in celis est.'*)": *The Commentary on the First Six Books of the 'Aeneid' Commonly Attributed to Bernardus Silvestris*, eds. Julian Ward Jones and Elizabeth Frances Jones (Lincoln: Univ. of Nebraska Press, 1977), 62, with the English translation of Earl G. Schreiber and Thomas E. Maresca, *Commentary on the First Six Books of Virgil's 'Aeneid'* (Lincoln: Univ. of Nebraska Press 1979), 61. As such, the *umbrosa silva* and its perils revealed by the Virgin here are to be connected with the savage world of the Papal Curia in "Eclogue IX" (lines 142–46, 158, and notes) and more obliquely with the creatures at the shaded whirlpool described by Batrachus in the tenth eclogue (lines 129–35 and notes).

cit., 131). Cf. III, 148.
115–17 Badius has a series of notes on these lines that, like his gloss on line 110, suggests how thoroughgoing an allegorical reading Mantuan's description encouraged in Renaissance scholars (as well as schoolmasters and their students): "**takes up the depths**: is always in the slime of carnal desires. **a mountain looms large**: that is, the difficulties and dangers in a life of excess. **Stygian waters**: that is, the hateful waters of hellish sorrow. (*ima occupat id est semper versatur in limo carnalium desideriorum. Mons plurimus id est difficultates & pericula quae sunt in luxuriosa vita. Latices stygios id est, obscœnas aquas tristitiae infernalis.*)" (The association of sorrow with the river Styx goes back to Servius' note, on *Aen.* VI, 134, on the Styx: see lines 107–19n.)
116 mons (mountain): a constant element in accounts of the Other World (Patch, *op. cit.*, 129–30).
118–19 Zabughin (**Z2** 272) sees the influence of Dante and perhaps the *Visio Tungdali* here (see H.R. Patch, *op. cit.*, 113).
125 Idalias i.e., of Idalium, modern Dalin, a town on Cyprus. With the fall of Acre in 1291, the community on Mount Carmel was extinguished, but the province of the Holy Land continued on Cyprus until 1570: *New Catholic Encyclopedia*, III, 118.
124–40 The familiar opposition of infernal regions (e.g., Boccaccio's tenth, fourteenth, and fifteenth eclogues) or shadowy forests (Dante's *selva oscura* in *Inferno* I, 2 and 77–78) to mountaintop paradises was sharpened in Mantuan's case by the particular significance attached to Mount Carmel by his religious order: see VIII, 44–46n. and "Introduction: Themes, Style, and Organization."
126 Carmelus cf. X, 70–73 and VIII, 13–59, esp. 44–46 and note.
129–31 Cf. X, 59 and note.
132–40 For the Virgin's description of Mount Carmel as the embodiment of two Arcadias, see "Introduction: Themes, Style, and Organization," esp. note 96.
138 Nymphs and dryads likewise dwell in Boccaccio's sylvan heaven (*Ecl.* XV, 187).
154–55: varied by Eobanus Hessus in *Bucolicon* VII, 47–48 (**V** 475).
156 For Mount Baldo, see II, 172n.

Eclogue VIII

Partly a continuation of the topic raised in the sixth eclogue (in which, despite its title, little was said about country life), this eighth eclogue also carries over many of the characters, images, and themes of the immediately preceding poem. The association of hills and mountains, for example, with monastic life (lines 52–55 and notes) and the Terrestrial Paradise (lines 44–46 and notes) contributes to the mountain symbolism at work in the eclogues as a whole (see "Introduction: Themes, Style, and Organization"). Pollux in this eclogue exemplifies a strain of Mariology, fundamental to the ideals of the Carmelite order, that recurs throughout Mantuan's poetry and prose.[23] Pollux's prayer to the Virgin (lines 122–51) makes an interesting synthesis of this devotional strain with what Zabughin (**Z1** 149) sees as elements of the local religion of Mantuan's day. Like Pollux, Mantuan composed several prayers and poems of thanksgiving addressed to the Virgin.[24] The brief *kalendarium*

[23] See Joseph Vicentius ab Eucharistia, "Libamentum Aesthetico-Marianum ex B. Baptistae Mantuani operibus," *AOCD* 20 (1948), 205-58.

marianum that concludes the eighth eclogue (lines 177–219) was to find its most ample expression in Mantuan's *De sacris diebus*, begun early in the sixteenth century with a poem on the Visitation (C65).

1 Cornix See X, 3n.
4–66 Cf. the dispute between Thomalin and Morrell on hills and plains in "July" 1–92 of Spenser's *Shepheardes Calendar* (**Var** VII[1], 326–31).
16–18 For the giving of drugs, cf. Virgil, *Ecl.* VIII, 95–96. Mustard quotes a passage from Burton's *Anatomy of Melancholy* (II, 4, 1. 2) testifying to the popularity of Mount Baldo among herbalists.
18 Valsasinus (from Val Sasina): on the east of Lake Como.
23 polenta See VI, 5n.
28–33 Badius was uncertain whether Mantuan was praising or mocking his subject in this passage.
40 Mustard notes the verbal echo of Virgil, *Ecl.* VIII, 43 (*duris in cotibus*), but readers might also recall the hard lot of Meliboeus' goat, who must abandon her new–born young "on the naked flint (*silice in nuda*)" (*Ecl.* I, 15).
44–46 Mantuan here reflects the medieval tradition, based on Ezek. 28:13–16, that placed the Terrestrial Paradise on a lofty mountain in the East (**M**). The equally traditional belief that the Garden of Eden almost touched the moon grew out of the description of St. Paul's rapture in 2 Cor. 12:2 f., coupled with the Greek Fathers' tendency to identify Paradise with the third, lunar sphere (Arturo Graf, *Miti, leggende e superstizioni del medio evo* [Turin: E. Loescher, 1892–93], I, 16–18; A. Bartlett Giamatti, *The Earthly Paradise and the Renaissance Epic* [Princeton, Univ. Press, 1966], 44–45; Joseph Duncan, *Milton's Earthly Paradise: A Historical Study of Eden* [Minneapolis: Univ. of Minnesota Press, 1972], 24, 79, 80). Cf. VII, 124–40 and notes; and see "Introduction: Themes, Style, and Organization," esp. note 96.
51–53 The Grande Chartreuse: the Carthusian monastery near Grenoble. **Carmel**: see " Introduction: Themes, Style, and Organization." **Gargano**: the site of the sanctuary of St. Michael, established after his appearance there ca. 490. **Athos**: located on a peninsula in northern Greece, Mount Athos gives its name to the famous collection of monasteries located there. **Loreto**: the hillside town near Ancona, famous for the house of the Virgin. **Alverno**: a mountain in the Tuscan Apennines, midway between Arezzo and Florence; St. Francis received the stigmata while making a retreat at a chapel located there. **Sinai**: in the sixth century Justinian established the Monastery of St. Catherine on the traditional site of the burning bush. **Soracte**: Mustard notes that in Mantuan's time there was a monastery of St. Sylvester on this famous peak. **Vallombrosa**: this forest southeast of Florence gave its name to the chief monastery of the Vallombrosans located on Monte Seccieta there.
54–55 Nursini senis (aged Nursian): St. Benedict, born at Nursia, a small town near Spoleto, died at Monte Cassino (**M**). **Camaldoli**: located in the Tuscan–Romagnole Apennines, the Abbey of Camaldoli comprises two monastaries associated with the Camaldolese congregation, a reform movement within the Benedictines.
80 Cf. VII, 110–14 n.
81 See *G.* I, 17 and esp. 338 f. where Virgil advises the farmer that, to avoid the destructive power of storms, he should reverence the gods and Ceres in particular.
85–86 Badius cites Rev. 12:1 (". . . a woman clothed with the sun, and the moon under her feet, and on her head a crown of twelve stars [. . . *mulier amicta sole et luna sub pedibus eius, et in capite eius corona stellarum duodecim*]"), a description often applied to

[24] E.g., *Ad divam Virginem pro recipienda sospitate post febrim acerrimam, votum* (*Opera* II, 54-55). and the unprinted poem edited by Graziano di Santa Teresa as "Un carme inedito del B. Battista Mantovano relativo alla S. Casa di Loreto," *Il Monte Carmelo*, 28 (1942), 19-20.

the Virgin Mary.
104–7 A reference to *G.* I, 335–36, the same pasage in which Virgil urges the husbandman to reverence the gods (see line 81n.). The details in Mantuan's description of Saturn's ill effects come from Servius' commentary (the house, in particular, catches fire because of lightning).
117 Ianni hircum (Jannus' goat): As Mustard notes, Jannus' goat of IV, 30 f.
123–24 Mustard quotes passages from the *Liber medicinalis* of Quintus Serenus and from Nicolò Perotti's *Cornucopiae* to substantiate acceptance of these beliefs.
137 An adaptation, as Badius notes, of Lycidas' description of the relationship between words and measures in Virgil, *Ecl.* IX, 45: "The measure I remember, could I but keep the words (*numeros memini, si verba tenerem*)."
150 Echoed in Euricius Cordus, *Ecl.* VII, 71 (**M** 55).
155 Cf. Euricius Cordus, *Ecl.* IV, 48 (**M** 54).
158–60 crates for **grates** (see "Introduction: Themes, Style, and Organization," note 88). Virgil at times (e.g., *Aen.* I, 600) speaks of "giving [or paying] worthy thanks (*grates persolvere dignas*)."
173 f. As Leonard Grant notes (*op. cit.*, 275–76), the prayers of a shepherd named Pius to Christ and the Virgin in Euricius Cordus' seventh eclogue have their basis in Pollux's devotion to the Virgin Mary here.
177–80 The Assumption of the Blessed Virgin, 15 August (**M**).
182 The Nativity of Mary, 8 September (**M**). In *G.* II, 394, Virgil uses similar langauge to describe a religious ceremony honoring Bacchus.
185–89 Loreto overlooks the Adriatic. Illyrian and Chaonian ships would come from the Dalmatian coast where the house of the Virgin, situated at Loreto, had originally been set down. For the pilgrims here as *laeti*, see X, 148n.
190–93 The Presentation, or entrance of the Virgin into the Temple, 21 November (**M**). The apocryphal gospel of the pseudo–Matthew tells how her parents took Mary as a young girl to the Temple and how she eagerly ran up the steps, remaining in the apartments there and never inquiring after her parents again. Long interpreted as a model of self–offering and dedication to the spiritual life, its theme is echoed in the early rule of the Carmelites (see "Introduction: Themes, Style, and Organization").
197 The Conception of the Blessed Virgin, 8 December (**M**).
199–200 As Mustard notes, long before the Virgin's immunity from original sin became accepted dogma in the mid–nineteenth century, Mantuan affirms it here and in his *Parthenice Mariana* (I, 223 f.).
205 The Purification, or the Presentation of Christ in the Temple, 2 February (**M**).
206 gregis princeps (the Lord of the flock): Apollo. Traditionally associated in ancient pastoral with the care of the herds and flocks, he often (as in, e.g., Theocritus XXV, 21) bore the title "Apollo of the pastures (*Apollo Nomios*)." See VII, 32–33.
209 paranymphus: in ancient times the friend of the groom who accompanied the latter when he went to fetch home the bride. Noting that the term appears in the same way in a poem formerly attributed to Venantius Fortunatus, Mustard quotes a passage from Mantuan's "Apologeticon" attached to his *Parthenice Mariana* in which he defends his use of the word by noting that in a sermon on the Nativity Augustine likewise used *paranymphus* to name the angel sent to Mary.
210 The Annunciation, 25 March (**M**).
213–14 See Matt. 1:18 and Luke 1:27.
214 No such feast established itself in the Calendar.
215–19 The Visitation, 2 July (**M**). Luke (1:56) states that Mary remained three months with Elizabeth, and as in his treatment of the Visitation in *De sacris diebus* (*Opera*, II, 316v–317) Mantuan here assumes that the feast falls on the date of her return.
223 Cf. *G.* II, 475 f., where Virgil mentions his aspirations to write a poem on the

movement of the heavens.

Eclogue IX

Candidus' journey southward to Rome echoes the expulsion of Menalcas and especially of Meliboeus in Virgil's ninth and first eclogues, as does Falcone de' Sinibaldi's role as Octavian, Tityrus' savior in Virgil's first eclogue (see lines 212–32, esp. 220–21 and notes). Mantuan was doubtless familiar with Petrarch's attacks on the Papal Court at Avignon in the sixth and seventh eclogues of his *Bucolicum carmen*. His own harsh criticism of the Curia at Rome, echoed again notably in *De calamitatibus temporum* and his sermon preached before Innocent VIII in 1488 (see "Introduction: Life"), made Mantuan's "Eclogue IX" a favorite during the Reformation. Matthias Flacius cites it in his *Catalogus testium veritatis* (Basel: Oporinus, 1556), 568, and an anthology of Mantuan's works printed at Nuremberg in 1571 (C426) quotes the eclogue at length to enlist the Carmelite reformer as a precursor of Luther. Before the Reformation its satiric–allegorical scheme was borrowed by Eobanus Hessus in *Bucolicon* I and IV (V 480-82). Spenser used "Eclogue IX" as a model for his attack on "Popish prelates" in the "September" eclogue (**Var** VII[1], 351, 354–57, 364–65), and it supplied a conspicuous precedent for Milton's attack in "Lycidas" on corruption within the English clergy.

18 Cf. the "*cariceam casulam*" in Euricius Cordus, *Ecl.* VIII, 109 and IX, 65 (**M** 55).
19 Cf. I, 1 (**M**) and II, 28–30n.
20–31 Along with lines 34–37, the basis for a discussion of drinking in Teofilo Folengo's sixth eclogue (B. Cotronei, "Il 'Contrasto di Tonin e Bighignol' e due ecloge maccheroniche di Teofilo Folengo," *GSLI*, 36 [1900], 293–94).
20–22 Badius notes that Candidus is invited to drink so that anything he says can be put down to the wine.
24–31 These lines are quoted and discussed by Ravisius Textor in his *Epistolae* (London: n. p. , 1683), 35, 36 (**M** 48).
31 Oenophili: see I, 161 and note.
35–37 As Mustard notes, a common refrain in Roman poetry (e.g., Tibullus I, 2, 1).
41 See VIII, 40n.
42 Badius notes the echo of Virgil's famous phrase *labor improbus* (*G.* I, 145–46).
50–52 A confusing adaptation, as Badius points out, of Moeris' premonition in Virgil, *Ecl.* IX, 15. According to Cicero (*Div.* I, 85), to confirm an omen the bird should appear on the left, a detail Mantuan observes only in describing how it settles on the left side of Candidus' roof.
67–70 A dense tissue of Virgilian echoes, as Badius first noted, of Meliboeus' rhapsodic description (*Ecl.* I, 53–58) of the homeland he is being forced to leave.
75–76 Tityrus' circumstance at the beginning of Virgil's first eclogue.
77 A further idyllic echo from Virgil's eclogues, this time from III, 92 (**B**).
78 An echo of Virgil's praise of the farmer in *G.* II, 458–59: "O happy husbandmen! too happy, should they come to know their blessings! (*O fortunatos nimium, sua si bona norint, / agricolas!*)."
90 Echoed in Euricius Cordus, *Ecl.* X, 123 (**M** 55).

102 Zabughin (**Z_1** 152) connects the sleek herd with the Riario and della Rovere families, whom Sixtus IV notoriously indulged. Lucia Gualdo Rosa notes that their influence, far from waning after his death, continued under Innocent VIII, whom Cardinal Giuliano della Rovere helped to elect: *Poeti latini del quattrocento*, 904–5. For Mantuan's use of biblical imagery here (cf. Ezek.34:18), see the discussion of early versions of the ninth and tenth eclogues in "Appendix I."
117–19 are echoed, as Mustard notes (49), in Barclay's fourth eclogue (lines 103–6).
130–31 Cf. the malign serpent of *G.* III, 425–34, esp. 434, and his counterpart in the Bible, an elemental image of deceit, abomination, and wickedness (Gen. 3:1, 14; Lev. 11:41; Rev. 12:9; et passim). Cf. X, 138–39.
133–35 The protective cap comes, as Mustard notes, from Calpurnius (I, 7); but the diction is close to Judges 8:7 and in general Mantuan's brambles echo the thorns and briars that in the Bible are often images of hardship and punishment (e.g., Gen. 3:18; Isaiah 5:6). Cf. VII, 111; also VI, 240 and note.
142–46 The metamorphosis into a wolf recalls, as Badius notes, a striking passage in Virgil's eighth eclogue: "These herbs and these poisons, culled in Pontus, Moeris himself gave me—they grow plenteously in Pontus. By their aid I have oft seen Moeris turn wolf and hide in the woods . . . . (*has herbas atque haec Ponto mihi lecta venena / ipse dedit Moeris (nascuntur plurima Ponto), / his ego saepe lupum fieri et se condere silvis / Moerim* . . . .)" (lines 95–98). The basis of the wolf image is, however, biblical, founded in the wolves that raven among the flocks in, e.g., Matt. 7:15. Cf. the hospice of wild beasts (*ferarum hospitium*) revealed by the Virgin Mary in VII, 107–8.
151–52 Cf. Acts 20:29–30: ". . . after [Christ's] departure, ravening wolves will enter among you, not sparing the flock. And of your own selves shall arise men speaking perverse things, to draw away disciples after them."
153–54 Badius and Mustard cite references to Egyptian animal worship in Cicero, *N.D.* III, 19; *Tusc. Disp.* V, 27, 78; Juvenal XV, 1–8; Arnobius I, 28; and Celsus, in Origen's *Contra Celsum* III. Nor should one forget biblical condemnation of such worship in Wisdom 11:16 and 12:24–25.
158 Badius cites God's blessing on Adam and Eve: ". . . fill the earth, and subdue it, and rule over the fishes of the sea, and the fowls of the air, and all living creatures that move upon the earth" (Gen. 1:28). Cf. also Mantuan's *De vita beata*: Gigo has just finished deploring corrupt prelates who, misleading others, cannot even guide their own actions, and Hadrianus, his pupil, concurs: "And with this of which you speak that poem of Ovid's agrees [*Met.* I, 84–86]: 'And though other animals gaze in a prone position upon the earth, [the world's creator] gave an uplifted face to man and bade him see the heavens and raise his countenance to the stars' (*huic quod dicis illud carmen Nasonis poetae convenit: 'Pronaque cum spectent animalia cætera terram, / Os homini sublime dedit cælumque videre / Iussit et erectos ad sydera tollere vultus.'*)" (*Opera* IV, ii, 183). See VII, 110–14 and note.
159–67 Badius rightly recalls Virgil's famous description of a plague in *G.* III. 478–566: cf. line 162 and *G.* III, 515–16; line 163 and *G.* III, 549–50. The sickness Faustulus describes here is perhaps to be associated with the snakes' venom of line 140.
185–91 Mustard compares II, 87–88.
188–90 **Athesis (Adige); Abdua (Adda)**: like the Po and Mincio, rivers in northern Italy.
192 Echoed in Euricius Cordus, *Ecl.* IX, 98 (**M** 55).
199–200 **Luna**: famous for its harbor, it was destroyed in 1016. **Hadria**: an ancient seaport between the Po and Adige, it was destroyed in a war with Venice in. 1017. **Salvia**: an island town in Picenum, it was a place of some commercial importance under the Empire but was completely destroyed by Alaric. (**M**)
200 **Umber**: see IV, 81n.

206 fontes (springs): Cf. VII, 129–31; X, 70–72n.
210 Vaurentinus notes the Virgilian echo of the exiled Meliboeus' mournful call: "Away, my goats! Away, once happy flock! (*ite meae, quondam felix pecus, ite capellae*)" (*Ecl.* I, 74).
213 Falcone de' Sinibaldi, the Falco of the title. See "Introduction: Composition and Publication of the *Adulescentia*," esp. note 52.
217–19 A rustic analogy: cf. Virgil, *Ecl.* V, 16–17; I, 26 (M); and see IV, 193–95n.
218 For the Adda, see 188–90n. The Magra flows between Liguria and Etruria.
220 Tityrus: see II, 8–9n.
221 A clear echo, as Badius points out, of Tityrus' grateful vow to his protector, Octavian, who in Virgil's first eclogue has shielded him from Meliboeus' fate (*Ecl.* I, 42–43).
223–25 i.e., Apollo.
225–27 After the Virgilian echoes of lines 210 and 220–21, a concluding modulation back into the language of Biblical pastoral (e.g., John 10:14). Rosa, *op. cit.*, 911, identifies Christ as the "master from Jerusalem (*Solymi magistri*)" and Peter, who forsook his fisherman's nets to become pastor of the flock that had its origins in Palestine (hence an "Assyrian flock [*Assyrii pecoris*]"), as the "father of old (*antiquo patri*)." Badius notes that Peter is called *pater* to underline his office as pope.
228–30 Cf. Petrarch's more guarded faith at the conclusion of his seventh eclogue (132–36) in the reforming potential of Angelo Acciaiuoli, bishop of Florence.

Eclogue X

A debate between Myrmix, spokesman for a mitigated rule within the Carmelite order, and Batrachus, like Mantuan a reformer of the order's wayward ways. The form of the eclogue, inherited from medieval debate literature, helps to distance Mantuan (lines 194–200 excepted, for which see note) and holds together the tensions represented by Myrmix and Batrachus, Bembus' concluding judgment serving to bring together, in terms favorable to the latter, the contending Carmelite factions. A reprise of themes and images developed in the other eclogues (e.g., lines 203, 59, 70–72, 131–33, 138–41 and notes), this tenth eclogue would seem a fitting conclusion to the revised collection of the poet and reformer of the Carmelite order. George Turberville, perhaps assuming that Protestants would have little interest in a quarrel among monks, excluded it from his English version; Thomas Harvey included the tenth eclogue in his translation, however, and in our century Bembus' judgment (lines 201–4) along with the passage on the origin of the order (lines 52–75) have once again been translated by Brocard Sewell of the Carmelite house at Aylesford (C541).

1 Bembe Bernardo Bembo, as Mustard first suggested: see "Introduction: Composition and Publication of the *Adulescentia*," esp. note 53.
3 Batrachus, Myrmix The names of Mantuan's characters are sometimes playful (e.g., "Cornix [crow]" and "Fulica [coot]"), but Badius is probably correct in thinking that Myrmix's name (Greek "ant") also refers to the black color of the non–observant Carmelite habit. His argument that Batrachus' name (Greek "frog") alludes to the grey inner tunic of

the reformed brethren is less convincing. Mantuan may have remembered the Batrachus of Boccaccio's ninth eclogue, a contentious spokesman for Florence against the Holy Roman Emperor. Mustard notes that the name *Myrmix* is used again in the second and fifth eclogues of the Danish poet Erasmus Michaelius Laetus. For Candidus' name, see IV, 105n.

3 certare parati: one of several phrases and motifs in this eclogue borrowed by Eobanus Hessus in the amoebean contest presented in his *Bucolicon* V (V 474).

6 pater vatum (father of prophets): like Bembus' familiarity with the Holy Land (lines 28–40), added in revision. As Badius notes, since Carmelites are often called "son of the prophets" because of their Elian heritage, in describing Bembus as a "father of prophets" Mantuan is suggesting that allegorically he represents the General of the order. Both revisions seem calculated to give Bembus' concluding judgment greater authority than would have been carried by Bernardo Bembo.

6–7 Badius notes that the phrasing here echoes that of Palemon in Virgil's third eclogue ("It is not for me to settle so high a contest between you [*Non nostrum inter vos tantas componere lites*]") (108), to which Mustard adds Nemesianus' eulogy for Meliboeus (I, 52–53): "With patient ear and soothing word for diverse plaints, you were wont to judge the disputes of the peasants. (*tu ruricolum discernere lites / adsueras, varias patiens mulcendo querellas.*)" (*Minor Latin Poets*, ed. and trans. J. Wight Duff and Arnold M. Duff, rev. ed. [London: Heinemann, 1935], II, 461, 460). Palemon and Meliboeus judge singing competitions, however, not (as here) debates.

8 Pierios liquores (Pierian waters): i.e., waters from the springs of Helicon.

10 Eurotæ campos, Phocidis arva Eurotas is the principal river of Laconia in Greece. Phocis, a region in Greece, includes Mount Parnassus, Mount Helicon, and the Castalian spring.

13–14 A variation of a pastoral motif also found in II, 28–30, for which see note.

31 fons (spring) The spring issuing from the fount of Elijah.

32–33 In *G.* III, 441 f. Virgil describes cures for scab; but, as Badius notes, the references here, as in line 99, are religious: the disease being original sin and the shepherd (in this case) being John the Baptist. Boccaccio draws a similar link between *scabies* and original sin in *Ecl.* XIV, 97–98.

34–39 The Jordan has its sources at the foot of Mount Hermon, not Lebanon (a common error, perpetuated as late as Charles Estienne's *Dictionarium historicum, geographicum, poeticum* [Geneva: J. Stoer, 1596], fol. 253), and after flowing through Lake Huleh and the Sea of Galilee (Tiberias was on its western shore), passes near Jericho and flows into the Dead Sea ("Asphaltites' flood"), a place commonly associated with Sodom and Gomorrah.

54 Elias (Elijah) According to Carmelite tradition, along with Elisha a founder of the order: see "Introduction: Themes, Style, and Organization."

54–55 A passage that troubled Badius, who wanted to substitute *arva* for *arma*. Mantuan seems to have meant no more, however, than that Elijah encountered his enemies in the garb of a countryman, having retreated from the city into rural seclusion (see *Opera*, IV, i, 242; S 279)—although, of course, with the fire of God (see 4 Kings 1:1–16).

59 A figurative adaptation involving the fount of Elijah mentioned in line 31. As Mustard notes, we should recall the Virgin's claim in Mantuan's seventh eclogue that "From this peak reverence for God comes, led off into your mountains, just as streams issue from an unceasing fount or many descendants from a single sire" (VII, 129–31).

70–72 Noting the threat of pestilence in southern Italy, Badius interprets the turning of the stream's course towards the south as signifying allegorically the perversion of sound teachings. Given the symbolic geography of "Eclogue IX" (e.g., lines 90–101), however, the south is also undoubtedly to be connected with Rome. In the Old Testament, the south is sometimes (e.g., Gen. 12:9; Vulg. Ps. 125:4) called the "dry country," for which cf. IX, 10, 23, 206, et passim.

73 Cf. the healing stream that flows eastward from the temple in Ezekiel 47:1–12 and its anagogic counterpart, the river of water of life in Rev. 22:1–5. **ortum**: it is one of Mantuan's untranslatable economies that in flowing "east" the stream would also be traveling back to its "source" (cf. lines 145–47).
79–82 As Badius first noted, this exchange on vineyards and yew trees alludes to Virgil, *G*. II, 112–13: "Bacchus [i.e., the vine] loves the open hills, and the yew tree the cold of the north wind. (*apertos / Bacchus amat colles, Aquilonem et frigora taxi*.)." The point of both passages is that no one climate suits the well–being of all things. As in "Eclogue IX" south and north here allude to Rome and to northern Italy with its Mantuan reform movement.
89–90 The modern Clitunno or la Vene, Clitumnus is a small river in Umbria in whose surrounding pastures were fed white steers sacrificed during a triumph in ancient Rome (see Virg. *G*. II, 146–48). Mantuan's point about the "sheep" of Modena is that they are not black but grey, the color of the reformed Carmelite habit: see "Introduction: Themes, Style, and Organization." Like Mantua, Modena had a reformed Carmelite community (S 193–94).
99–100 See 32–33n. Petrarch employs a similar religious adaptation of Virgilian imagery in his *Ecl*. VII, 187–88.
106–9 See "Introduction: Themes, Style, and Organization."
116–18 See I, 68–69n.
124–27 These lines are imitated in the eleventh idyl (lines 68–74) of Eobanus Hessus (M 53).
131 gurges (whirlpool): cf. VII, 117–19; Virgil, *A*. VI, 296; Juvenal III, 266; and see VII, 107–19n. *Gurges* is substituted in revision for *lacuna* to link this passage with the imagery of VII, 117–19 (the addition of *densa spineta* at line 132 serves the same function [cf. VII, 111; also X, 101]).
133 Badius interprets these venomous creatures allegorically as misshapened traditions and wicked customs. See VII, 107–19n.
138–41 coluber (serpent): cf. Virgil, *G*. III, 419–21; and see IX, 130–31n. The basis for the other images in this passage is Biblical: for scorpions, cf., e.g., the faithless Judeans in Ezek. 2:6; for toads, the deceitful spirits resembling frogs in Rev. 16:13. As Mustard notes (49), Alexander Barclay adapts these striking lines in his fourth eclogue (lines 107–10).
140 ventrosus bufo Cf. Eobanus Hessus, *Id*. V, 55 (**M** 53).
143–44 grege diviso (having divided the flock in two) A reference to the quasi–autonomy granted to the Mantuan Reform by Eugene IV in 1442 (for which, see S 71–81).
145–53 Cf. VII, 126–31 and 126*n*; and see "Introduction: Theme, Style, and Organization."
148 pascua laeta (rich are the pasturelands): Cf. Virgil's description of abundant fields in *G*. I, 101–2: "*laetissima . . . farra, / laetus ager*." As T. E. Page notes of this passage, "the adjective *laetus* is commonly used in Latin of crops which are abundant and bountiful . . . . Nonetheless we must not suppose that 'abundant' is an adequate translation of the word, which, at any rate in Virgil, is always used to describe actual 'joy': so here the crops are 'joyous' because they are flourishing, and the field 'rejoices' in its crops: the 'joy in harvest' (Isaiah 9:3) is not confined to men but extends to inanimate nature." (P. Vergilius Maro, *Bucolica et Georgica* [London: Macmillan, 1898], 194). In Mantuan's allegorical landscape the line between subject and object is less sharply defined. True piety engenders joy, as it does among the pilgrims to Loreto, the *laeti*, of VIII, 188–89.
152 Badius explains this as an allusion to the dimensions of the separate cells within which the early Carmelites lived.

175–76 Mustard understands these lines as meaning that the Mantuan Reform is still not close enough to the original rule of the order. But the desert or wilderness, the place designated in Saint Albert's rule for the foundation of monestaries (*The Rule of Saint Albert*, 80), also became a symbol in Carmelite thought of contemplative withdrawal from the world (*Dictionnaire de spiritualité*, II, 1, 162).
180 cuium pecus As Mustard notes, an imitation of Virgil, *Ecl.* III, 1, *cuium* itself being a subliterary word used by the Roman poet to convey the flavor of rustic speech (Col 25). For Mantuan's style here, see "Introduction: Themes, Style, and Organization," note 88.
194–200 Added in revision. For Candidus, see IV, 105n.
201–4 For the relation of this passage to the unprinted version of "Eclogue X," see the discussion in "Appendix I."
203 lustra ferarum (haunts of wild beasts): Cf. III, 144; VII, 107–8 and note; IX, 142.
204 antiquis campis (fields of old): Cf. I, 2 (*antiquos amores* [loves of old]).

APPENDIX I AND II

APPENDIX I

The first text printed below, extracts made by John Bale from Mantuan's *Suburbanus* and the information supplementing them,[1] have been transcribed from fols. 34v–36 in a manuscript compilation in scribal hand,[2] MS. Selden supra 41, now at the Bodleian Library, Oxford. For the second item, a text of an early version of Mantuan's ninth eclogue, I have chosen a late fifteenth or early sixteenth century manuscript in two italic hands—MS. 1/4, now in the library at the Collegio di Sant' Isidoro, Rome—that is unique in preserving Mantuan's original letter of dedication.[3] The third item, a transcription of the manuscript version of the tenth eclogue, is based on a unique copy preserved in an early sixteenth–century manuscript in italic hand—MS. Ottob. lat. 2280—now in the Vatican Library.[4] The title and headnote of Mantuan's eclogue, which I have transposed to the beginning of the text, appear as a fortunate afterthought copied out on folio 178v, an otherwise blank page. In all the transcriptions I have retained the spelling and word division of the original texts. Punctuation has likewise been preserved, modern punctation marks within brackets having been inserted in a few places for clarity. For the same reason a few capital letters

1 Of the glosses (all apparently by Mantuan), the note on Giorgio Tifernate provides no new information about Mantuan's teacher or about Giorgio Merula. Antimachus is unknown, unless he is related to the Mantuan humanist Marcantonio Antimaco (1473–1551). Hadrianus Ciniber, likewise unknown to history, perhaps left his stamp on Hadrianus, the inquisitive novice in Mantuan's *De vita beata*.

2 Stage two in the evolution of Bale's hand, according to Leslie Fairfield *op. cit.*, 159–60, the entries dating from some time just before 1523.

3 The existence of Mantuan's ninth eclogue in this manuscript was first recorded by Paul Oscar Kristeller in *Iter Italicum: A Finding List of Uncatalogued or Incompletely Catalogued Manuscripts of the Renaissance in Italian and Other Libraries* (Leiden: Brill, 1963–), II, 134. With minor variants, copies of this eclogue, all in italic hand, are also contained (as Kristeller notes in ibid., II, 54, 55, 168, 436) in the following:

MS. C 61, fols. 56v –59v, Biblioteca Comunale Augusta, Perugia.
MS. F 5, fols. 1v –5v, Biblioteca Comunale Augusta, Perugia.
MS. J IX 13, fols. 64–67v, Biblioteca Comunale degli Intronati, Siena.
MS. Ottob. lat. 2280, fols. 173v –178, Bibliotheca Apostolica Vaticana, Rome.
MS. Lat. Misc. c. 62., fols. 76v –79v, Bodleian Library, Oxford.

4 Likewise first recorded by Kristeller in *Iter Italicum*, II, 436.

have been inserted within brackets. Superior letters have been lowered, *v* has in all cases been distinguished from *u*, and all abbreviations have been expanded (*e* being rendered as *ae* only when accompanied by an abbreviation mark). Textual variants, for the most part few and minor, between the Sant' Isidoro text and the other copies have been left unrecorded. The Vatican copy of "Eclogue IX" has several variants sufficiently suggestive of a slightly different version of the poem, however, that I have incorporated them, bracketed in italics, into my transcription.

****

In the dedicatory letter to his revised version of the *Adulescentia*, Mantuan complains that much in the original poems was too youthful (*multa nimis iuvenilia*), and that he had partly in mind their style is indicated by the fact that fewer than fourteen lines from Bale's extracts survive recognizably in Mantuan's printed version of the *Adulescentia*.[5] (Small wonder that he felt free to rededicate what must have seemed to him virtually a new work![6]) All three texts reveal Mantuan's care in replacing metrically defective lines[7] and awkward diction;[8] and beyond this, they show him reigning in a verbal prolixity that was to be a besetting vice throughout his career.[9]

So little survives in Bale's excerpts from the eclogues that generalizations as to the nature of Mantuan's original collection must be tentative. Nonetheless, granted Mantuan's interest in stylisic revision and elaboration, a further meaning might be seen in his objection to the youthfulness of the poems in *Suburbanus*. Bale's extracts are all taken from what became in the final version the first four eclogues, on erotic love and women. His selections reveal a disturbing tendency to view women as an almost supernatural cause of all men's woes in love.[10] Touches of this attitude remain in the printed version (e.g., II, 111–14), but in the *Adulescentia* much of this material has been placed in Umber's attack on women.[11] Especially in depicting Amyntas' love in the second and third

5 Cf. Bale, lines 59–60 and IV, 221–22; Bale 61 and IV, 110; Bale 62 and IV, 117; Bale 62–63 and IV, 119–21; Bale 64–65 and IV, 118; Bale 69–70 and IV, 150–51; Bale 82–83 and IV, 177–78; Bale 101–3 and IV, 236–38; Bale 104–6 and IV, 239–41.

6 H. W. Garrod discusses the common practice of rededicating works in "Erasmus and his English Patrons," *The Library*, 5th ser., 11 (1949), 2.

7 E.g., MS. X, 17; MS. X, 29; MS. X, 31.

8 E.g., *verba . . . gramenque nocent* (Bale 72); *mittit in incertum tristes sine lege sagittas* (Bale 37); *perone pedem vesti* (MS. IX, 106); *est animus nobis . . . ascendere mortem* (MS. X, 106)

9 Cf., e.g., MS. IX, 48–52 and IX, 66; MS. IX, 132–34 and IX, 171; Bale 101–10 and IV, 236–41.

10 Thus within ten lines in the extracts Mantuan slips from warning that the lover will languish in love (Bale 41) to the unwarranted assertion that women are the cause of all his hardships (Bale 51).

11 The prose gloss on Gregorio Tifernate (Bale, fol. 35v) doubtless accompanied the description

eclogues Mantuan puts a good deal of stress in the printed text on deliberation and choice, Amyntas being urged to consider how foolish he looks (III, 53–55), how destructive love is to his fortunes (II, 115–19), and so forth. The effect of Mantuan's revision is to tone down and place the misogyny that to some extent disfigures even the revised version of the poems. As a title, *Adulescentia* may describe the time in his life when Mantuan first drafted many of the eclogues. Nevertheless, the intelligence that shaped their final form seems to have been not only artistically more sophisticated but morally more alive to the factors that govern human actions and choice.[12]

****

From manuscript evidence we now know that the span of more than twenty years separates the pastoral poems excerpted by Bale from the eclogues dedicated to Falcone de' Sinibaldi and Bernardo Bembo. The first eight eclogues, as the title of the printed collection suggests, date from Mantuan's *adulescentia,* from his years of admiration for the Latin elegiac poets and deep personal turmoil affecting his family and eventually leading him to a life within the cloister. The ninth and tenth eclogues come, in contrast, from the time when, as spokesman for the Mantuan Reform movement in northern and central Italy, he was involved in recalling his religious order to its ancient ideals and deeply concerned with the corruption that he saw overtaking the Papal Court. Shepherds have become *pastores* in Mantuan's ninth and tenth eclogues, religious allegory being placed in the service of ecclesiastical satire. His decision to yoke the two poems together for publication with his earlier eclogues immediately brought him face to face with a number of potential difficulties. Especially in the first four eclogues, Mantuan had pushed strains of rustic realism to limits unprecedented in previous Latin pastoral, and in uniting his two allegorical pastorals with this first group of poems, he wisely attempted to correlate the world of his *pastores* with the lives of his more worldly shepherds.

This accommodation is most clearly evident at the beginning of his ninth eclogue. The original version opens simply and sparely with Faustulus' pastoral offer of a consoling glass of wine: "Wine lessens thirst and shields us from painful thoughts (*Vina sitim minuunt : animique doloribus obstant*)," he says, to which the oppressed Candidus laconically responds, "Wine lessens thirst, but sadness and pain both remain (*Vina sitim minuere : manet moerorque dolorque*)" (lines 21–22). In the revised version this exchange has been considerably expanded. Faustulus begins by describing

of Umber (IV, 95–103 in the 1498 printed text) that prefaces his attack on women. Much of the material—not only the language but the themes (e. g., Bale 61–67 and IV, 110–21; Bale 80–84 and IV, 177–84)—of Bale, lines 40–86 which, on the evidence of the printed text, would have described erotic love, seems therefore to have been transferred in revision to Umber's speech.

12 For further discussion of Bale's excerpts, see my article on "Mantuan on Women and Erotic Love: A Newly Discovered Manuscript of the Unprinted Version of His Eclogues," *Renaissance Studies*, 3 (1989), 13-28.

a sort of seven–stage conquest of thirst that, commencing with a sip or two of wine, ends in the triumph of Bacchus. The jest, he says, came from Oenophilus—a reference, of course, intended to take us back to the conclusion of the first eclogue, where in a long and memorable passage (lines 161–71) the shepherd Faustus describes how Oenophilus, the "wine lover," along with Tonius, the drunken bagpiper of *bergerie*, had led the celebration of Faustus' marriage to squint–eyed Galla.

But if Oenophilus' jest and the reference to him in the ninth eclogue link Candidus and Faustulus with the earthy world of the opening poems, the motivation behind Faustulus' offer betrays a complexity and worldliness that is also reminiscent of the earlier eclogues. In the final version Faustulus dwells too long and loudly on the benefits of the grape. Repulsed in his claim that wine will sooth Candidus' cares, he urges him to drink the wine unmixed. This will be the antidote for your heartache, Faustulus claims; with this potion Rome cures a troubled mind. Badius long ago recognized the true meaning of what is going on here: that Faustulus is openly urging Candidus to drink so that his subsequent attack on the corruption he has found in Rome can be set down by anyone overhearing it simply as an expression of drunken intemperance.

Indeed, Candidus and Faustulus move within a fearful, malevolent world, a realm that in its uncertainty has a good deal in common with the difficult, often dangerous lives that Mantuan's shepherds lead in his first eight eclogues. To strengthen this link, in revising the ninth eclogue Mantuan substantially expanded his portrait (*Adulescentia*, lines 85–89) of the figure, Fortuna, whom the shepherds in his first group of poems often blame for their troubled lives. Both her features and thoughts are changeable; according to Faustulus in the revised poem; she cares for nothing, all goes by chance. Mantuan's language here intentionally echoes the famous tirade against women in his fourth eclogue (e.g., *Ad.* IV, 111, 114–15 and IX, 85, 88; *Ad,* IV, 141–43 and IX, 87–88): the agents, he strongly implies in the opening poems, through whom Dame Fortune works her greatest harm. In "Eclogue IX," however, Fortuna by no means distributes her afflictions blindly; rather, she has turned her back on Candidus, according to Faustulus, to teach him a lesson because he valued her gifts too lightly. At the beginning of Mantuan's third eclogue, the source and role of earthly hardships and suffering are dismissed as unknowable. In the clearer air of his allegorical ninth eclogue, the workings of the world seem to be more open to view.

That such certitude is possible is justified in the final version by Mantuan's organization of the eclogues. As noted in my introduction,[13] "Eclogue VII" is the hinge on which the development of his collection turns. Written, as its headnote indicates, "when the author is already aspiring to enter the religious life (*cum iam auctor ad religionem aspiraret*)," the vision of the Virgin Mary presented in this climactic eclogue radically alters and defines the direction of the rest of Mantuan's collection. Most immediately,

---

[13] See "Style, Themes, and Organization" and further P_2 578–79.

erotic love, the subject of the first four eclogues, disappears, being replaced in the eighth eclogue by Pollux's devotion to the Virgin Mary. It is in the last two eclogues, however, that his vision exercises its full effect. Here, as appearances are sifted in light of it for the truth behind them, mimesis gives way decisively to allegory, Mary's words extending outwards through the quest of the *pastores* Faustulus, Batrachus, and Candidus (the last, in particular, a refraction of the implied author "after his entry into religious orders (*post religionis ingressum*)"[14] for an earthly Carmel preparatory to their heavenly one.

At crucial points in both eclogues Mantuan returns to the language and imagery of Mary's revelation in the seventh eclogue, strengthening the connection in revision. Among the many dangers in the allegorical Roman landscape of "Eclogue IX" there are brambles whose *spicula longis dentibus* in Mantuan's final version (*Ad.*, lines 134–35) recall the thorny thickets, described by the Virgin Mary, that maim and transform their helpless victims (*Ad.*, VII, 111–12). And likewise among the monsters in the tenth eclogue Batrachus discovers a scorpion whose *cornua* (MS X, 76), a term used exclusively of animals, are metamorphosed in revision into plurisignificant *bracchia* (*Ad.*, X, 140).[15] Expanding a suggestion in the first version of the ninth eclogue (MS. IX, 96–98), Mantuan in a *fabula* makes Rome itself into an owl that entices and traps its victims (*Ad.*, IX, 120–28); and a Virgilian adaptation (cf. Virgil, *Ecl.* VIII, 97–99) that portrays Papal predators as men who transform themselves into wolves to slaughter their flock (MS. IX, 114–17) leads in revision to a satiric excursion on Rome as the exemplar *par excellence* of animal worship (*Ad.*, IX, 153–58).

The most conspicuous reflection of Mary's vision occurs, however, in the tenth eclogue. Here Batrachus, fleeing eastwards from the monsters he found in Myrmix's company, comes upon rich pasturelands, untainted waters, sweet springs without fault. These are the fields where his forefathers dwelt, he tells us; even traces of their cells remain (MS X, 81–89; cf. *Ad.*, X, 145–53). It is, of course, Carmel; and after much wandering Batrachus has at last reached his goal: the liminal dwelling described by Mary in the seventh eclogue.

****

All this seems quite sensible, weaving as it does the last four eclogues together to form a unit coherent in theme and figure. And yet at the end of the tenth eclogue Mantuan made an important revision that would seem to qualify this strategy. Both versions of "Eclogue X" conclude with Bembus' judgment on the proper course of action for the Carmelite order. In both cases Bembus' speech begins with a call to "walk in the footsteps of your forefathers (*ferte per antiquos patrum vestigia gressus*)." But then in the first

14 See also the headnotes of the manuscript versions of the ninth and tenth eclogues.

15 Lewis and Short, *A Latin Dictionary*, s. v. "*cornu* ."

version, Bembus' words open out into an allegorical vision of an achieved Carmelite ideal (MS X, 122–35) that echoes Batrachus' earlier description (79–89) before closing in again with the words that also conclude the printed version of the eclogue: "Call back flocks wandering among the valleys and rocks, among the haunts of wild beasts. Build your huts again in the fields of old."[16]

At least two reasons suggest themselves for this change. Most immediately, within the dialogue form, Mantuan's alteration displaces Batrachus' point of view from the central position it had held by being affirmed within the first version in Bembus' concluding judgment. Mantuan was writing the eclogue, it would now seem, in the late 1480s, after the most conspicuous point of dispute between the two Carmelite factions, the controversy over the order's habit (S 98–106), had officially been settled. Although he elaborated allegorical details recalling this dispute—most notably Batrachus' comparison of the black and white fleece of the reformed and non–observant Carmelite "flocks" (*Ad.*, X, 88–90)—Mantuan's tone in the conclusion of the revised tenth eclogue stresses accommodation and unity in pursuit of a shared goal: a spirit also evident in Candidus' admonition, added in revision, that the two factions recognize the foolishness of their quarreling and listen in peace to Bembus' judgment (*Ad.*, X, 194–200).

Beyond this rhetorical strategy, Mantuan's excision also shifts the emphasis of his conclusion away from possible achievement to evangelistic struggle to win back flocks wandering *per lustra ferarum* of this world. To grasp the significance of what he has done here, we must keep clearly in mind the workings of the biblical pastoral imagery that Mantuan had inherited from the allegorical eclogues of Petrarch, his chief model for religious pastoral and ecclesiastical satire. In Petrarch's sixth eclogue, Pamphilus (Saint Peter) returns to lament the disregard for the flocks shown by Mitio (Clement VI), who has allowed innocent lambs to die and he–goats to ravage the woodlands and crops. In the concluding lines Pamphilus leaves, warning Mitio that, amidst his ease and false sense of security, Christ, their common master, will come again to change Mitio's joy to sorrow. Given that Petrarch has been justly accused[17] of being purposely enigmatic in his *Bucolucum carmen*, in its general outlines "Eclogue VI" can nonetheless be considered willful or riddling only if we confine him to Graeco–Roman pastoral imagery instead of allowing him the use of biblical pastoral images that had long since become an accepted and familiar part of his literary heritage.[18] But, more than this, we must bear in mind that along with this imagery the Bible brought to pastoral its own view of the future and its own way of seeing things. As an alternative to Virgil's picture of the coming Golden Age, the Old and New

16 ". . . *revocate vagantes / per valles per saxa greges[,] per lustra ferarum[.] / Figite in Antiquis iterum magalia Campis*," (lines 136–38).

17 by, e. g., Leonard Grant, *Neo–Latin Literature and the Pastoral*, 92.

18 Enrico Carrara, *La poesia pastorale* (Milan: F. Villardi, 1909), 40–67.

Testaments, as the Middle Ages and Renaissance understood them, offered to Petrarch and Mantuan a composite, evolving view in which (to pick immediately relevant details) Yaweh and later Christ would come to punish wicked *pastores* (Jeremiah 23:1–2; Ezekiel 34:10), separate the sheep from the he–goats (Matthew 25:32–33; cf. Ezekiel 34:17), and lead the flocks into rich pasturelands on the high mountains of Israel (Ezekiel 34:13–14; cf. Isaiah 40:11). Such imagery must surely be described as a legitimate extension of the age–old pastoral motif (e. g., Virgil, *Ecl.* I, 12–15) of the shepherd's concern for his flock. But, as Northrop Frye has reminded us,[19] images like these are at the same time radically visionary and prophetic: anagogic and, in the last passage, also tropological.[20]

The sleek herds that ravage the fields in Mantuan's ninth eclogue are, like the wanton heifers in Petrarch's poem (VI, 45), descended from the herds in Ezekiel that tread down the pastures and foul the waters (34:18) and that are to be subjected along with the he–goats to divine judgment at the end of time. But in neither of his last two eclogues does Mantuan open tropology out towards the anagogy of Petrarch's concluding apocalyptic threat. Rather, at the end of his ninth eclogue Mantuan invokes a Virgilian framework, making Falco into an Octavian figure able to cure all the ills besetting Candidus in Rome. Contemporary rumors suggest that Falcone de' Sinibaldi aspired to become a cardinal (**S** 130); but Faustulus' assurance that Falco is worthy to succeed the *magister Solymus* (Christ, the good shepherd) and the *Assyrii pecoris pastor* (Peter, whose flock had its origins in Palestine: hence "Assyrian") can do little, especially within the framework of the printed

---

19 *The Great Code: The Bible and Literature* (New York: Harcourt, 1982), 29.

20 As B. D. Napier remarks, "in view of the very nature of the sheep—affectionate (II Sam. 12:3), unaggressive (Isa. 53:7; Jer. 11:19; John 10:3–4), relatively defenseless (Mic. 5:8; Matt. 10:16), and in constant need of care and supervision (Num. 27:17; Ezek. 34:5; Matt. 9:36; 26:31)—and the corresponding relationship between the sheep and the shepherd, it is not at all surprising that in figurative–theological language the sheep and the shepherd are repeatedly, and often movingly, employed" in the Bible: *Interpreter's Dictionary of the Bible*, eds. George Arthur Buttrick, et al. (New York: Abingdon, 1962), IV, 316. Renato Poggioli's assertion that there can be no heavenly paradises in successful pastoral (*The Oaten Flute: Essays on Pastoral Poetry and the Pastoral Ideal* [Cambridge: Harvard Univ. Press, 1975], 19) would doubtless have puzzled Mantuan—or Boccaccio and Milton, for that matter. Cf., e.g., Nicholas of Lyre on Ezekiel 34:13–14 (God's promise to lead his flock into rich pasturelands) cited above: "That is, in the church militant through a gift of grace and in the church triumphant in the gift of glory. These things are described here by means of most fertile pasturelands and other physical objects because in the Old and New Testaments things of the spirit are often described by means of corporeal similtudes, so that (according to what Gregory writes in his thirty–seventh homily) 'the mind might rise from things known to things unknown and, through what it knows, might learn to esteem highly and love what is unknown to it.' (*Id est in ecclesia militante per dona gratiae, et in triumphante per dona gloriae, quae designantur hic per pascua uberrima et caetera corporalia: quia spiritualia sub similitudinibus corporalium in scriptura veteris ac novi testamenti frequenter designantur, ut secundum quod Gregorius, Hom. XXXVII. Surget animus ex his quae novit ad ea quae non novit, ac per hoc quod novit, diligere discat, et incognita amare.*)" (*Biblia sacra cum glossa . . . ordinaria, Nicolai Lyrani Postilla et Moralitatibus. . . .* [Lyons: Gaspar Treschel, 1545], vol. IV, fol. 259).

collection, to divert us from seeing that, no matter how sincere or well grounded Mantuan's hopes in Falcone might have been, we are being asked in the final analysis to put our faith in the Pope's treasurer.

Batrachus' Carmelite pastoral goal in the tenth eclogue, a more balanced ideal with which to conclude Mantuan's collection, is likewise tropological, looking outwards only by implication to the anagogic link between two Mount Carmels of the seventh eclogue. More than this, however, in the revised version Mantuan glances only fleetingly at this earthly goal, the *campi antiqui* in defense of which he had raised his standards. Like his tropological focus, Mantuan's concluding stress on the need for struggle within this life represents a distinct turning away from the anagogic focus of Petrarch's sixth eclogue. The revised conclusion to Mantuan's tenth eclogue would moreover seem a better reflection of the spirit and style of his printed collection. Puttenham and Drayton quite rightly speak of "moral Mantuan." But deeper than this insistance on right action, from the first to the last line of Mantuan's eclogues there lies a recognition of decay and human fallibility and of the constant need to protect what one has gained or been given. At the same time Mantuan's Batrachus also holds out, couched in visionary imagery, the possibility of an achievable eremitic paradise on earth. In the interplay between Batrachus' Carmelite pastoral vision and the revised version of Bembus' concluding judgment, Mantuan in effect kept true to the claims lying behind the blending of allegory and corporeal realism that so strikingly characterizes his collection of eclogues:[21] the claims, that is, of body and spirit, and of struggle and vision that run throughout the final, printed version of his *Adulescentia*.

****

Idem [B]aptista [M]antuanus edidit librum metricum (cui [S]uburbanus tytulus est) [fol 34v]
ad Johannem Baptistam [R]efrigerium / prohemium incipit[:] excerta ex hoc prohemio

Pauperis es domini modico contentus amictu
 Ibis et incompto parve libelle sinu.
Peccat quisquis opes cultu mentitur inani[;]
 Proventus debent sumptibus esse pares.

et infra[:]

pluris apud multos [V]enus est quam [P]alladis artes[,]
 Cecus [A]mor pluris quam tua [P]hebe lira.
Tubicenas nusquam superest [A]ugustea virtus
 Occidit ac [C]rassus imperat atque [N]ero.
Non est equali qui ponderat omnia lance
 Nec bona sed que sunt commoda quisque probat.
Spreta fugit virtus : et pro virtute libido
 Regnat. in hoc vicium femina virque ruunt.

21 Whence, e. g., Fontenelle's attack on their earthiness and Alexander Pope's condemnation of their use of religious allegory (see "Introduction: Themes, Style, and Organization").

Alloquitur postea librum suum jdem [M]antuanus[:]

I felix tenere proles mea prima iuvente.
I felix animi conscia carta mei.
I precor. I felix fausto precor omine vade.
Parve libelle [mea?] munera prima tege.
Astra tibi faveant. faveant tibi numina teque
Dent precor longa posteritate legi.

et infra[:]

Que modo vulgamus pedibus sunt edita senis[;]
Imparibus restant plurima facta undis[.]
Nostra sinu servat plures [E]leg[i]a tabellas
Absconditque suas callida delicias[.]
Ipsa suas depromet opes non invida quando
Se sciet auctori posse placere suo[.]
Interea tristes solancia carmina sensus
Perlege. dum spei nobile crescit opus.

Argumentum libri videlicet [S]uburbani vel fragmenti incipit /

Faustus adit segetes et [F]ortunatus easdem
Ambo pastores . annis gravioribus ambo[.]
Gesta domi positis recitant iuvenilia veris et cetera

Faustus et [F]ortunatus sunt collocutores in [S]uburbano.

Sequitur in prosa / Amencie cognicio sanioris mentis est argumentum.

et infra[:] Non puerilia hec ederem : nisi iam et apud multos vulgata et sub nomine meo [fol. 35]
legi certe scirem[.]

[E]t infra metrice[:]

Ut doceam [V]eneris nil esse nocencius igne[.]
Heu[,] funesta lues[,] durum et crudele venenum[;]
Pectora letiferis populans mortalia flammis[,]
In furias agitans homines[,] in proelia mittens[,]
Sevus [A]mor bellis et fuso sanguine gaudet[,]
Quem merito cecum fixit cordata vetustas[.]
Nulli etenim parcit[,] nullum puer iste veretur[:]
Mittit in incertum tristes sine lege sagittas
Ignicomasque faces[;] si [J]upiter obvius iret[,]
Figeret iste [J]ovem.

[E]t infra[:]

Sed ne te per multa vagans sermone fatigem[,]
Accipe quae nisi contempnas mandata. [S]enesces
liber agens dulcem sua sollicitudine vitam
Candida lascive cum videris ora puelle[;]

Et nam luctifici sunt vera [C]upidinis arma[.]
Illius a facie bellum tibi crede parari[.]
[F]lecte alio vultus[,] alio vestigia flecte[:]
Non secus ac trepidans conspecto cerva leone[,]
Non secus ac viso fugit angue viator inermis
Qui contra capud attollens sperasque resolvens
Sibilet accelerans sinuosum in pulvere gressum[.]
[F]eminea sub fronte latet genus omne malorum[:]
Inde dolor[,] cure[,] clamor[,] convicia[,] rixe[,]
Dedecus atque mine[,] labor et sine fine querele.
Mens vaga[,] blandicie ficte[,] mutabile pectus[,]
Os mendax[,] lachrime iusse[,] risusque dolique[,]
Et fuco picta facies[,] oculique procaces[,]
Composite fraudes . hec sunt mulieribus arma[.]
[F]emineum genus est nobis hoc utile tantum
Quod parit et partum nutrit . temptare recusa
Dum licet . hic fragilis quot habet fastidia sexus[.]
[F]emineum crudele genus[,] moderamina nescit[:]
Aut amat aut odit nimium. facilisque videri
femina si studeat[,] fiet lasciva procaxque[.]
Si gravis esse volet[,] si frontis amica severe[,] [fol. 35v]
[T]rux fiet . servare modum[,] cohibere furorem[,]
Et freno racionis agi[,] fedusque fidemque
Custodire velit si femina[,] nesciet[;] omne
Labitur in vicium semel ut pudor excidit . et quod
Non est ausa scelus mulier[?] quae crimina non sunt
Feminea tentata manu[?]

[E]t infra[:]

Nil magis est hominum quod possit vertere mentes[:]
Verba minus gramenque nocent[,] minus efficit hostis[,]
Tela minus fulmenque nocet[,] minus efficit ensis[,]
Saxa minus ledunt eris [i.e., imis?] quae impacta cavernis
Sulferis et clausi violencia proicit ignis[.]
Nec tantum est tenere segeti sus noxia nec tam
Dente caper viti . neque grandinis impetus uve
Quantum feminei venus insidiosa veneni
Mentibus infirmis iuven[i]um viridique iuvente[.]
Audisti ne viros plures inferna petisse
Tartara et ad patrios iterum rediisse penates[?]
Dic michi quae tristem mulier descendit ad [O]rchum
Et rediit.

[E]t infra[:]

Femineos fuge congressus[,] fuge rethia[,] pastor[.]
Si qua dee veniet dubia sub ymagine contra[,]
Esse negato deam[,] fallacem respice formam.

Sequitur in prosula / Que sequuntur in laudem [G]regorii [T]ipherni / viri utriusque lingue et omnium liberalium arcium supra omnes quos etas nostra habuit periti : preceptoris quondam mei [M]antue composui. [H]ic post peragrata [G]recie (quae tota tunc Christianorum erat)

[Y]talieque et [G]alliarum gimnasia [V]enecias [i.e., Venetiae?] concesserat scribendo et docendo reliquum vite sue tempus illic consumpturus : sed superis visum est aliter[.] [N]am antequam annum [V]eneciis complevisset[,] subita morte sublatus est. Morienti illi astabant Matheus [A]ntimachus [M]antuanus et Hadrianus [C]liniber [(]qui eamdem mecum religionem professus est[)] fidissimi eius discipuli[.] [I]n sanctorum [J]ohannis et [P]auli cimiterio sepultus est . In mortui locum successit Georgius [M]erula[,] doctissimus eius discipulus inter illustres gramaticos et rhetores annumerandus : qui nunc utramque linguam [V]eneciis (ut audio) florentissime tradit.

Et sequitur post multa[:] [fol. 36]

Noxia feminei fugito contagia sexus[,]
Nam cute sub moli[,] sub purpureoque colore
Bella latent.

[E]t infra[:]

Robore non animi[,] non ullis viribus aude[.]
Nulla tibi pugne dabitur victoria[;] tantum
Spem tibi pone fuga[,] [P]arthos imitare fugaces[.]

Et infra habetur de Helia [C]armeli principe[:]

Quid referas te[,] magne pater[,] quem flammea biga
Sublimen rapuit[,] quid te[,] sanctissime vatum[,]
Cui gemino sacros madefecit flumine crines[,]
Optimus immensi Jhesus moderator [O]limpi[,]
Femineas artes passi[?] cognoscitis ambo
Tincta gerat quanto mulier precordia felle[!]
Prode[,] precor[,] pater omnipotens[,] immite nocensque[,]
Prode[,] genus satis et dampni satis atque laborum
Intulit. [H]arpie sunt he quae ventre soluto
Proluvie fetida thalamos[,] cenacula[,] mensas[,]
Compita[,] templa[,] vias[,] agros[,] mare[,] flumina[,] colles[,]
Inficiunt. He sunt (verum si dicere fas est)
Gorgones extremis [L]ibie quae finibus olim
Aspectu vertisse viros in saxa feruntur[.]
Perde genus pater invisum[,] da [P]ersea nobis
Alligerum[,] [L]ycie da [B]ellorophonta [C]himere
Victorem[,] qui trans [T]auri iuga maxima transque
Caucaseas rupes abigant hec impia monstra.

Et infra prosaice / Sicut ultima vite pars tota in religionem solet esse conversa : ita [S]uburbanus meus in beatissime virginis [M]arie (a qua ordini meo peculiare cognomen est inditum) laudes exit et religiose terminatur.

Expliciunt extracta quedam notabilia a [L]ibro suburbani bucolicorum [B]aptiste [M]antuani. Quod totum transcripsit ex exemplari actoris magister Hadrianus de [E]chout / doctor Carmelita [B]ononiensis anno domini 1476°. [Q]uo eciam anno doctor [P]adue effectus est . et decanus theologorum in eadem alma universitate . [H]ic obiit [G]andani in conventu.

[Baptista Mantuanus published a book of verse, entitled *Suburbanus*, which he dedicated to Giovanni Battista Refrigerio. The proem begins:

You are content with your poor master's moderate dress and will go forth, my poor little book, with your breast unadorned. That person errs, whoever he may be, who by means of vain finery misrepresents his wealth. Our income should equal our expenses.

And further on:

Among many persons, Venus is of greater worth than the skills of Minerva, blind Love is valued more highly, Phoebus, than your lyre. On your trumpet you proclaim that nowhere does Augustan virtue survive, moreover that Crassus is ruined and Nero reigns supreme. No one weighs all matters equitably; everyone approves not what is good but what is convenient. [11] Having been spurned, virtue flees and lust rules in her place. Both men and women rush headlong into this vice.

Afterwards Mantuan addresses his book:

Go auspiciously, my first offspring of tender youth. Go auspiciously, page privy to my thoughts. Go, I pray you; go auspiciously, I pray that you depart under a lucky omen. Poor little book, shelter [my?] first offerings. May the stars be well disposed towards you, may the gods be propitious to you and may they grant, I pray, that you be read by many ages to come.

And further on:

What I now publish came forth six feet at a time. Much remains that was written in unequal waves [i.e., in elegiac verse]. [21] My Elegy keeps many pages of verse close to her bosom and skillfully conceals her delights. She herself will yield up her riches ungrudgingly when she knows how she can please her author. Meanwhile read over these unhappy poems that console the emotions while the noble product of my expectation continues to grow.

The argument of *Suburbanus*—or rather of the fragment—begins:

Faustus and Fortunatus—shepherds both, both of graver years—neared the same fields. They recounted the deeds of their youth, the truth having been left at home. . . .

Faustus and Fortunatus are speakers in *Suburbanus*.

Mantuan goes on, in prose: a more sensible mind's knowledge of love's madness is the argument of the eclogue.

And further on: I would not publish these childish pieces if they were not already widely spread abroad and if I didn't know that they are being read as having been written by me.

And further on, in verse:

[30] Would that I might teach you that nothing is more harmful than Venus' flames. Alas, it is a deadly pestilence, a harsh and cruel poison. Ravaging mortal breasts with its deadly flames, driving men into a frenzy and sending them into battle, intemperate Love delights in war and spilled blood. With good cause judicious antiquity represented him as blind. For that boy spares or fears no one. He lets fly his grim darts and fieryhaired brands indefinitely and without order. If Jupiter opposed him, that boy would pierce him with his arrows.

And further on:

[40] But lest by wandering on in lengthy discourse I weary you, hear (unless you scorn them) my injunctions. You grow weak, idly living a life agreeable in its anxiety, when you have viewed the fair countenance of a wanton girl. And to be sure her looks are the true weapons of doleful Cupid. Believe that her beauty is preparing war against you. Turn your face and your step in another direction: just as a deer flees, trembling at the lion he has seen, or as an unarmed traveler flees when he has seen a snake that, raising its head and uncoiling itself opposite him, hisses while hastening its sinuous pace through the dust. [51] Behind a woman's countenance lurks every kind of evil: thence spring anguish, care, shouting, insults, and brawls; thence arise shame and threats, toil and endless complaining. Wandering thoughts, feigned blandishments, a changeable heart, false words, forced tears, deceitful laughter; a painted face and wanton eyes; carefully planned deception—these are a woman's weapons! The female race is useful to us only in this: that they bear children and rear them. While you are able, don't put to the test how much scorn this brittle sex possesses. [61] A woman is cruel, she knows no self–control: she either hates you or loves you too much. Should she try to seem open, she becomes wanton and skittish. Should she wish to be serious, a friend of severe mien, she becomes pitiless. Should a woman wish to observe due measure and control her emotions, to be guided by reason and keep her agreements and promises, she would be ignorant of how to do so. Once her sense of shame has been lost, she lapses wholly into vice. What crimes have not been attempted by the hands of women?

And further on:

[71] There is nothing greater that can subvert the minds of men. Words and grasses are less harmful, the sword less effective. Less injurious are rocks that, having become wedged [deep?] within holes in the earth, are hurled skyward by the violence of pent up sulphurous fires. A sow is not as harmful to a tender crop, a goat's tooth to the vine or a hailstorm to the vineyards as the treacherous love of a woman's poison is to the immature thoughts of young men and the first flower of youth. [80] You have heard of many men who have sought out infernal Tartarus and returned to their ancestoral homes? Tell me, what woman ever descended into gloomy Orcus' realm and returned.

And further on:

Shepherd, flee the company of women, flee their snares. Should some girl, in the doubtful likeness of a goddess, come face to face with you, deny that she is a goddess and take heed of her deceptive form.

Mantuan continues in a brief passage of prose:

What follows I wrote in praise of Gregorio Tifernate, a man expert above all others of our generation in both Greek and Latin and in all the liberal arts, and at one time my teacher at Mantua. After travelling through Greece (which was then wholly in Christian hands) and Italy and traversing the schools of France, he retired to Venice to spend the rest of his life writing and teaching there. But the matter seemed otherwise to the gods above. For after he had lived a year at Venice, he suddenly died. At his side when he was dying were his very loyal students Matheus Antimachus of Mantua and Hadrianus Ciniber, who entered the same religious order with me. He was interred in the cemetery of SS John and Paul. After he died, Giorgio Merula moved up into his place. A very learned pupil of Gregorio's to be counted among famous grammarians and rhetoricians, Merula now (as I hear) teaches both Greek and Latin with great repute at Venice.

And after many things Mantuan continues:

Flee the harmful infection of the female sex, for beneath their soft skin and radiant complexion women conceal their warfare.

And further on:

[90] Do not rely on the strength of your thoughts or on any other strength. No victory in battle will be granted to you. Only put your hope in flight. Imitate the fleeing Parthians.

And later on, Mantuan contends, concerning Elijah, our founder on Mount Carmel:

Oh, mighty father whom a fiery chariot raised on high, and you, most sacred of the prophets, for whom Jesus steeped his holy locks in the twofold river (Jesus the most high, the ruler of mighty Olympus)—why do you report that you endured the wiles of women? Because both of you found that women have hearts tainted with so much bile! [99] Come forth, almighty Father, come forth, I pray you! This cruel and harmful sex has caused enough deprivation and toil. They are harpies that loosening their bowels, taint with a foul–smelling flood bedchambers, dining rooms, banqueting tables, crossroads, churches, highways, fields, seas, rivers, and mountains. They are (if I might speak truly) Medusas: Medusa who once in far–off Lybian lands is said to have turned men to stone by her glance. Destroy, oh Father, this hateful race! Grant us a Persius, grant us a winged Bellerophon, conquorer of the Lycian Chimera: a Persius and Bellerophon to drive those impious monsters over the highest Taurian ridges and over Caucesian crags.

And later on, in prose:

As the most recent part of my life is usually directed wholly to a life of devotion, so my *Suburbanus* is terminated and piously concluded in praise of the most blessed virgin Mary, by whom the title particular to my religious order was conferred.

Thus conclude certain notable extracts from Baptista Mantuanus' *Book of the Rustic's Eclogues*. Adrien van Eckhoute, a Carmelite doctor from Bologna, made a complete transcription of this book from the author's copy in 1476. Furthermore, in the same year he received his doctorate at Padua and became dean of theologians at the university there. He died in the convent at Ghent.]

Reverendo in Christo patri ac Domino Falconi Sinibaldo
protonotario ac Thesaurario apostolico/
Frater Baptista Mantuanus Carmelita salutem ac foelicitatem dicit.

Scio te hominem propter excellentes animi tui virtutes accuratissimum lectionibus indigere que recreare et honestam possint asservare voluptatem. Ingenia enim nostra ut cultellorum acies exercitio retunduntur : et opus est ea sicut cultellos cote / iocis et salibus exacuere. Hoc precipue videtur anni principio id est sacratissimae domini nostri Jesu Christi nativitati convenire. Erant namque maioribus nostris celeberrimi dies Natales : Et in anni principio reintegrande charitatis et reconciliande amicitae gratia depositis curis hilarius vivebant. iocis indulgebant. munuscula mittebant. quod equidem et in hominibus christianis laudaverim modo nulla pars careat officio. Huius igitur naturam temporis admonitus Æglogam quam egrotans meditatus sum Tibi dono / dico / et mitto Ut sit / pro anni principio xenium / pro mea servitute tributum / curarum tuarum medicamentum / et apud dominatum tuum nostri memoriale[.] Vale[.]

Fratris Baptistae Mantuani Carmelite
ad Dominum Falconem Sinibaldum ægloga.

Collocutores Candidus et Faustulus. Candidus autoris personam gerit. Conqueritur sibi et gregi non esse prosperam fortunam in Latio.

FAUSTULUS
Candide quo casu patriis procul actus ab oris
Hec in rura venis? hic pascua nulla nec amnes.
Nec liquidi fontes nec ovilia tuta nec umbre.
Et tamen assiduos gregis hec pascuntur in usus.
CANDIDUS
Faustule me noster Corydon qui plurima quondam
His armenta locis habuit : magnamque peculi
Congeriem fecit : pecori me credere adegit
Esse salutares istis in montibus erbas.
At postquam segnes agros et inertia saxa
Vidimus : et siccis arentem fontibus oram[*undam*][,]
Poenituit. longeque viae patrieque relictae.
FAUSTULUS [fol. 118]
Postquam te incolumem saltus intrare latinos
Contigit. antiqui potes hec mea tecta subire
Iure sodalitii. sunt hic mihi pauperis agri
Iugera pauca mee vix sufficientia vitae[,]
Quidquid id est comune puta[.] tibi forsitan ulla
Prospera sors aderit. Fortuna simillima vento est.
Cariceae succede casae dum preterit aestus.
Dum grex in gelida procumbens ruminat umbra[*herba*][.]
Pone pedum ut mihi sit tecum / cape pocula / sermo[.]
CANDIDUS
Pocula quis tanta demens aestate recuset?
FAUSTULUS
Vina sitim minuunt : animique doloribus obstant.
CANDIDUS
Vina sitim minuere : manet moerorque dolorque.
Non madet imbre dies. nec habet nox humida rorem
Crescere nec duris possunt in cotibus erbae.
Importuna fames / Labor improbus / aeris ardor
Confecere gregem macie[.] vix debile corpus
Spiritus eger agit : vacua cute porrigit ossa
Clunis et exilis cava contrahit ilia venter.
Hic aries qui fronte lupos cornuque petebat
Nunc ove debilior pavidoque fugacior agno est.
Hec mihi / sed mea tunc nimium me vota ferebant
Prescia non dubio predixerat omine cornix.
Vix egressus eram limen quom vocibus illa
Ter quater expressis tecti de culmine nobis
Infaustum garribat iter casusque sinistros. [fol. 118v]
Heu[,] heu[,] grex qui prolis eras et lactis habundans
Dum patrie licuit pingues decerpere campos[.]
Gramina dum queris : succi plus perdis eundo

Quam pastu referas. miserum tabescit in horas.
Paupertate pecus[,] pre sollicitudine pastor.
[FAUSTULUS]
O nostre regionis opes[,] o florida prata
O campi virides[,] o pascua leta feraxque
Et numquam sine fruge solum. currentia passim
Flumina labuntur / rivi per rura / per ortos.
Hinc pecus[,] hinc tellus pinguis[;] sub sydere cancri
Arva virent[,] texte lento de vimine sepes
Poma ferunt[,] redolent incluse sepibus erbe[:]
Hysopi[,] mentheque[,] come roris marini[,]
Acer Thimum / serpilla / rose / crinesque marathri[.]
Hinc coryli[,] crispeque nuces[,] et amigdala crescunt[,]
Cornaque[,] et ex humili nascentia stirpite fraga[.]
[CANDIDUS]
O[,] nemorum dulces umbre mollesque susurri
Quos tecum memini gelidis carpsisse[*traxisse*] sub umbris
Turturis ad gemitus argute ad carmina prognes.
Aura strepens nemorum foliis veniebat ab euro[.]
Rivus agens tenues sonitu[*cursu*] applaudebat arenas[.]
Illic multa cave formam testudinis arbor
Fecerat et densis arcebat frondibus aestum[,]
Terraque sub ramis semper frigebat opacis.
FAUSTULUS
Vivere tum foelix poteras diuque beatus[;]
Sed quia non fueras sortem perpessus iniquam[,]
Prospera nescivit tecum fortuna manere[.] [fol. 119]
Quando iterum veniet[,] si forsitan unquam[,]
Sicut capreolis vites serpentibus herent
Atque suas crebris retinent complexibus ulmos[,]
Sic illam tu stringe manu nec desere coeptam [i. e., captam?].
CANDIDUS
Delitias patrii quoties reminiscimur agri
Ferre tot erumpnas animo non possumus aequo[.]
Sed quo mente feror? casu afflictatus amaro
Unde magis crucier foelicia tempora volvo[?]
Maius adest. florent vites humilesque geniste[;]
Iam spicata seges[*ceres*][,] malus iam punica multo
Flore rubet[,] redolent sepes albente sabuco[.]
Hii vero nec dum incipiunt pubescere montes[.]
Quod si vere solum torpet : quid frigora brume
Solstitiumque feret? gelidas quom terra pruinis
Albicat et rapido quom coelum incantuit estu?
Sunt tamen hic armenta quibus cutis uvida / cervix
Non signata iugis / gemino frons ardua cornu
Luxuriansque toris pectus[;] nisi pabula carpant :
Non fuerit tanta gravidum pinguedine tergus.
FAUSTULUS
Hec armenta quibus caput a tellure levatur
Cuncta vorant[:] erbas primum[,] mox ore supino
Arboreas frondes[,] tenereque cacumina silve[.]
Hoc imbelle pecus quod humi nascentia tantum
Gramina decerpit : vacuis ieiunat in arvis.

CANDIDUS [fol. 119v]
Quid verbis opus est? cunctis animantibus una est
Condicio : semper maiora minoribus obsunt[*obstant*][.]
Agna lupo[,] mites aquilae sunt preda columbe[,]
Innocuos delphin venatur in aequore pisces.
Unde fit? hec certe res prodigiosa videtur.
Hec loca[,] si procul hinc videas e rupibus altis[,]
Pingue solum et multo vestitum gramine dicas.
Quo magis approprias[*appropriant*] : tanto magis omnia sordent.
FAUSTULUS
Hoc est Roma viris : avibus quod noctua. visco
Capta perit. si quae laqueos evadere possunt :
Attonite fugiunt. et nota pericula vitant.
CANDIDUS
Ecce[!] procul coluber tortos in pulvere gressus
Flectit et exertis sitiens ferit aera linguis[.]
FAUSTULUS
Candide que moneo memori sub pectore serva[.]
Quando rubos inter graderis[,] defende galero
Lumina. Nam dure pretendunt lumina[*spicula*] sentes.
Nec depone pedum[,] multaque armare memento
Cote sinum[,] ne te subito novus opprimat hostis[.]
Et perone pedem vesti : spineta colubris
Plena ferunt gelidam furtivo vulnere mortem[,]
Et nunc longa dies aestu facit acre venenum.
Mille lupi / totidem vulpes in vallibus istis.
Nec solum in tenebris sed aperta in luce vagantur
Insidiasque parant[;] et quod mirabile dictu est :
Se in formas hominum vertunt humanaque sumunt [fol. 120]
Ora[.] sed his longe graviora pericula dicam[:]
Ipse : homines (huius tanta est violentia coeli)
Saepe lupi effigiem moresque assumere vidi
Inque suum servire gregem multaque madere
Cede sui pecoris[;] factum vicinia ridet
Nec scelus exhorret : nec talibus obviat ausis[.]
Saepe canes tantam in rabiem vertuntur : ut ipsos
Vincant cede lupos / et qui tutela fuerunt
Hostiles ineunt[*induant* (sic)] animos et ovilia mactant[.]
Saepe etiam morbosa estas et pestifer annus
Ingruit : et passim languens pecus omne per arva[*agros*]
Sternitur[;] extincte dum balat ad ubera matris
Agnus obit : moritur sub duro vomere Taurus.
Et gemit in nuda moriens tellure iuvencus[.]
Nec modus est morbo. non est medicina veneno.
Sed vicina domus vicino a limine mortem
Accipit : infecte spargunt contagia caulae[.]
CANDIDUS
Heu[,] heu[,] quo preceps miserum me insania traxit[?]
Credere fallaci gravis est dementia fame[.]
Romuleos colles / tiberim romanaque tecta[,]
Auratasque trabes[,] solidoque ex aere columpnas[,]
Atque peregrino vivos in marmore vultus

Audieram et studio mens est accensa videndi
Ducendique bonis in tot prestantibus evum[.]
Propterea sedem pecori ratus esse quietam[,]
Accessi cum parte gregis[.] tentoria demens
Integrumque larem cum pastoralibus armis
Trans iuga summa tuli[;] sed iam sperata negantur [fol. 120v]
Pabula[,] circumstant recitata[*memorata*] pericula : cogor
In veteres remeare casas et coepta fateri
Consiliis exorta malis iterumque per aestus
Et montana pati duros per saxa labores[.]
Heu pecus infoelix / o[*heu*] / levo sidere pastor
Huc avecte : fuit multo praestantius istud
Ignorasse solum : patrioque in limine tutos
Consumpsisse dies. placidis quievisse[*sedisse*] sub antris[,]
Atque padi circum ripas athesisve[*atesisque*] per agros
Aut ubi per virides campos et pascua laeta
Mincius it. vel qua vitreo natat abdua cursu[*tergo*]
Et gregis et propriae curam tenuisse salutis.
FAUSTULUS
Te tua credulitas[,] et me mea fallit in horas[.]
Vidi ego suppreme qui prosperitatis habebant
Culmina dum laudata petunt : cecidisse. nec unquam
Emersisse malis : quos experientia cautos
Reddidit : explorant / et non laudata sequuntur
Pascua : laude carent que sunt meliora[.] fuerunt
Que celebrem famam retinent. sic luna vetusque
Adria nomen habuent clarum. nam saepius istas
Carminibus nobis laudabat tytyrus urbes
Tuque etiam meminisse potes[;] sed nomina praeter
Nil superest. Patriae minor est modo gloria meae[,]
Res melior. famae tenet immortalis honorem
Roma : sed utilitas iam pridem antiqua recessit[.]
Ipsi prisca quibus maduerunt pascua fontes
Nunc umore carent[,] Tiberis non irrigat agros[,] [fol. 121]
Nulla pluit nubes : est interceptus aquarum
Cursus. et exusto gemit arida gramine tellus.
Tempus aqueductus veteres contrivit / et arcus
Longa dies minuit. procul hinc[,] procul ite capelle[.]
Hic ieiuna fames. et languida regnat egestas.
Hic tamen [(]ut fama est : et nos quoque vidimus ipsi[)]
Pastor adest : quadam ducens ex alite nomen[,]
Lanigeri pecoris dives[*custos*] / Ditissimus agri[,]
Carmine qui priscos vates atque orphea vincat
Orphea qui traxit sylvas et saxa canendo[.]
Hic alios omni tantum virtute latinos
Exuperat / quantum Tyberim padus[,] Anser anatem[,]
Lenta salix iuncum[,] tribulos rosa[,] populus algam[.]
Credimus hunc illi similem cui Tytyrus olim
Bissenos fumare dies altaria fecit[.]
Hic ovium custos ipso vigilantior argo
Daphnide nec[*non*] solum sed eo[*illo*] qui dicitur olim
Admeti pavisse boves per thessala rura
Doctior : innumeras solymi curare magistri

Dignus oves. dignus magno succedere patri
Qui fuit Assyrii pecoris post retia pastor.
Ipse[*iste*] potest servare gregem / depellere morbos /
Humectare solum / dare pascua / solvere fontes /
Conciliare Iovem / fures arcere luposque.
Si favet iste : mane. Quod si negat iste favorem :
Candide : coge pecus melioraque pascua quere.

[To Reverend Father in Christ and my Most Esteemed Lord
Falcone de' Sinibaldi, Protonotary and Papal Treasurer,
Baptista Mantuanus, Carmelite, Wishes Health and Happiness.

I am aware that, as a man of meticulous tastes due to your outstanding intellectual abilities, you require reading matter that is able to revive the spirits and preserve honorable pleasure. For like a knife's edge, our mental powers are dulled by exercise, and they need jests and quips, just as a knife needs the whetstone. This seems especially befitting at the beginning of the year, that is, at the most holy nativity of our Lord Jesus Christ. For among our ancestors birthdays were very festive occasions. And to restore charity and reestablish friendship at the beginning of the year, they lived more merrily, having put aside their cares, and they indulged in jests and sent presents—all of which I should also praise in Christian men, provided that there be no dereliction of one's obligations. Prompted therefore by the nature of the season, I am dedicating and sending as a gift to you this eclogue which I composed when I was ill, so that it might be a new year's present, a tribute to my indebtedness to you, a balm for your cares, and a memorial of me with your lordship. Farewell.

**An Eclogue by Baptista Mantuanus, Carmelite,
Dedicated to my Lord Falcone de' Sinibaldi.**

Candidus and Faustulus are the speakers. Candidus stands for the author. He laments that he and his flock are not favored by fortune in Latium.

Faustulus By what misfortune, Candidus, driven far from your fathers' lands, have you come into these fields? Here are no pasturelands or rivers, no clear springs, secure sheepfolds, or shade. Yet flocks constantly pasture in these lands.

Candidus Corydon, our fellow—who once kept many herds in this region and heaped up his savings—led me, Faustulus, to believe that the grass in those hills there would be wholesome for my flock. But after I saw the listless fields, lifeless stones, and dried-up springs, I regretted my long journey and leaving my homeland behind me.

Faustulus [12] Since it has befallen you to enter safe and sound into these Latin groves, by the right of our fellowship of old, you may enter my house here. My few acres of poor land yield me barely enough for my living. Yet such as it is, consider it yours. Perhaps some favorable destiny will befall you: Dame Fortune is much like the wind. Enter my hut of reeds until the heat of the day has passed, while the cattle, sunk down within the cool shade, are chewing their cud. Lay aside your sheephook—and have a drink—so that we can talk.

Candidus Crazed by so much heat, what man would refuse?

Faustulus [22] Wine lessens thirst and shields us from painful thoughts.

Candidus Wine lessens thirst, but sadness and pain both remain. The days here are not drenched by rain, damp night has no dew, nor can grass grow among the hard stones. Relentless famine, ceaseless toil, and the heat of the air have all wasted my flock. Their diseased breath scarce causes their weakened frames to move. Their haunch bones stick out, and meager bellies contract their hollow entrails. Here's a ram that used to attack wolves with his forehead and horns. Now he is weaker than a ewe and more apt to flee than a fearful lamb. All this (but at that time I was carried away too much by my burning desires) a prescient crow foretold by a sure sign. [34] I had scarce stepped from my door when from a rooftop it spoke repeatedly in its cawing of my ill–starred journey and baleful misfortunes. Alas, alas, my flock that used to abound in offspring and milk when you were allowed to pasture in the rich fields of our homeland. While you are looking for grass, you lose more vigor in journeying than you gain in pasturage. From hour to hour we are wretchedly wasting away: the flock oppressed through want, their shepherd through worry.

Faustulus [42] Ah, the wealth of that land of ours! its flowery meadows and green fields! its pastures rich and fertile and its soil forever fruitful! Its rivers flow, running here and there, throughout the land; channels flow through fields and gardens! On this side flocks, on that side rich earth. Under the sign of Cancer the fields are green, hedges woven of pliant branches support their burden of fruit, and wild herbs enclosed within the hedgerows diffuse their fragrance: shoots of hyssop, mint, and rosemary; pungent thyme, wild thyme, roses, and fennel's feathery foliage. On this side grow hazel, walnut, almond, and cornel trees, and wild strawberries are springing from their lowly stems.

Candidus [53] Ah, the sweet shade and soft murmuring of the groves! I remember gathering the delights of these with you in the cool shade close by the turtledove's sighs and the songs of the whistling swallow. A breeze, rustling among the leaves in the groves, came from the east. Carrying along scattered grains of sand, a stream rippled in its channel. Over there, a large tree had shaped itself in the form of a hollow tortoise shell. With its dense foliage, it drove off the heat, and the ground underneath its shady branches was always cool.

Faustulus [61] You were able to live as a man who enjoyed good fortune then and had been blessed for a long time. But because you had not experienced bad luck to the full, good fortune was unwilling to remain with you. When she comes again (if by chance she ever returns), as vines cling with their twisting tendrils to elm trees and hold them fast in their numerous embraces, just so bind her fast with your hand and, once you have seized her, don't let her go.

Candidus [68] Whenever I remember the delights of my fathers' fields, I am unable to endure so many troubles with a composed mind. But where are my thoughts bearing me? Struck down by bitter misfortune, why, to torment myself further, am I pondering happier times? May has come. The vine and lowly broom are blooming there. The fields having already bristled with wheat, the pomegranates are red with flowers and the hedges are fragrant with blossoming elder. But the hills here have not yet begun to put on their foliage. If in spring the soil here is languid, what will winter's cold or the summer solstice bring, seasons when the earth is white with icy hoarfrost or the sky glows with consuming heat? Yet here there are herds with sleek coats and necks unmarked by the yoke, cattle whose foreheads are lofty with twin horns and whose breasts ripple with muscle. If they didn't graze on good fodder, their backs would not be heavy with so much fat.

Faustulus [83] These cattle, their heads raised high off the ground, devour everything: first the grass, then, their mouths uplifted, the leaves and tops of the tender trees. And this peace–loving herd here, who crop only the grasses growing on the ground, is left to fast in barren fields.

Candidus But why speak more of such things? For all living creatures the condition is the same: the larger ones always harm the smaller ones. Lambs are the wolf's prey, gentle doves are the eagle's booty. In the sea the dolphin hunts the harmless fishes. And how does this come about? (Indeed, this seems a monstrous thing.) If you viewed this place at a distance from some high cliff, you might call it rich land thickly arrayed with grass. But the nearer you approach it, the baser everything becomes.

Faustulus [96] Rome is among men what the owl is among birds. Caught in birdlime, a bird dies. And if any are able to evade her snares, stupified they flee and shun the dangers they know by experience.

Candidus But look! over there a serpent is making its winding way through the dust and in its thirst smites the air with its outstretched tongue.

Faustulus [101] Candidus, keep the warnings I am giving you, holding them close within your thoughts. When you walk among brambles, protect your eyes with a hat: for the briars stretch forth pitilessly towards your eyes. Don't put down your sheephook; and remember to arm your pockets with many stones lest some new enemy suddenly take you by surprise. Put boots on your feet: thorn hedges filled with serpents bring chill death by their secret wound, and now the heat of the long days makes their venom keen. A thousand wolves and as many foxes dwell in those valleys there. Not only within the shadows but in broad daylight they roam about and prepare their ambushes. And (what's wondrous to tell) they transform themselves into the shapes of men and take on human features. But let me speak of dangers far graver than these. I myself have often seen men (so violent is this region) often assume the shape and ways of a wolf and rage among their own flocks, drenching themselves with the slaughter of their sheep. Their neighbors laugh at what is done, neither trembling at the crime nor preventing such bold acts. [117] Often dogs are transformed by so great a rage that they better even the wolves in slaughter, and those who were guardians take on a hostile intent and kill their own flocks in the sheepfold. Moreover, the heat of the year's pestilential season often strikes, and the entire flock is laid low, sickening here and there throughout the fields. The lamb, while it bleats near the udders of its dead mother, is dying, the bull perishes under its hard burden, and the calf groans, dying on the bare earth. Nor is there a limit to the disease nor an antidote against the poison. A house receives death from its neighbor, and infected sheepfolds spread the infection.

Candidus [130] Alas, whither has this madness drawn me headlong in my wretchedness? Grave madness it is to trust deceptive rumors. I had heard about Romulus' hills, the Tiber, and the roofs of Rome, about the gilded beams, columns of solid bronze, and lifelike faces carved from foreign marble, and my mind burned with zeal to see and lead my life among things excellent in so many ways. [137] Therefore, having reckoned the site to be a peaceful one for the sheep, I drew near with part of my flock. In my madness over mountain ridges I bore my tents and all my household goods along with the tools of my shepherd's trade. But now I am denied pastures I hoped for, and all around are the dangers you have described to me. To my huts of old am I forced to return, to confess that my venture arose from bad counsel, and once again in the heat and among the rocks in the mountains must I endure a life of hard toil. Alas, unfortunate flock! Oh, shepherd borne hither by an unlucky star! More excellent far were it not to have known of this land; better to have passed my days securely in my father's house; better to have rested from toil within peaceful caves; and on the banks of the Po or in the Adige's fields or where the Mincio glides among green plains and luxuriant pasturelands, or where the Adda floats along in its glassy course, better far were it to have kept my mind on attending to my flock and my own well-being.

Faustulus [153] Your credulity deceives you and mine deceives me from hour to hour. I myself have seen men who used to dwell on fortune's peak fall when they sought things of praise and never rise from their troubles—experience has made these men cautious. They investigate and seek out unpraised pasturelands: for those things that are better are wanting in praise. There were cities that preserve a distinguished reputation. Thus Luna and old Hadria had famous names, for Tityrus quite often used to praise those cities in his songs, and you too even now are able to remember them. But beyond their names nothing remains of them. Only my homeland's glory is less; in reality, it is a better place than they are. Rome has the honor of immortal fame, but her former usefulness has long since passed away. [166] Those very springs by which the ancient pastures used to be moistened now lack water; the Tiber does not irrigate the fields; clouds pour down none of their rain; the flow of the rainwater has been diverted, and the parched earth groans, its grasses burnt dry. Time has worn down the old aqueducts, and the arches have been reduced to fragments by the long lapse of time. Hence, you goats, get you hence. Here reign lean famine and dull poverty!

[173] And yet here (for such is the rumor, and I have seen him myself) there is present a shepherd to help us, a shpeherd who takes his name from a certain bird, a man rich in woolbearing flocks, most rich in land, a man who might overcome in song the bards of old and even Orpheus—Orpheus who drew the trees and rocks when he sang. This man exceeds other Latians in every virtue as much as the Po exceeds the Tiber or a goose a duck, the pliant willow the rush, the rose the thorn, or the poplar seaweed in the ocean. I think this man to be like him in whose honor Tityrus once long ago caused an altar to smoke twice six days. [184] This guardian of the flock is more vigliant than Argus himself, more skilled not only than Daphnis but him who is said once to have pastured Admetus' cattle in the fields of Thessaly; worthy to watch over the countless sheep for that master from Jerusalem and worthy to succeed that father, great of spirit, who, forsaking his nets, was shepherd of the Assyrian flock. This man has the power to protect the flock, dispel sickness, moisten the ground, bestow pasturelands, release springs, appease Jupiter, and keep away thieves and wolves. If he smiles with favor, stay. But if he denies his favor, drive forth your flock, Candidus, and seek greener pastures.]

Fratris Baptiste mantuani Carmelite
ad clarissimum ac regalis magnificentie virum
dominum Bernardum Bembum
Venetorum ad Innocentum VIII summum pontificem Oratorem :
Egloga

Candidus auctor est : Batrachus partes eorum tuetur qui integritatem antique vite conantur observarare : Myrmix vero defensor est eorum / qui maiori cum licentia vivunt. Bembus arbiter est :

Cand: Maxima pastores agitat discordia[,] Bembe[,] [fol. 171]
Pascere qui Solymos colles et pinguia letae
Littora Phoenicis[i.e., Phoenices][,] galilaeaque rura colebant.
Batrachus hinc[,] Myrmix illinc certare parati
Iudice te paucis (si non audire recusas
Et nisi te revocant maiora negocia) dicent.
Tu pacare nos[,] Tu scis componere lites :
Te quoque pierios fama est potasse liquores :
Et videsse deas / quibus est custodia sacri
Fontes : et Eurotae campos et phocidis arva :
Et lauro cinxisse comas : Phebique tulisse
Munera[,] vocales citharas et eburnea plectra[.]
Bemb: Dicite[,] quandoquidem tepidos admovit ad ignes
Nos hyberna dies : Dum non sinit ire per agros
Bruma gregem : flatu Boreas dum sevit acuto[,]
Dum riget omne solum : tectis dum plurima pendet
Stiria. dum torpent undis glacialibus amnes.
Ocia damnantur quae nulla negocia tractant[.]
Myr: Pastores genus infelix : aestate vagamur
Pro grege solliciti : sed cum nos frigidus imber
Continet in stabulis / lites et iugria surgunt.
Batr: Qui veteres audent ritus mutare : suoque
Arbitrio nullis ducunt sub legibus aevum[,]
Hi[,] fateor[,] rixas et bella domestica gignunt.

Bemb: De veteri ritu / de consuetudine patrum [fol. 171v]
Lis igitur vobis? Patres meresque[i.e., moresque] paternos
Batrache dic. et cur nostrum venistis in orbem.
Nonne ferax propriaque madens uligine tellus?
Nonne Laurus illic? gelidisque e fontibus amnes?
Batr: Bembe[,] genus nostrum generisque exordia paucis
Accipe. Nos genuit primum Helios [i.e., Helias] : Helion[,] inquam[,]
Qui postquam patrios implevit ovilibus agros[,]
Dicitur ardenti translatum in aetera curru.
Hic ovium primus custos : hic tradidit artem
Qua curare greges : qua noxia pabula fas est
Discere : et occultos imbres ventosque latentes
Quique salutaris foret / et qui pestifer annus
Signa dedit : Summo Carmeli in vertice montis
Fons vetreis[i.e.,vitreas] emanat aquas : Modo currit in austrum[,]
Sed prius (extat adhuc vetus alveus) ibat ad eurum[.]
Hi cursus fecere alios : liquere priores[.]
Myr: Quid tibi sive novo currat seu tramite prisco
Dummodo per campos fluat uberioribus undis?
Et quid de caeli querimur regione? per austrum
Solis iter[,] melior vitis quae respicit austrum :
Et legitur melior libycis de vitibus uva[.]
Batr: Pastor es. et cura pecoris malesane relicta
Sermonem de vite facis : quasi legibus hisdem
Grex et vitis eant : quod sit discrimen in undis [fol. 172]
Graminibusque miser nescis : Precepta parentum
Temnis : et errorem vis tali ambage tueri.
Bembe[,] mihi tecum sermo est : Dum viximus una
Dum commune pecus nobis fuit : hei mihi quantum
Dedecus : heu quot sunt pecudes incommoda passae[!]
Nec mersare gregem fluvio : nec velera certis
Temporibus (sicut mos est) tondere licebat.
Nudabant spineta pecus : nudata secabat
Terga rubi : Scabie cutis aspera : Tabidus humor
Pestis : et in totum serpebant ulcera corpus.
His animadversis egre tot damna ferentes
Venimus ad fontem : rivumque a vertice summo
Scrutari mihi cura fuit : Tu[,] provide Myrmix[,]
Interea nidos avium vel dorcada parvam
Venabare : tue que dona darentur Asile.
Alveus excelsa labens de rupe Lacunam
Fecerat : et ripis gyrum facientibus undam
Saltus obumbrabat[,] Silveque annosa vetuste
Brachia frondoso prohibebant tegmine solem.
Mille venenorum species in gurgite vidi :
Mille secus ripas in opaco margine : mille
Per nemus ad silvas sinuoso serpere gressu[.]
Obstipui[,] et rapido rediens ad ovilia cursu
Incipio paleas furca versare tricorni[.] [fol. 172v]
Ecce[!] caput tollit Coluber : linguaque minaci
Sibilat[,] inflantur fauces : Nepa livida tendit
Cornua : ventrosus profert vestigia bufo.
Vipera per stipulam gradiens strepit / [']o / loca[',] dixi[,]

[']Non pecori tantum / verum et pastoribus ipsis
Noxia['] : mox grege diviso de gregibus illis
Pascua quesitum tristis meliora recessi :
Perque iter antiquum fontis nova flumina duxi
In campos : ubi prima suos Aurora colores
Explicat : et croceos [P]hoebi nascentis ad ortus[.]
Hic mihi phoecunde pecudes / hic pabula loeta[i.e., laeta] :
Et sine labe liquor : dulces sine crimine lymphe[.]
Hec loca primevi patres coluere : supersunt
Signa case veteris[,] puteus cariosaque ligna
Fixa solo seiuncta pedum discrimine septem
Et focus et lacera quae cingitur area sepe[.]
Myr: Cura viris levibus rerum solet esse novarum[;]
Propterea certe nova pascua quaeris / et amnes
Fingis inauditos / et vis novus auctor haberi[.]
Batr: Hec novitas[,] Myrmix[,] est instaurata vetustas
Quam tua currupit veritas : et nota tuorum
Segnities. Igitur siquis labentia tecta
Erigat : et sterilem qui mansuefecerit agrum
Iudice te damnandus erit? Non ponitur arbor [fol. 173]
Altera / sed veteri inseritur bona virgula trunco[;]
Segne prius lignum nostro fit fertile cultu[.]
Myr: Quamvis pingue tuo pecori sit gramen : et unda
Defecata : tamen multe cum matribus agne
Interiere : Lupi et paste meminere volucres.
Batr: He[,] fateor[,] que dira tue Contagia pestis
Aspiciunt : etiam procul aspicientibus obsunt.
Propterea magis atque magis discedere semper
Est animus nobis : ipsumque ascendere montem
Atque viam cursumque tuo restringere zino [zelo?] .
Ut loca consumptum pecus in meliora reducas.
Myr: De grege multa meo soli tibi cognita narras :
Cur mihi / qui pasco cuium pecus / ista tueri
Non licuit? solis ne domus mea cognita vobis?
Batr: Aethiopes una quoniam nigredine sordent[,]
Ille color nulli vitio datur : omnibus idem
Vultus : et alterius siquis reprenderet ora[,]
Et sua damnaret : pecori pecorisque magistro
Fex eadem : scabies eadem : cutis et color idem.
Bemb: Parcite[;] iam satis lis est intellecta : diesque
Inclinata cadet[i.e., cadit]. litem sententia claudat.
Myr: Batrache, me audaci tociens sermone lacessis[!]
Bemb: Parcite : Iam satis est : et me patientius audi[.]
Ferte per antiquos primum vestigia gressus : [fol. 173v]
Et veteres servate vias : Laudata parentum
Pascua / laudati fontes : pinguissimus illis
Caseus / et lane que vellera serica vincunt[.]
Illis semper erat (seu nix seu stringent aestus[)]
Lac niveum : semper spumabant Cymbia : semper
Et foetura recens et plena sub ubere mulctra.
Cura vigil[,] solers studium defendere multum
Res divina magis pecudes et minima possunt.

Crebrius antiqui superos in vota vocabant
Sacraque reddebant maioribus Orgia donis[.]
Propterea grex omnis erat foecundus : ubique
Graminibus laetis Tellus innoxia : fontes
Undique securi. quod si submittere vultis
Iudicio lites diuturnaque prelia nostro[,]
Observate primum leges. revocate vagantes
per valles per saxa greges[,] per lustra ferarum[.]
Figite in Antiquis iterum magalia Campis[.]

[An Eclogue by Baptista Mantuanus, Carmelite, dedicated to that most celebrated man of regal magnanimity, my Lord Bernardo Bembo, Venetian orator to Pope Innocent VIII.

Candidus is Mantuan, the author. Batrachus defends the side of those striving to adhere to the purity of their ancient way of life. Myrmix, on the other hand, defends those living under a mitigated rule. Bembus is their judge.

Candidus The greatest discord, Bembus, now stirs shepherds who used as pasture Jerusalem's hills and the fertile shores of joyful Phoenicia, shepherds who used to dwell in the fields of Galilee. On one side Batrachus, on the other side Myrmix say they stand ready to contend briefly against each other for your judgment, unless you refuse to hear them or greater business recalls you. You have the skill to reconcile us. You know how to lay quarrels to rest. Also, they say that you have drunk of Pierian waters and have seen those goddesses who watch over the sacred fount, Eurotas' plains, and Phocian fields. It is said that you have crowned your locks with laurel and have borne away Apollo's gifts: his tuneful citharas and ivory plectra.

Bembus [13] Speak, since we are led to our warm fires by the winter's days, a time when the weather forbids the flock to roam the fields and the north wind rages with its keen breath, when the ground freezes solid, when icicles hang thick from the roof and the streams' icy waters flow sluggishly. Leisure is condemned when it has no tasks to perform.

Myrmix We shepherds, a hapless race, range about in the heat of summer, anxious for our flocks. But when chilly rain keeps us among the sheepfolds, then quarrels and disputes arise.

Batrachus [22] Those who dare to change the old ways and who live at their own discretion under no rules—those, I confess, are the men who are causing this brawling and these wars within our own house.

Bembus So you are quarreling about the long–established rite, the customs of your forefathers? Tell me, Batrachus, about them and their ways. And tell me, why you have entered our part of the world? Your ground is fertile (is it not?) and watered by its own marshlands? Aren't laurel trees there? and rivers sprung from ice–cold springs?

Batrachus [30] Bembus, hear in brief of our race and its beginnings. Helius [i.e., Elijah] first begat us—Helius, I say, who after he had filled the countryside with our forefathers' sheepfolds is said to have been borne up into the sky in a fiery chariot. He was the first to watch over the sheep. He bequeathed to us the art that enables us to care for our flocks and know which pasturage is harmful. He gave us the signs to discern lurking storms and winds and to foresee wholesome and pestilent times. On the peak of Mount Carmel, a fount pours forth its glassy waters. Now they flow towards the south, but before (the old channel can still be seen) they flowed towards the east. These men have made other watercourses and have abandoned the previous ones.

Myrmix [42] What is it to you if the stream runs in a new course or an old one, so long as it flows through the fields with more plentiful waters? And why complain about the direction?

The sun's course is through the south. Better is the vine that looks to the south, better the grape gathered from Libyan vines.

Batrachus You are a shepherd, and yet, having rashly abandoned the flock's care, you speak of the vine as if the same rules governed the flocks and vineyards. About the distinctions of waters and grasses you are pitifully ignorant. You scorn the precepts of our forefathers and want to maintain your deviation by evasions such as these. [52] But Bembus, I must talk to you. While we lived together and shared the flock—alas! how much disgrace, how many vexations the sheep endured! I wasn't permitted to dip my flock in the river or (as is our custom) to shear off their fleece at the appointed times. Thorn hedges stripped the sheep and brambles cut their bare backs. Their coats were rough with scab, their bodies' moisture was dried up by sickness, sores crept throughout their frames. Having pondered so many losses and enduring them with great difficulty, we came to that fount. My task it was to explore the stream from its highest reaches. Meanwhile you, prudent Myrmix, were hunting birds' nests or a small gazelle to give to your Asila. [65] Tumbling down from a high cliff, the stream's channel had made a pool. On the encircling banks a woodland shaded the waters, and the aged branches of an ancient forest kept off the sun with their leafy covering. A thousand kinds of venomous things I saw in that watery abyss, a thousand sorts of creatures on the shady margins along its banks, a thousand things that wound sinuously towards the densely wooded parts of the forest. I was struck with terror, and running back to the sheepfold I began to turn over the straw with my three-pronged pitchfork. [74] And, lo! a serpent raised its head, hissed with its menacing tongue, and swelled open its jaws. A scorpion stretched out its spiteful claws. A big-bellied toad advanced towards me, and a viper rustled, moving through the straw. "Oh place," said I, "harmful not only to the flocks but to the shepherds themselves!" Directly, having divided my flock from those flocks, I departed in sadness to seek out better pastures. And through the fount's old channel I led new streams into rising fields where Aurora first unfurls her colors and towards the golden sunrises of ascending Phoebus. Here my sheep are fertile in fleece, and rich is the pasturage. Here the waters are without taint, the sweet springs without fault. [86] In this place our forefathers dwelt in their youth. The traces of their ancient cells still remain: the well, the decayed logs driven in the ground seven feet apart, the hearth, the torn-up plot surrounded by a hedge.

Myrmix Frivolous men are wont to busy themselves with newfangled things. Surely it is for this reason that you have sought out new pastures, invented unheard-of streams, and want to be thought our new founder.

Batrachus This newness, Myrmix, is a restored antiquity which your "truth" and the well-known sloth of your fellows have corrupted. If then a man is raising buildings that are falling down and has tamed unfruitful fields, judge you that he should be condemned? We aren't planting a second tree; rather, a healthy slip is being engrafted on the trunk of the old one, wood dormant before is becoming productive again under our care.

Myrmix [100] Though the grass might be made luxuriant for your flock and the waters be cleansed, nonetheless many lambs have perished with their mothers. Wolves and birds gorged with prey remember them well.

Batrachus 'Tis true—of those sheep who consider your fearful pestilence! Even from afar it harms those who think about it. For this reason I am always minded to depart further and further from you, to ascend that mountain itself, and to restrict the way and course [of your hatred?] so that you might lead your wasted flock back into better pasturelands.

Myrmix [109] You describe many things—known to you alone—about my flock. Why couldn't I, who pasture anyone's flock, look after these things? Is my house known only to you?

Batrachus Since Ethiopians are all soiled by blackness, that color is thought no blemish. It is the same among all of them, whether one visage condemns itself or another. Shepherd and sheep have the same impurity, the same scab, the same skin color.

Bembus Cease! Now I understand your quarrel well enough. Moreover, the day is ending. Let my judgment close up your dispute.

Myrmix Batrachus, you provoke me so often with your bold talk!

Bembus [120] Cease! 'Tis now enough! Listen to me more patiently. First of all, walk in the footsteps of your forefathers and keep up the old ways: the renowned pasturelands and springs of your ancestors; their cheese richer than these and the wool of their sheep, wool surpassing silken fleece. They always had snow–white milk (neither snow nor heat confined it from coming); their cups always foamed with frothy cream; they always had new offspring and pails filled with milk under the udders of their ewes. Watchful care, skilled diligence, and, more truly, worship of the gods (no matter how little it is)—these things can make a mighty defense of our sheep. [130] More often than we do, men of old used to invoke the gods in prayer and perform the sacred mysteries with larger offerings than ours. As a result, their whole flock was productive of offspring; their earth, covered with lush grass, did no harm; and in all aspects their founts were secure. Wherefore, if perchance you wish to submit your quarrels and longstanding battles to my judgment, then first of all abide by the laws. Call back flocks wandering among the valleys and rocks, among the haunts of wild beasts. Build your huts again in the fields of old.]

APPENDIX II

To the 128 entries at present accepted[1] from Edmondo Coccia's list on pages 113–15 of his *Le edizioni delle opere del Mantovano,* the following printings of the Latin text of Mantuan's **Adulescentia**, with their *fontes,* should be added[2] (cited, unless otherwise noted, by entry number):

From Philippe Renouard. *Bibliographie des impressions des œuvres de Josse Badius Ascensius.* 1908; rpt. New York, Burt Franklin, n. d. Vol. II, pp. 110–24:

Lyons: Claude d'Aoust, 1507 (G9)
Paris: Jean Barbier for Denis Roce, 1511 (G15)
Paris: Jean Marchant for Jean Petit, 1513 (G18)
Lyons: Jacques Mareschal, 1514 (G19)
Lyons: Jacques Myt for Simon Vincent, 1515 (G22)
Deventer: Albert Paffraet, 1515 (G23)
Antwerp: widow of Jean Loë 1569 (G42)

From *Index aureliensis: catalogus librorum sedecimo saeculo impressorum.* Printed by the Fondation Index Aureliensis, Geneva. Distributed by B. de Graaf, Nieukopp, 1965– . Vol. III, pp. 71–125:

Strasbourg: Getz and Prüss, 1506 (112.425)
Deventer: per Iacobum de Breda, 1508 (112.462)
Deventer: per Iacobum de Breda, 23 March 1509 (112.473)
Milan: Lignanorum fratrum impensa, ca.1512? (112.329/112.559; cf. **GW**3245)
Leipzig: ex officina Melchioris Lottheri, 1516 (112.636)
Strasbourg: Matthias Schürer, 1518 (112.664)
Deventer: Albert Paffraet, 1519 (112.674; cf. 112.675)
Turin: Pietro Paolo Porro, 1520 (112.697)

From Giulia Bologna. *Le cinquecentine della Biblioteca Trivulziana.* Milan: Castello Sforzesco, 1966. Vol. II:

Brescia: per Ludovicum Britannicum, 1525 (133)

---

[1] C23, C90, C132, C341, and C419 are all unrecorded in the *Index aureliensis.* In addition, C182=C334, according to the *Index aureliensis* (112.692), and C44=C54 (ibid., 112.391).

[2] *Carmina Illustrium poetarum italorum* (C489), which contains the Latin text of all ten eclogues (vol. 6, pp. 184–240), should also be included.

From H. M. Adams. *Catalogue of Books Printed on the Continent of Europe, 1501–1600 in Cambridge Libraries*. Cambridge Univ. Press, 1967. Vol. I, p. 707:

Limoges: per Paulum Bertonem expensis Leonardi Fardelet, 8 August 1520 (M393)

Lyons: per Ioannes Crespin, [7 August] 1526 (M394)

From Louis Degraves, ed. *Répertoire bibliographique des livres imprimés en France au seizième siècle*. Baden–Baden: Librairie Heitz, 1968–79:

Poitiers: Jean Bouyer and Guillaume Bouchet, ca. 1504 (vol. V, p. 8)

Caen: Laurent Hostingue(?) for Michel Angier, not after 1518 [ca. 1511, according to Adams M392] (Vol XXVII, pp. 78–79, 44)

Limoges: per Paulum Bertonem. Expensis . . . Leonardi Fardelet, 11 May 1526 (Vol. III, p. 21)

From Elly Cockx–Indestege and Geneviève Glorieux. *Belgica Typographica 1541–1600*. Nieukoop: de Graaf, 1968– . Vol. I, pp. 19–20; vol. II, p. 18:

Antwerp: Joannes Latius for Johann Steelsius, n. d. (5147) (cf. C398)

Antwerp: widow of Jean Loë, 1567 (250)

From *The National Union Catalogue: Pre–1956 Imprints*. London: Mansell, 1968–81. Vol. XXXIV, pp. 216–27; vol. DCXCV, pp. 5–9:

Lyons: device of Jean Robion, 151–? (NB0100954) (cf. C209)

Lyons: per Claudium Nourry, 1510 (NB0100979)

London: J. Y. pro Societate Stationariorum, 1646 (NB0101002)

London: E. F. pro Societate Stationariorum, 1672 (NSB0016731)

London: T. B. pro Societate Stationariorum, 1697 (NB0101008)

London: T. Ilive pro Societate Stationariorum, 1707 (NB0101010)

From W. A. Jackson, F. S. Ferguson, and Katherine F Pantzer. *A Short–Title Catalogue of Books Printed in England, Scotland, and Ireland . . . 1475–1640*. 2nd ed. London: Bibliographic Society, 1976. Vol. II, p. 349:

London: Thomas Marsh, 1576 (22982.3)

London: Thomas Marsh, 1577 (22982.5)

London: Thomas Marsh, 1580 (22982.7)

London: Garrat Dewes & Henry Marsh, ex ass. Thomas Marsh,1584 (22983.5)

London: Robert Robinson, 1593 (22984.1)

London: Robert Robinson for Robert Dexter, 1598 (22984.3)

London: Robert Dexter, 1601 (22984.4)

London: pro Societate Stationariorum, 1606 (22984.5)

London: Felix Kingston, ex. typ. Societate Stationariorum, 1613 (22984.6)

London: John Beale? ex typ. Societate Stationariorum, 1617 (22984.7)

From *A Short–Title Catalogue of Books Printed in France and French Books Printed in Other Countries from 1470 to 1600 Now in the British Library: Supplement*. London: British Library, 1986. Page 69:

Paris: Ambroise Girauld, 1528

From Donald Wing, John J. Morrison, et al. *A Short–Title Catalogue of Books Printed in England, Scotland, Ireland, Wales, and British America and of English Books Printed in Other Countries 1641–1700*. Revised ed. New York: Modern Language Association of America, 1972–1988. Vol. III, pp. 412–13:

London: E. T. pro Societate Stationariorum, 1663 (4787B)
London: R. D. pro Societate Stationariorum, 1665 (4787C)
London: J. C. pro Societate Stationariorum, 1667 (4787D)
London: ________[?]________, 1667 (4787E)

INDEX

Some Titles in the Series

JAMES J. WILHELM
General Editor

1. Lars Ahlin, *Cinnamoncandy*.
   Translated from Swedish by Hanna Kalter Weiss.

2. *Anthology of Belgian Symbolist Poets*.
   Translated from French by Donald F. Friedman.

3. Ariosto, *Five Cantos*.
   Translated from Italian by Leslie Z. Morgan.

4. *Kassia: The Legend, the Woman, and Her Work*.
   Translated from Greek by Antonia Tripolitis.

5. Antonio de Castro Alves, *The Major Abolitionist Poems of Castro Alves*. Translated from Portuguese by Amy A. Peterson.

6. Li Cunbao, *The Wreath at the Foot of the Mountain*.
   Translated from Chinese by Chen Hanming and James O. Belcher.

7. Meïr Goldschmidt, *A Jew*.
   Translated from Danish by Kenneth Ober.

8. Árpád Göncz, *Plays and Other Writings of Árpád Göncz*.
   Translated from Hungarian by Katharina and Christopher Wilson.

9. Ramón Hernández, *Invitation to Die*.
   Translated from Spanish by Marion Freeman.

10. Edvard Hoem, *The Ferry Crossing*.
    Translated from New Norwegian by Frankie Denton Shackelford.

11. Henrik Ibsen, "*Catiline*" *and* "*The Burial Mound.*"
Translated from Dano-Norwegian by Thomas Van Laan.

12. Bāṇabhaṭṭa, *Kādambarī: A Classic Sanskrit Story of Magical Transformations*. Translated from Sanskrit by Gwendolyn Layne.

13. *Selected Poems of Lina Kostenko.*
Translated from Ukranian by Michael Naydan.

14. Baptista Mantuanus, *Adulescentia: The Eclogues of Mantuan.*
Translated from Latin by Lee Piepho.

15. *The Mourning Songs of Greek Women.*
Translated from Greek by Konstantinos Lardas.

16. *Ono no Komachi: Poems, Stories, and Noh Plays.*
Translated from Japanese by Roy E., Nicholas J., and Helen Rebecca Teele.

17. Adam Small, *Kanna–He Is Coming Home.*
Translated from Afrikaans by Carrol Lasker.

18. Federigo Tozzi, *Ghisola.*
Translated from Italian by Charles Klopp.

19. *The Burden of Sufferance: Women Poets in Russia.*
Translated from Russian by Albert Cook and Pamela Perkins.

20. Chantal Chawaf, *Mother Love, Mother Earth.*
Translated from French by Monique Nagem.

For Product Safety Concerns and Information please contact our EU
representative GPSR@taylorandfrancis.com
Taylor & Francis Verlag GmbH, Kaufingerstraße 24, 80331 München, Germany

www.ingramcontent.com/pod-product-compliance
Lightning Source LLC
Chambersburg PA
CBHW071407100726
47908CB00004B/1091

* 9 7 8 0 3 6 7 1 8 0 3 1 7 *